THE TRIUMPH OF MERCY

The Reconciliation of All through Jesus Christ

by
George Sidney Hurd

Copyright © 2017 George Sidney Hurd.

All rights reserved.
Except for brief quotations in critical publications or reviews, no part of this book may be reproduced in any manner without prior written permission from the publisher.

Contact: http://www.triumphofmercy.com

All texts are quoted from the New King James Version unless otherwise indicated.
Other versions cited from are listed below with their abbreviations:

ASV	American Standard Version
CLV	Concordant Literal Version
Darby	Darby Bible 1889
KJV	King James Version
NIV	New International Version
MKJV	Modern King James Version
PLT	Personal Literal Translation
TEV	Today's English Version
WNT	Weymouth New Testament 1912
YLT	Young's Literal Translation

Contents

Acknowledgments 7

Preface to the Second Edition 8

INTRODUCTION 9

   How I Discovered the Immensity of the Mercy of God 9

Chapter one: **The Universal Inclusiveness of the Gospel** 23

   The Savior of the Whole World 26

   The Purpose of God in Election 32

   The Manifestation of the Sons of God 37

   The Universal Restoration 41

   Universal Reconciliation 45

   The Destiny of Fallen Spirits 47

Chapter two: **Christ the Last Adam** 57

Chapter three: **Does God Get What He Wants?** 67

   Two Traditional Opinions 67

      The Arminians 67

      The Calvinists 72

   The Common Denominator between Arminians and Calvinists 74

   Free-Will? 75

Chapter four: **God's Nature and Hell** 79

   God's Holiness and His Love 79

   A Divided God? 81

   When Righteousness and Peace Kissed each other 83

   Righteous Justice is a Just Measure 84

   God's Hatred 85

      Hate Defined 89

      The Temporal Nature of God's Hatred 91

      The Relative Nature of Godly Hatred 93

   Becoming Rooted and Grounded in the Knowledge of God's Love ... 96

   Preachers' Depictions of Eternal Punishment 98

- *Jonathan Edwards* 99
- *Pedro Lombardo* 100
- *Gerhard* 100
- *Samuel Hopkins* 101
- *Sermon by Father John Furniss* 101
- **The Fatherhood of God** 102
- **Created Out of Nothing or Out of God?** 107
- **Does God show Favoritism?** 113
- **The Inclusion of Children and the Mentally Handicapped** ... 116
  - *Jonathan Edwards* 117
  - *Jeremy Taylor* 117
  - *Reverend J. Furniss* 117

Chapter five: **The Duration of Punishment** 123
- **OLAM** 124
  - *1. Indefinite Past Time:* 125
  - *2. Indefinite Future Time:* 126
  - *3. Indefinite Past and Indefinite Future Time combined* 126
  - *when referring to God:* 126
  - *Examples of where Olam was mistranslated.* 127
  - *Olam and Beyond* 130
  - *The Shame and self-Contempt is for olam and No More.* .. 130
- **AIÓN, AIONIOS** 132
  - *Aión* 134
  - *Aionios* 136
  - *What the Linguists Say* 137
  - *Aión and Aionios in Greek Literature* 141
- **AIDÍOS** 142

Chapter six: **The Bible and Hell** 145
- **The Lack of Emphasis on Post-mortem Punishment in the Scriptures.** 145

- **Gehenna Fire** 150
  - *The Unquenchable Fire* 155
  - *Fire for Christians?* 157
- **Gehenna and the Destruction of Soul and Body** 164
- **Death, Destruction and Annihilation** 167
- **The Furnace of Fire** 169
- **The Rich Man and Lazarus** 171

Chapter seven: **The Two-Edged Sword** 175

Chapter eight: **Texts used to Prove Eternal Punishment** 181
- **"They will go away into Everlasting Punishment"** 181
- **Temporal vs. "Eternal" in 2Corinthians 4:1** 192
- **Eternal Destruction** 193
- **"Shall not see Life"** 199
- **Are there few who are saved?** 200
- **Forever and Ever** 206
- **Tormented with Fire** 211
- **Fire and Sulfur** 216
- **Eternal Fire** 218
- **The "Unpardonable" Sin** 220
- **Better for Judas Not to have been born** 225

Chapter nine **The Testimonies of Near-Death Experiences** 227

Chapter ten: **Her Gates are Always Open** 237

Chapter eleven: **The Age of Ages** 245
- **The ages of the ages** 249

Chapter twelve: **Universalism in the History of the Church** 251
- **Universalism – The Doctrine of the Majority until Saint Augustine and the Dark Ages** 252
- **Clement of Alexandria AD 150 to AD 215.** 256
- **Origen AD 184 to AD 254.** 257
- **Theofilus of Antioch AD 186.** 257

- Irenaeus AD 182. ... 258
- Ambrose of Milan AD 340 to AD 397. ... 258
- Gregory of Nyssa AD 330 to AD 394. ... 259
- Gregory Nazianzen AD 328 to AD 389. ... 260
- Marcellus of Ancyra AD 315 to Ad 374. ... 261
- Titus of Bostra AD 338 to AD 378. ... 261
- Theodore of Mopsuestia AD 359 to AD 429. ... 261
- Ambrose of Milan AD 340 to AD 397. ... 262
- Marius Victorinus AD 300. ... 262
- Jerome AD 347 to AD 420. ... 263
- Theodore the Blessed AD 387 to AD 458. ... 264
- Theodore Olympiodorus AD 495 to AD 570. ... 264
- Summary of the History of Universalism ... 265
  - *1. In The Early Centuries.* ... 265
  - *2. In Modern Times.* ... 268
  - *3. In America* ... 272
  - *Conclusion* ... 273

Chapter thirteen: **The Unadulterated Gospel** ... 275
- The Leaven of the Pharisees - The Good News, Bad News Gospel .. 277
- The Leaven of the Sadducees ... 281

INDEX OF PASSAGES IMPLYING A UNIVERSAL RESTORATION ... 287
- Passages that imply a Total Restoration: ... 287
- Passages which indicate that Punishment is Not Eternal: ... 303

CONTACT THE AUTHOR ... 313

Acknowledgments

I am truly grateful to my dear wife, Norma who has shared the same vision and has always supported me in spite of having to sacrifice so much as I dedicated myself to writing. Also, my daughter Monica has been a tremendous help with the proofreading of my Spanish translations.

I am especially indebted to my dear friends Paul and Betty Wetselaar, who have shared the spiritual journey with me since the beginning of our walk with the Lord in the '60s. They have greatly assisted me in editing all of my books.

Preface to the Second Edition

Since I originally published *The Triumph of Mercy* in 2014, I have made several additions, including chapter 13: *"The Unadulterated Gospel."* Some of the additions are further discoveries I have made over the last four years, while others are clarifications added in response to questions made by my readers. Although the primary substance of the first edition has not changed, this addition contains some fifty additional pages of further information which I considered to be relevant material which justified announcing this new edition. *(May, 2018)*

INTRODUCTION

In the Scriptures, we find repeated over and over *"The Lord is good, for His mercy endures forever."* Yet, how many of us really believe this in our heart of hearts? Could an omniscient God and Creator of all things really be called *"good"* if He were to initiate a plan, creating man in His own image and likeness, knowing all along that the final outcome for the great majority of mankind would be an eternal punishment infinitely more horrible than anything that Ivan the Terrible, Adolf Hitler and Pol Pot together could have dreamed up? I believe that the God revealed in the Bible and in Jesus Christ really is **good**, without any shadow of turning.

Also, we see that *His mercy endures forever.* In your opinion, how long is "forever"? If an infant were to die at birth would you allow that *forever* extends beyond its last breath? What about a child who dies at eleven years of age? What about thirteen years of age? Many would say that twelve years of age is the "age of accountability" and therefore marks the limit of God's mercy after death; even for those who have never heard the gospel and for that reason haven't believed. But, where in the Scriptures do we find stated such a limitation to divine mercy? Do we really believe that the mercy of the Lord endures *forever*, or do we tempt God, *limiting the Holy One of Israel? (Ps 78:41).*

Most of us adopt our beliefs concerning our destiny, and that of others, without much thought or reflection. Normally when one receives Christ, they join a church, learn its distinctive doctrines and even defend them without questioning their scriptural validity. But God has called us to grow in our personal knowledge of Him and His Word; He calls upon us to test all things; searching the Scriptures, carefully examining all things, retaining the good and abstaining from all appearance of evil. He calls us to be experts in the Word, having our senses trained to discern between good and evil *(Acts 17:11; 1Thess 5:21; Hebrews 5:13,14).*

How I Discovered the Immensity of the Mercy of God

I was raised in a denomination that taught immortality was conditional and only the just receive immortality in the resurrection.

The unjust, according to their doctrine, are resurrected for the final judgment and then burned up in the lake of fire for a length of time, longer or shorter, according to their works. The most severe punishment will fall upon Satan, who I was taught would burn for a thousand years. According to their belief, after being consumed in the lake of fire they will all cease to exist – they will be annihilated.

At around ten years of age I began to realize I had a bent towards sinning, although at that time my sins were mostly minor infractions - like stealing my classmate's pencil, lying to my parents or fighting with my brother and two sisters. Nevertheless, I couldn't stop doing it.

I remember asking my teacher at the Christian school I attended how many times I could be forgiven for the same sin. When he told me that God would forgive me two or three times, but only if I was truly sincere, I knew there wasn't any hope of salvation for me, since I had already greatly exceeded the limit of God's mercy. Also, I figured that I wasn't truly sincere when I asked God to forgive me, otherwise I wouldn't repeat the same sin over and over.

I came to a crisis in my life on the 27th of December, 1962, four days after turning twelve. Taking advantage of the Christmas holidays, we went from Escondido, California where we were living, to Fort Bragg, California, visiting relatives. My brother, Leslie, who was only fifteen, was at the wheel. He only had a learner permit and was driving much too fast for someone just learning to drive. There were six of us crammed into our 1949 Volkswagen bug. The engine had been rebuilt and it had a new metallic blue paintjob, and to us it was like new. Just five minutes outside of Ft Bragg my brother lost control of the car and we flipped end on end five times before coming to a stop. When I regained consciousness, the first thing I saw was my brother on the pavement with a pool of blood around his head. The ambulance driver assured me he was going to be okay, but in the morning they broke the news to me that he had died during the night.

Leslie's death was devastating to me. My father had left us and was living far away in New York State. To me, Leslie was not only my elder brother, but also my father and best friend. Why had God taken him from me? In my mind it was confirmation that God had abandoned me. To make things worse I knew that my brother had stolen a crossbow from a neighbor's house. The owner of the house hadn't been there for several months, and out of curiosity we broke in to explore. When he took a crossbow from the house, I told him that he was stealing, but he said that he was only going to borrow it for a while and then return it, but he never had the opportunity. After his death, when my dad discovered what he had done he blamed my mom, saying that, because she wasn't more attentive, Leslie wouldn't go to heaven since he had stolen something without making restitution.

At that stage of my life I couldn't see the mercy of God. I only saw a God who demanded perfection to such a degree that 99% of those He had created in His own image and likeness would end up being incinerated – reduced to ashes, just because they were born contaminated by a sinful nature they had inherited from Adam. Didn't God know before He began to create us that His plan would end so tragically for all, except for a few of the strongest and most privileged? How could a God of love plan such a thing? I felt like an orphan, abandoned by my Father and Creator, and without hope.

Since I was raised by a very devout mother, I had an acutely sensitive conscience and felt the need to seek the Lord. But since I felt it was impossible for me to live up to His expectations, I decided to do all I could to drown out the voice of my conscience. When I was alone and felt the emptiness of not having God in my life, I would look up into heaven and curse God out loud. I would intentionally do things against His will, because I felt a mixture of pain and rage against Him. Before I turned thirteen, I had already been sent to a correctional institution for insubordination to my father. He had returned and remarried my mother, but I was not the same boy I was before the accident. I quickly sank into the world of drugs and delinquency. By the age of 18 I had already accumulated more than three years' time in correctional institutions, and my health was failing due to drug abuse. I weighed only 145 pounds, which is not much for someone five foot ten inches tall. Due to sharing needles with other drug addicts I had become infected with hepatitis A,B,C and hepatitis Delta, although medical science only knew about hepatitis A and B at the time.

For years I had said that I no longer believed in God and actually had myself convinced that I was an atheist - that is until I found myself in a situation in which I thought I was dying of an overdose. At that moment, being only 18 years old, and feeling my life draining from me, I realized that deep down I had always known God existed;

I just didn't feel worthy of Him and so I tried to erase Him from my mind. Someone who was with me at the time told me to cry out to God for help. I tried to pray, but finally responded saying: "It is no use. God will not hear me after all I have done." There are no words to describe the fear and anguish I felt in those moments.

I was taken to a hospital, and after leaving intensive care I was placed in a room shared with an elderly man. He was a Christian who reflected the love of Jesus in a way I could feel – even in my drugged state. A nurse covered the tracks in my veins, saying that they were no sight for the man of God sharing the same room with me. Nevertheless, I felt no rejection or repulsion from him – only a love without conditions. When he invited me to receive Christ, I confessed that I was tired of living as I was but didn't feel that God would accept me after all I had done. He then told me the words of Jesus: *"Those who are well have no need of a physician, but those who are sick. I did not come to call the righteous, but sinners, to repentance." (Mk 2:17).* I had never thought of Jesus (not to mention God the Father), as being a *loving* God, *full of mercy* towards His rebellious children even though they have turned away from Him and destroyed their lives in the far country.

The love I felt in this man of God and his words awakened a new hope in me. But after leaving the hospital I realized that I was incapable of freeing myself from the chains that held me fast to my old way of life. After a weekend spent on drugs and a rock concert in San Francisco, I found myself crying out to God early Monday morning at work. I said, "God, I really want to live for you, but I can't." For the first time in my life that I can remember, I heard the voice of God speaking to me. He said: "I have been waiting to hear you say, 'I want to, but I can't'. Now you are going to see what I will do for you." From that moment on it was like a veil had been removed from my eyes. I could see, as never before, how good is good and how evil is evil. I had violated my conscience so many times that I could no longer distinguish between good and evil until that moment.

The next Sunday was the 16th of November, 1969. I visited the "First Free-will Baptist Church" which, as with many churches at that time, was experiencing revival. That evening a missionary from Africa was sharing. At some point during his sermon, the Holy Spirit came upon me in a very beautiful way. It was like liquid love being poured all over me, and yet at the same time penetrating my whole being. He revealed to me that I was now a part of God's family. I no longer felt like an abandoned orphan child. I felt so clean and free from the stains of my past. The chains of addiction fell from me. I was so captivated by His presence that I didn't even realize until weeks later that the addictions I couldn't overcome before no longer had any attraction to me. I had come to know the love of God that never ceases and the mercy that never comes to an end, and I no longer needed drugs to fill the void.

Since the church I was attending was experiencing a powerful move of God, and the pastor's messages seemed so anointed and backed up by Scripture, I adopted all the doctrines taught by him and the denomination without questioning them. I considered the presence of God as sufficient confirmation that all their doctrines were flawless. I didn't stop to consider at the time that God was also visiting other churches with differing doctrinal emphasis. (It was the time now known as "The Jesus Movement"). I didn't realize that God visits us by His pure grace because He loves us and not because we've got it all right-on doctrinally.

Since it was a church that emphasized the free-will of man to choose or reject God, they unwittingly ended up limiting the free-will of God *"who will have all men to be saved and to come to the knowledge of the truth."(1 Ti 2:4 MKJV)*. They affirmed that God loves everyone equally, but at the same time believed that if one died without hearing the gospel and believing in Jesus within the brief window of time between "the age of accountability" (12 years), and death, he would be subjected to the "eternal wrath of God" in hell, which, (according to them), was created by God for the sole purpose of tormenting forever all who failed to accept Christ during their brief life-time.

I turned twelve the 23rd of December, 1962. That means that if I had died with my brother Leslie on the 27th, my window of opportunity to receive the mercy of God would have only lasted four days. At that time, I had heard a lot about Christ but had no concept of the good news of the gospel. On the other hand, Chairman Mao of China, who was responsible for the murder of millions of Christians because they refused to renounce Christ, lived nearly 83 years. What system of justice on earth would give the same sentence to a young boy who dies just four days after his 12th birthday as that of an antichrist dictator who lived 71 years beyond the "age of accountability," being responsible for the death of some 70 million people?

They argue that His justice and holiness are infinite and therefore His judgment – even for the least offense, requires infinite punishment. But where in the Scriptures do we find that concept put forth? On the contrary, as we will see further along, the judgment of God is measured in proportion to the offense and not according to the prominence of the person offended. The story and movie "Les Miserables" was set in a time when one would receive a life sentence for simply stealing a loaf of bread if it happened to be stolen from the king's palace instead of an ordinary home, because it was an offense against the king. People are moved to indignation by the story because of the inequity and injustice of such a severe judgment solely on the basis of the prominence of the person offended.

Even justice without mercy in the Bible would be *eye for eye, tooth for tooth, hand for hand... (Ex 21:23-25)*. Any punishment beyond that would be unjust according to the law of God, just as it would also be according to human justice - even in Muslim countries. The Lord limited the severity of punishment permitted for an offense to 40 lashes in Deuteronomy 25:1-3:

*"If there is a dispute between men, and they come to court, that the judges may judge them, and they justify the righteous and condemn the wicked, 2 then it shall be, if the wicked man deserves to be beaten, that the judge will cause him to lie down and be beaten in his presence, **according to his guilt, with a certain number of blows.** 3 **Forty blows he may give him and no more**, lest he should exceed this and beat him with many blows above these, and your brother be humiliated in your sight."*

Is it possible that the God of all mercy, who put limits on punishment permitted, saying that anything beyond that would be excessive and inhumane, would Himself beat His children unceasingly for all eternity? Jesus made it clear that the lashes measured out in God's judgment will also be according to the offenses of each individual and not infinite:

*"And that servant who knew his master's will, and did not prepare himself or do according to his will, shall be **beaten with many stripes**. 48 But he who did not know, yet committed things deserving of stripes, shall be **beaten with few**. For everyone to whom much is given, from him much will be required; and to whom much has been committed, of him they will ask the more." (Lu 12:47-48)*

Just judgment is always in proportion to the offense. No judge on earth would have the right to give a sentence of life imprisonment to a person just for "J" walking. How much less would the God of all mercy commit such an injustice; not to mention an eternal, never-ending punishment!

We also find in Scripture that His *"mercy triumphs over judgment"* (Jas 2:13). It is His *wrath* that is just for a moment – not His mercy *(Ps 30:5). "The Lord is merciful and gracious; slow to anger, and **abounding in mercy**. 9 He will not always strive with us, **nor will He keep His anger forever."** (Ps 103:8-9).* It is His mercy, not His wrath which endures forever: *"Oh, give thanks to the Lord, for He is good! For **His mercy endures forever."** (Ps 107:1).*

Initially after my salvation experience, I simply rejoiced in my own personal salvation without much reflection upon the destiny of others. I was concerned about the salvation of my brother Leslie and other departed loved ones, but I comforted myself in the hope that they may have repented and accepted Christ while they were between life and death. In my mind, death marked the limit of the mercy of God, but even in cases of suicide I reasoned that perhaps there existed the possibility of repenting before actually abandoning the body.

A few years later I moved to another city and joined a Calvinistic Baptist church. The Calvinists follow the doctrine of John Calvin, who taught that all who God wants to save will be eternally saved, in contrast with the Arminians who insist that salvation only comes through the free-will response of man to the gospel. The Calvinist insists that salvation is not dependent upon the free-will of man. Since God is sovereign and all powerful, they say that all whom He desires to be saved will be saved. According to them, He simply does not want all men to be saved. They teach that Christ only died for the elect whom God loved and chose from before the foundation of the world. The rest come into this world being, by default, predestined to an eternal hell. When I asked why God didn't save all mankind since it is in His power to do so, they told me I was asking the wrong question. They said I should be asking God why He saved me, and that I should be grateful for my own salvation without questioning the limitations of God's goodness towards others.

To me, some Scriptures seemed to support the Arminians while others seemed to support the position of the Calvinists. For many years I tried to maintain an equilibrium between the Scriptures presented by both sides, taking a position that was neither Arminian nor Calvinistic. Even then, I recognized that there was no possible way to reconcile the Scriptures entirely with any scheme that included damnation for the vast majority – especially if it included *eternal, never-ending* torment. On one hand the Arminians insisted that since God is love He loves all men equally, and He desires their salvation. However, according to them, He cannot accomplish the salvation of all as He desires because of the free-will of man. On the other side were the Calvinists who insisted that God is sovereign and accomplishes all He desires but doesn't love all men and therefore doesn't desire the salvation of all. The Bible is very clear in affirming that God loves all without partiality and desires the salvation of all mankind as the Arminians affirm *(Jn 3:16; Acts 10:34; 1Ti 2:4, etc.)*. But the Bible is also clear in establishing what the Calvinists teach; that God is sovereign and omnipotent and accomplishes all He desires *(Ps 135:6; Isa 46:10; Isa 14:27, etc.)*.

For many years I was in a tension between these two undesirable doctrinal options concerning my God: 1) God *desires* but cannot, and 2) God *can* but doesn't want to. I was unable to resolve this tension until I made the discovery of the third piece of the puzzle which fit perfectly with the first two truths: 1) God *desires* the salvation of all, 2) God *can* accomplish what he desires, and 3) He *will do it* in His time. I began to discover in the Scriptures abundant declarations that God wants to save all and that He is able to do all that He desires, but no Scriptures indicating that He cannot save all or that He doesn't want to save all. What I discovered is that there are also abundant passages affirming that He will indeed save all in His own time. Then, I was able to remove the second phrase from the first two equations and add the third equation: *He will do it* in His time. Finally, it all fell together, revealing a marvelous plan for the ages with a conclusion that truly results in the praise of the glory of His grace:

1) God ***desires*** ~~but cannot~~.

2) God ***can*** ~~but doesn't want to~~.

3) God ***will*** do it in His time.

I did not arrive at this conviction concerning the ultimate salvation and restoration of all overnight. There were moments when certain passages seemed to be proclaiming the salvation of all, but each time I would go to authors presenting the traditional doctrine of eternal punishment. They argued that the verses didn't mean what they seemed to mean, since according to their assumption, not all will be saved. As time went on, I began to discover an ever-increasing number of verses that seemed to teach universal reconciliation, yet each time I would retreat to the security of the majority position.

I didn't know at the time that the majority position of the early Church, during the first five centuries before the Dark Ages, was universal salvation, which I was now also beginning to see in the Scriptures. [1] Even though I had specialized in the *koine* Greek of the New Testament and was conscious of many errors in the King James Version, as well as other versions, I had never reflected upon the extent of the influence that the traditions and dogmas of the Dark Ages had had upon the translators. Also, King James of England prohibited the translators from translating in any way contrary to the established doctrine of the Church. For example, since the Church didn't baptize by immersion, they didn't dare translate the Greek word *baptizo* according to its meaning, "submerse," so they simply transliterated the word to avoid having to reveal its true meaning. Therefore, even if they may have wanted to translate faithfully the meaning of the original text, in many cases they were forbidden to do so. Also, they approached their work of translation, either consciously or unconsciously, with their own doctrinal biases and traditional influences, which had much influence upon their renditions of many words in the text. More recent translations have corrected many of these errors, although one can still identify renderings of words that are actually interpretations according to the doctrinal positions of the translators. There are now several *literal* versions available that - even though harder to read, avoid most of the interpretive renditions of many translations.

About three years before the writing of this book I was going to preach a message based upon Acts 3:21 which says: *"whom heaven must receive until **the times of restoration of all things**, which God has spoken by the mouth of all His holy prophets since the world began."* I intended to use it for a message concerning the restoration of the Church and applying it to the doctrine of justification by faith, the five-fold ministries and the gifts of the Spirit. But while I meditated

---

[1] See chapter eleven, *Universalism in Church History*

on the meaning of the text, it became evident that the passage was making reference to a total restoration of *all* things – something much beyond the restoration of the Church in this age. I saw that the restoration begins at the time of the Second Coming of our Lord, because it states that heaven will receive Him *until* the restoration begins. It was also obvious that it didn't have application to the restoration of the Church, since at the time Peter spoke these words, the Church didn't need restoration, since it was just in its infancy. Also, I saw that it was something predicted by the prophets since the world began. As I continued reading, I saw in verse 25 that the restoration of all things prophesied since the beginning included all the families of the earth:

*"You are sons of the prophets and of the covenant which God made with our fathers, saying to Abraham, 'And in your seed **all the families of the earth shall be blessed**." (Acts 3:25)*

Another important observation is that in the phrase, *"the restoration of all things,"* the word *"things"* does not exist in the Greek. It was added by the translators, giving the impression that "all" (Gr. *pas*) has reference to inanimate things rather than people. It became evident to me that it was speaking of times in which there will be a total restoration, including all the families of the earth, and not simply future families, but all families that have existed or will exist from Adam up to the last generation, in the same way that the promise that God gave to Eve that her seed would gain the victory over Satan has application to every generation. The promise wasn't only for Adam and Eve; it wasn't only for those living in the time of Christ or those living in the time of the Second Coming, but rather for all who have ever lived since Adam's fall.

When I discovered the scope of this passage, I was very ill because the hepatitis C I had been infected with 40 years earlier had destroyed my liver. Even though the doctors had given me only months to live in 1998, God had given us the promise that this sickness was not unto death, but for His glory. God was faithful to His promise. On June 29 of 2012 I received a liver transplant in Bogotá, Colombia. In 1998 the doctors told me that my days on this earth would be shorter than the waiting list for a transplant. However, upon receiving my liver transplant in 2012, I had remained alive, serving the Lord as a missionary in the Colombian Amazon Jungle for more than 12 years. I received my liver transplant only 6 days after being put on the waiting list for a transplant in Colombia. Upon examining my damaged liver after removing it, they found cancer. They told me that, because of the cancer, I wouldn't have lived much longer if I hadn't received the transplant when I did. God has perfect timing!

Taking advantage of my convalescence between 2011 and 2014, I determined to seek greater clarity on what God had begun to show me concerning universal restoration. I examined anew what the Bible had to say about hell and carefully analyzed the usages of *olam* in the Old Testament and *aión* (with its adjective *aionios*) in the New Testament – words which definitely refer to measurements of time but have been rendered "everlasting," "forever" and "eternal" in many instances by traditional translators. I also read what the early Church fathers, who spoke koine Greek as their first language, had to say and discovered that most believed in a universal restoration until Augustine of Hippo (AD 354 to AD 430). He popularized the doctrine of eternal punishment, and the institutionalized Church eventually imposed the doctrine upon Christianity, declaring restorationism (the restoration of all), and annihilationism (the annihilation of the unjust), anathema.

In every area I investigated: both in the Old and New Testaments, in the meanings of words in the original languages, and also in Church history, I discovered that all of it put together taught that the plan of God for the ages was *"that in the dispensation of the fullness of the times He might **gather together in one all things in Christ**, both which are **in heaven** and which are **on earth** — in Him." (Eph 1:10).*

I discovered that everything was in agreement with what Paul said - that the time would come when Christ, having submitted all things to Himself, will then submit Himself to the Father *that God may be all in all (1Cor 15:22-28).*

As I hope to demonstrate in the following chapters, universal reconciliation is not some new doctrine. Neither did it find its origins in the teachings of modernist liberals. Quite to the contrary, it was foreseen by the prophets since the beginning of time, and further clarified in the teachings of Jesus and the Apostles – especially Paul, to whom were revealed, as to none other, the mysteries of God's plan for the ages.

It is necessary to distinguish biblical and evangelical universalism from syncretistic universalism which says that all roads lead to God. The Bible is very clear in stating that there is only one way to God and that way is Jesus. The universalism presented in these pages does not minimize the importance of the cross. On the contrary it magnifies the centrality and efficacy of the work of Christ on the cross in a manner that is not possible with the traditional belief that the majority of those for whom Christ died will be eternally lost without benefitting from His salvation. A famous phrase of Martin Luther was *"sola scriptura" (only Scripture).* My conviction and hope in the final salvation of all is based upon that same theme. By that I do not mean to say that we should discount our God-given capacity of reason, but our final authority for faith and doctrine should be based solely upon the Scriptures. I do not believe that one can be a true disciple of Jesus and not have the same respect for the authority of Scriptures that He demonstrated.

It is my conviction, as I hope to demonstrate from the Scriptures, that the restoration of all is the missing piece in the puzzle that reveals God's plan for the ages – a piece that was lost to the traditional Church entering into the Dark Ages. This truth confirms that He who began a good work in the creation will bring it to perfection. Of course, with any doctrinal position there will always be some texts that, at first glance, seem to be in tension with it. There are texts that seem to teach the annihilation of the unjust and others that seem to teach eternal torment. But, taking into account the overall theme of Scripture, I believe that as a whole the Scriptures harmonize with universal restoration in a way that the doctrines of eternal punishment or annihilationism are not able to do. Also, I hope to demonstrate that the reconciliation of all is what best reflects the nature of God as revealed in the Scriptures.

I do not presume here to write a book that would equal other works already written on this theme. I have read many books and articles on this subject from all three major perspectives, but the two I would most highly recommend are *"Hope Beyond Hell"* by Gerry Beauchemin and *"Patristic Universalism"* by David Burnfield. They can both be obtained on Amazon.com. Also there is a great wealth of information that has been made available by Gary and Michelle Amirault on their website Tentmaker: http://www.tentmaker.org [2]

---

[2] Gary and Michelle Amirault http://www.tentmaker.org

Other books and materials on the subject can also be found on my website: www.triumphofmercy.com

My motives for writing this book are to present my discoveries in written form while I have the time to be focused on the subject, and also to make available a work on this subject in Spanish. After I had already begun to write this book, Gerry Beauchemin's *"Hope Beyond Hell" (Esperanza Más Allá del Infierno)* became available in Spanish and can be obtained on the internet. It is my hope that this effort will be of as much benefit to my readers as the writing of it has been to me.

It is not my intention to be offensive in any way to those who hold to the traditional beliefs. If I come across as indignant at times, or mockingly, please keep in mind that I am also indignant with myself and mocking myself since I once held and defended those positions. If it is the first time you have examined this subject, I would anticipate that many objections will arise in your mind as you read this book. Paradigms founded on tradition are very difficult to overcome, but I would encourage you to carefully examine all the scriptural arguments presented here before putting it aside. The renewal of one's mind is a process; not an event. Many times we can become convinced in our minds but our emotional responses are harder to bring in line with the truth. This is especially true with the dogma of eternal punishment since it is so deeply rooted in fear.

Most Christians are more emotionally oriented than intellectually oriented. We need both, but our convictions should be based upon the Word of God and not upon our emotions. The Church has used fear to control and motivate the people of God for more than a millennium, keeping the people from the truth that would make them free. Even to the present we can see this tendency in many churches.

Many in the Church today are more convinced by "testimonies" of individuals who tell of visions of hell than what the Scriptures themselves actually teach. We need to be renewed in our understanding and not tossed to and fro by subjective experiences and even doctrines of demons designed to seduce us by appealing to our emotions. The Scriptures speak clearly of hell but whatever testimony that adds to the Scriptures or limits the inclusiveness of the redemption which is in Christ Jesus needs to be confronted and cast aside - no matter what our emotions or the "testimonies" of hell would tell us. In chapter eight we will examine more closely the phenomenon of visions of hell and near-death experiences.

Chapter one
The Universal Inclusiveness of the Gospel

*"And behold, an angel of the Lord stood before them, and the glory of the Lord shone around them, and they were greatly afraid. 10 Then the angel said to them, "Do not be afraid, for behold, I bring you **good tidings of great joy** which will be **to all people**… 13 And suddenly there was with the angel a multitude of the heavenly host praising God and saying: 14 "Glory to God in the highest, and **on earth peace, goodwill toward men!**" (Luke 2:9,10; 13,14)*

Just how inclusive is the *good tidings of great joy*? When the angel said: *"all people,"* did he really mean "all" or just some? Some would say that it only applies to the people of Israel. However, we know that the good news of the gospel is not limited to the Jews but is also for the Gentiles. In the very same chapter of Luke, seven days later when Joseph and Mary presented Jesus in the temple, Simon prophesied concerning Him using the same word, "people" *(Gr. laos): "Lord, now You are letting Your servant depart in peace, according to Your word; 30 For my eyes have seen Your salvation 31 Which You have prepared **before the face of all peoples** (laos), 32 a light to bring revelation **to the Gentiles**, and the glory of **Your people Israel**." (Luke 2:29-32)* Here, in the same chapter, the Holy Spirit makes it clear that *all people* includes both Israel and also the Gentiles. A few verses later He makes it even clearer when He says: *"And **all flesh** shall see the salvation of God." (Luke 3:6)*.

The Calvinists would say that it is only good news to the elect, but John emphasizes that the good news is not something exclusive of the elect of this age but rather encompasses *all,* when he says: *"And He Himself is the propitiation for our sins, and not for ours only but also for **the whole world**." (1John 2:2)*.

The Arminians would say that it is only good news for those who hear and believe it in their lifetime, but Paul says in 1Timothy 4:10 that God *"is the Savior of **all men, especially of those who believe**." (1Tim 4:10)*. In other words, Jesus is the Savior of *all men* – even those who have not yet believed in the good news of great joy for *all people*. Blessed are those who believe now. They are submitting themselves to the sanctification of the Holy Spirit in this life in order to be able to go directly into the presence of the Lord without the need of being hurt by the second death *(Rev 2:11; 20:6,14)*. But some day every tongue will have confessed that Jesus Christ is Lord, to the glory of God the Father *(Phil 2:10,11; Isa 45:22,23)*, because He is the Savior of all men, especially (not exclusively) of those who believe.

Some would say that it is only good news to those who hear and believe the gospel in this life. But what about those who died before the angel's announcement and before the cross? Is it not good news for them also? Some would say yes, but only for those who believed in Jehovah and practiced the Jewish ceremonies. But is it not good news also for those who were disobedient and died before Christ's victory on the cross? If it is not good news also for them, then why did Jesus descend into Hades to preach the good news *to them?* Many would insist that there is no good news for them, but the Scriptures indicate otherwise:

> *"For Christ also suffered once for sins, the just for the unjust, that He might bring us to God, being put to death in the flesh but made alive by the Spirit, 19 by whom also* **He went and preached to the spirits in prison***, 20 who* **formerly were disobedient***, when once the Divine longsuffering waited in the* **days of Noah***, while the ark was being prepared, in which a few, that is, eight souls, were saved through water." (1Peter 3:18-20)*

> *"For this reason* **the <u>gospel</u> was preached also to those who are dead***, that they might be judged according to men in the flesh, but live according to God in the spirit." (1Peter 4:6)*

If Christ's proclamation of the good news to those imprisoned in Hades wasn't for their salvation, then what purpose did it serve? Was it just to make them feel worse for missing out? No! He is the Savior of all – especially of those who believe, to be sure, but also of all the rest. In His triumph over Satan He obtained the keys of Hades. *(Rev 1:18)* Why did He obtain them if it wasn't in order to set the captives free? It is true that everyone, including believers, will be salted in fire in the judgment, and beyond, if necessary *(Mark 9:49; 1Cor 3:13-15; Rev 20:15, etc.)*, but as will be demonstrated later in this book, the fire will not last forever.

In Ephesians 4:8-10 Paul says the following concerning Christ:

"When He ascended on high, He led captivity captive, and gave gifts to men.' 9 (Now this, 'He ascended' — what does it mean but that He also first descended into the lower parts of the earth? 10 He who descended is also the One who ascended far above all the heavens, that He might fill all things.)"

I understand this to be telling us that when Christ descended into the lower parts of the earth, He released those who were in captivity and ascended with them on high, that He might fill all things. This is the idea expressed in Today's English Version: *"When he went up to the very heights, he took many captives with him; he gave gifts to mankind." (Eph 4:8 TEV)* He took the keys of Hades from Satan, preached the good news to those who were in captivity, and took them with Him when He ascended. Paul here is quoting from Psalms 68:18. There we see that He not only took with Him those who had lived saintly lives but also those who once were disobedient:

*"Thou hast ascended on high, thou hast led captivity captive: thou hast received gifts for men; yea, **for the rebellious also**, that the Lord God might dwell among them." (Ps 68:18 KJV)*

So we see that the gospel is good news of great joy **to all people**, not only for those who believe now, but also, in His time, for all. Even the rebellious will someday dwell in the presence of Jehovah God (Let us not forget that the rebellious would also include all of us before we came to know Christ).

We see comments by the Early Church Fathers that indicate that they also believed Ephesians 4:8-10 to be saying that Jesus freed the captives held in Hades. Athanasius (AD 296- AD 373), Bishop of Alexandria said: *"While the devil thought to kill one, he is deprived of all, cast out of Hades and sitting by the gates, sees all the fettered beings led forth by the courage of the Savior."* [3] Gregory Nazianzen (AD 330- AD 390), wrote: *"Until He loosed by His blood all who groan under Tartarean chains."* [4] And again he says, *"Today salvation has been brought to the universe to whatsoever is visible and whatsoever is invisible...the gates of Hades are thrown open."* [5]

---

[3] Athanasius. De pass. et cruce Darn.

[4] Gregory Nazianzen, Carm. xxxv. (ed. Lyons, 1840.

[5] Gregory Nazianzen, Or. xlii.

Most of us have been taught that this life is the only window of opportunity that we have to receive the gospel, although it's not even a nanosecond in comparison with eternity. It doesn't matter that the majority of human-kind have never even had the opportunity to hear the gospel – much less believe in it. But where did we learn this - from tradition or from the Bible? The only text presented in support of this belief is Hebrews 9:27: *"And as it is appointed for men to die once, but after this the judgment."* But this passage only says what we are all in agreement with – that men will face judgment after death. This passage does not exclude the possibility of repentance and salvation after death. It only indicates that all will have to face judgment.

The Savior of the Whole World

Something we see repeated several times in different ways is that Christ is the Savior of the whole world and not just a chosen remnant.

*"And we have seen and testify that the Father has sent the Son as **Savior of the world**." (1John 4:14)*

*"this is indeed the Christ, the **Savior of the world**." (John 4:42)*

*"Behold! The Lamb of God who **takes away the sin of the world**!" (John 1:29)* [6]

*"...the bread that I shall give is My flesh, which I shall give **for the life of the world**." (John 6:51)*

*"And He Himself is the propitiation for our sins, and **not for ours only** but also **for the whole world**." (1John 2:2)*

*"who gave Himself **a ransom for all**, to be testified in due time" (1Tim 2:6)*

The Calvinists must do tremendous mental gymnastics with these and many other passages in their attempt to limit the scope of the atonement of Christ to the elect. They say, in spite of the obvious

---

[6] Note that *sin* is in singular. Jesus not only bore our *sins* on the cross but took away the *sin* which came upon the whole world through Adam.

sense of these and many other texts, that Christ is only the Savior of the elect. On the other hand, the Arminians, just as the Universalists, affirm that Christ is the Savior of all, just as the Scriptures plainly state.

The difference between the Arminians and the Universalists is that the Universalists believe that Christ will indeed accomplish His mission to save the whole world *in due time,* while the Arminians maintain that, although it is the mission of Christ to save the whole world, His sacrifice will ultimately only save a few. His sovereignty, according to them, is frustrated by the sovereignty of man's "free-will." The "free-will" of God, who desires that all be saved, ends up being limited by the "free-will" of man. Nevertheless, they are quick to point out that man loses forever his "free-will" to choose God the instant his heart stops beating, and at the same moment God also somehow loses forever His "free-will" to save them.

But is it possible for Him to be called the Savior of *all* without actually saving *all?* What would we think of someone who called himself a lifeguard but only managed to save ten percent of those needing to be rescued? Arminians say that He wants to save everyone but only saves those who know about Him and receive Him before they die; this in spite of the fact that the vast majority never even knew in life that He was their Savior or for that matter that He even existed. What would we think of a lifeguard that observes those who are drowning but remains seated without intervention because those drowning don't see him or don't ask for help, and if they go under for the last time without crying out to him, he just leaves them to die? If you see that your son has lost his way and becomes so depressed that he attempts to jump from a high building to his death; being in your power to save him, would you intervene, or would you say that out of respect for his free-will you won't do anything for him? Any loving father would say that his son isn't in his right mind, otherwise he wouldn't want to die, and would intervene, even against his free-will and would care for him until he recovered. Are we better fathers than our Father God? Does the sacrifice of Christ have no power to save beyond the grave? Is it true that there is no more opportunity to draw near to God after death? Does Christ's priestly intercession cease at the moment of death or does it continue? What does the Bible have to say about this?

> *"but He, on the other hand,* **because He abides forever, holds His priesthood permanently***.* 25 Hence, also, **He is able to**

save forever those who draw near to God through Him, *since He always lives to make intercession for them." (Heb 7:24-25 NASB)*

The priestly intercession of Christ exists for the benefit of sinners who desire to draw near to God; not for those who are already in the presence of God and free from sin. This passage is a promise to those who, still being sinners, repent and need an intercessor in order to have access to God. Jesus will always be available as the intercessor priest as long as there are sinners needing access to God.

The Calvinists recognize that God is sovereign and *can* save all, but they don't believe that God *desires* to save all. In fact, many of them would say that God hates everyone except for the elect. On the other hand, most Arminians insist that God is love and therefore loves all, and desires the salvation of all, but since He must respect man's free-will, His hands are tied.

Nevertheless, in the Scriptures we see that God is sovereign and is not limited by the "free-will" of man. In fact, the term "free-will" is never used in the Scriptures in the sense that we understand it theologically. God is fully capable of arranging circumstances and exercising sufficient influence upon the will of man to cause every man, in His time, to voluntarily bow the knee to Him and confess Him as Lord for His glory.

Jonah is a good example of how God is capable of changing an individual's "free-will." Jonah was determined not to do the will of God and what did God do? Did He say: "Well I guess I'll just have to respect Jonah's free-will?" No. He prepared a great fish and sent it to swallow Jonah whole. After three days in the great fish, which seemed to him like an eternity, Jonah, with his own "free-will" chose the will of God. Jonah is a good example of what Paul says in Philippians 2:

*"Therefore, my beloved, as you have always obeyed, not as in my presence only, but now much more in my absence, work out your own salvation with fear and trembling; 13 for **it is God who works in you both to will and to do for His good pleasure**." (Phil 2:12-13)*

As we learn from Jonah, it is better to obey sooner rather than later, because sooner or later He will produce in us both the desire and the doing according to His will. As Jesus said: *"And whoever falls on this stone will be broken; but on whomever it falls, it will grind him to powder." (Matt 21:44).* It is better to be broken doing His will now than to be ground into powder (or swallowed by a great fish) later for resisting His will.

Saul (Paul) offers us another good example of the way in which God can produce in us the will (free-will?) to do what He wills:

*"when Saul, still **breathing threats and murder against the disciples of the Lord**, went…. 3 As he journeyed he came near Damascus, and suddenly a light shone around him from heaven. 4 Then he fell to the ground, and heard a voice saying to him, 'Saul, Saul, why are you persecuting Me?' 5 And he said, 'Who are You, Lord?' Then the Lord said, "I am Jesus, whom you are persecuting. It is hard for you to kick against the goads." 6 So he, trembling and astonished, said, '**Lord, what do You want me to do**?" (Acts 9:1-6)*

One moment we see Saul *breathing threats against the disciples of the Lord.* Moments later he said: *"Lord, what do you want me to do?"* From one moment to the next God is able to cause everyone – even a Saul or a Jonah, to do His will; and in His time, He will do just that in the life of each and every individual. Jesus said:

*"And I, if I am lifted up from the earth, **will draw all ~~peoples~~ to Myself**." (John 12:32)* [7]

*"And I, if I am lifted up from the earth, I **will draw all to Myself**." (MKJV)*

The Word "draw" is *helkô* which expresses something much stronger that a simple attraction. Strong's Dictionary defines it: *"drag (literally or figuratively)."* It appears eight times in the New Testament and in each case, it expresses the idea of being drawn by a force greater than the resistance of the one being drawn:

---

[7] The word *"peoples"* is not in the Greek text but was added by the translators, allowing Calvinists to say it only refers to *"all peoples"* or *"people groups"* rather than everyone.

*"Simon Peter went up and **dragged** the net to land, full of large fish, one hundred and fifty-three; and although there were so many, the net was not broken." (John 21:11)*

*"... they seized Paul and Silas and **dragged them** into the marketplace to the authorities." (Acts 16:19)*

*".... Do not the rich oppress you and **drag** you into the courts?" (James 2:6)*

*"Then Simon Peter, having a sword, **drew** it and struck the high priest's servant, and cut off his right ear." (John 18:10)*

The other occurrence indicates that none of us would come to him if we weren't irresistibly drawn:

*"No one can come to Me unless the Father who sent Me **draws** him...." (John 6:44)*

Man, separated from God, is so lost that he must be drawn/dragged to Christ. Otherwise he would not come to Him. Our "free-will" is of no use if we can't even see or comprehend the glorious gospel, and that is the situation in which God finds every individual. They are incapable of going to Him until He, in *their day of visitation* draws them to Himself, which He will do for every man *in due time (1Peter 2:12; 1Ti 2:6 KJV)*. In His time, He will remove the veil from the eyes of every individual. Until then they remain blinded and incapable of finding Him:

*"But if our gospel be hid, it is hid to them that are lost: 4 In whom **the god of this world hath blinded the minds of them which believe not**, lest the light of the glorious gospel of Christ, who is the image of God, should shine unto them." (2Cor 4:3-4)*

*"What then? Israel has not obtained what it seeks; but the elect have obtained it, and **the rest were blinded**. 8 Just as it is written: 'God has given them a spirit of stupor, eyes that they should not see and ears that they should not hear, to this very day*.*"* *(Rom 11:7-8)*

Israel, and many other nations, are under the judgment of God, and He allows the god of this age to blind their eyes *to this very day*. If one were to stop reading here it would seem that only a remnant of Israel will ultimately be saved. But Paul afterwards asks the question:

"So I ask, ***have they stumbled so as to fall?*** *By no means! But through their stumbling salvation has come to the Gentiles, so as to make Israel jealous. 12 Now if their stumbling means riches for the world, and if their defeat means riches for Gentiles, how much more will their* ***full inclusion*** *mean!" (Rom 11:11,12 NRSV)*

Because of Israel's stumbling they were blinded, but there awaits them, in the *day of their visitation, their full inclusion* or restoration. Do not think, even for a moment, that their stumbling results in their eternal exclusion. Paul goes on to reveal a mystery in the plan of God for the ages in verses 25 thru 27:

"For I do not desire, brethren, that you should be ignorant of ***this mystery****, lest you should be wise in your own opinion,* ***that blindness in part*** *has happened to Israel* ***until*** *the fullness of the Gentiles has come in. 26 And so* **all Israel will be saved***, as it is written: 'The Deliverer will come out of Zion, and He will turn away ungodliness from Jacob; 27 For this is My covenant with them,* ***when I take away their sins.****" (Rom 11:25-27)*

The mystery that Paul reveals is that the blindness happened to Israel in order to open the way for the inclusion of the Gentiles (something the Jews would have never allowed). But then it says that *all Israel will be saved* because God will *take away their sins.* That *"all Israel"* here includes all Israel's descendants and not just the end-time generation living at Christ's Second Coming is made evident in Old Testament prophecies such as Isaiah 45 where it says:

"In the Lord **all** *the descendants of Israel shall be justified, and shall glory." (Isa 45:25)*

All the *descendants of Israel* is inclusive of all who have descended from Jacob, past, present and future. Ezekiel prophecies the time when they will all be raised from the graves and made alive, receiving the Spirit, in fulfillment of the New Covenant:

"Then He said to me, "Son of man, these bones are ***the whole house of Israel****. They indeed say, 'Our bones are dry, our hope is lost, and we ourselves are cut off!' 12 Therefore prophesy and say to them, Thus says the Lord God: 'Behold, O My people,* ***I will***

*open your graves and cause you to come up from your graves, and bring you into the land of Israel. 13 Then you shall know that I am the Lord, when I have opened your graves, O My people, and brought you up from your graves. 14 **I will put My Spirit in you, and you shall live**, and I will place you in your own land. Then you shall know that I, the Lord, have spoken it and performed it,' says the Lord." (Ezek 37:11-14)*

Paul, in Romans 11, not only reveals that all Israel will ultimately be saved; he also says that their full restoration will be followed up by an even greater blessing for the rest of the Gentile world than what we have seen in this present age:

*"Now if their stumbling means riches for the world, and if their defeat means riches for Gentiles, how **much more** will **their full inclusion** mean!" (Rom 11:12 NRSV)*

What he is here presenting is nothing less than the final restoration of all, promised since the beginning of time. Paul concludes by saying:

*"For God has committed ~~them~~ [8] **all to disobedience**, that He might have **mercy on all**. 33 **Oh, the depth of the riches both of the wisdom and knowledge of God**! How unsearchable are His judgments and His ways past finding out! 34 'For who has known the mind of the Lord? Or who has become His counselor?' 35 'Or who has first given to Him and it shall be repaid to him?' 36 **For of Him and through Him and to Him are all things**, to whom be glory forever, Amen." (Rom 11:32-36)*

I think we can also add an Amen to that!

The Purpose of God in Election

When God chose (elected) Abraham, He promised that all the nations would be blessed through his seed. Israel was chosen to represent God to the nations, but they misunderstood their election to mean that only they, the chosen people of God, would be saved. In the same way, the Church today, who are God's chosen people of this age, have come to believe that they are the only ones God plans

---

[8] *"them"* is not in the original Greek text but was added by the translators.

on saving. We, as the Church, the called out elect people of God, have fallen into the same error as the Israelites. We have misunderstood God's purpose in election.

Just as it was with Israel in the past, many in the Church today think that they were chosen *in preference* to others. But God chooses a people with a purpose for each age. His purpose in choosing Israel was to be a light to the nations but very few of them recognized that purpose. Even after the Spirit had been poured out on the Day of Pentecost, the Church continued to think that salvation was just for the Jews. God had to repeat the vision to Peter three times saying: *"What God has cleansed you must not call common,"* in order to get Peter to obey and enter the house of Cornelius, a Gentile. And even then he wasn't anticipating that God would save them and pour out His Spirit upon them, because they weren't Jews. To Paul it was revealed that in these times God is forming a Church made up of Jews and Gentiles. Are we only called to be saved, or does God have a purpose in our election as He did with the Jews before us? I believe that in Ephesians we find stated the great purpose of God for our election in this age:

"Blessed be the God and Father of our Lord Jesus Christ, who has blessed us with every spiritual blessing in the heavenly places in Christ, 4 just as **He chose us** *in Him before the foundation of the world, that we should be holy and without blame before Him in love, 5 having predestined us to adoption as sons by Jesus Christ to Himself, according to the good pleasure of His will, 6* **to the praise of the glory of His grace***, by which He made us accepted in the Beloved. 7 In Him we have redemption through His blood, the forgiveness of sins, according to the riches of His grace 8 which He made to abound toward us in all wisdom and prudence, 9* **having made known to us the mystery of His will***, according to His good pleasure which He purposed in Himself, 10* **that in the dispensation of the fullness of the times He might gather together in one all things in Christ, both which are in heaven and which are on earth — in Him***. 11 In Him also we have obtained an inheritance,* **being predestined according to the purpose of Him who works all things according to the counsel of His will,** *12 that* **we who first trusted** *in Christ should be* **to the praise of His glory***." (Eph 1:3-12)*

Here, contained in just a few verses, we discover God's glorious purpose in His election of us, the Church (the assembly of His elect).

What were we chosen for? *"For the praise of the glory of His grace" (v.6).* Our lives, transformed by His presence and grace, is going to result in the praise of the glory of His grace to the rest of mankind, and not only them but also those who are in heaven and below the earth; both visible and invisible *(2Cor 5:18-20; Col 1:16,20; Rev 5:13).* We will be light to the nations, revealing the true nature of the God of all grace.

When will this take place? At present the Church in general is a poor reflection of the grace of God with all our legalism, tradition, religiosity and carnality. The harsh reality is that the Church has fallen into the same error as the people of Israel before us, thinking that we are chosen to the *exclusion* of others, rather than seeing that we are chosen for the *benefit* of the rest of creation.

The time of the fulfillment of His purpose in our election awaits *the dispensation of the fullness of time*, when He gathers *together in one* **all things** in Christ *(v.10)*. The phrase translated "all things," as we have already seen, is just the Greek word *pas,* which simply means "all." Even when it appears in the neuter form the context alone determines whether it refers to persons, things or places. In this passage it would be best to leave out the word "things." The primary focus of God in restoration is not upon "things," as the translation "all things" would lead us to think, but upon individuals – to bring together *all in Christ*. That the restoration includes things would be secondary. In other passages we see that *pas* is sometimes used in reference to a combination of both people and things. One example is 1Corinthians 3:21-23:

> *"Therefore let no one boast in men. For* **all ~~things~~** *(pas) are yours: 22 whether Paul or Apollos or Cephas, or the world or life or death, or things present or things to come — all (pas) are yours. 23 And you are Christ's, and Christ is God's." (1Cor 3:21-23)*

Some justify the addition of our English word "things" when *pas* appears in the neuter form in Greek. However, the neuter form in Greek does not necessarily make the subject an inanimate object as in English. For example, "Holy Spirit" is neuter in Greek, as is "the Lamb", but we know that they are persons. In English "things" always exclusively refers to inanimate objects and therefore it is misleading to insert the word "things" into the translations from Greek to English, since we only associate "things" with inanimate objects in English.

It is evident that the Greek Fathers, who spoke Greek like we speak English, didn't see the neuter form of *pas* as primarily referring to things. They took "the restoration of all (pas) in Acts 3:21 as a term to represent their belief in the ultimate restoration of *all rational beings* and they used the Greek word *apokatastasis* - "restoration" as a title for their doctrinal position. In this book, I usually strike out the word "things" when people are obviously the primary focus in order to avoid confusing the real issue in salvation.

In Ephesians 1 verse 12 we see that the elect of this age, the Church, are only those **who first trusted** in Christ. This is a further indication that the rest will follow in the coming ages. James also states that we are just the first of many to follow:

*"of His own will He brought us forth by the word of truth, that we might be **a kind of firstfruits** of His creatures." (James 1:18)*

We are just the firstfruits of His new creation, chosen for the praise of the glory of His grace. The rest of the harvest follows us. We are the **Church of the firstborn** *(Heb 12:23)*. "Firstborn" is in plural form in the Greek, referring to us as the Church, and it is the word *prototokos* which, though most often used to refer to the first-born, can also mean *the first in rank, first of a kind, first production,*[9] and therefore *a mold for production, or a prototype.* Actually, our word "prototype" was derived from *prototokos.* Christ is said to be the *prototokos* of creation *(Col 1:15).* Some have mistaken this to mean that the Son was somehow born of the Father, but we know that He is equally eternal with the Father. To say that He is *eternally generated* of the Father is an anomaly. What I believe we are being told in Colossians 1:15 is that He is the "prototype" of all of creation, and we, having been made in His image, are *"the Church of the prototypes"* of His new creation. The end result is that all will ultimately be gathered together in one in Christ – one with Him – just like Him who is the prototype of prototypes. Glory to His name!

In chapter 2 of Ephesians, Paul clarifies even more what he already said in chapter one concerning God's purpose for us in the coming ages:

---

[9] *Exegetical Dictionary of the New Testament* © 1990 by William B. Eerdmans Publishing Company.

*"But God, who is rich in mercy, because of His great love with which He loved us, 5 even when we were dead in trespasses, made us alive together with Christ (by grace you have been saved), 6 and raised us up together, and made us sit together in the heavenly places in Christ Jesus, 7 **that <u>in the ages to come</u> He might show the exceeding riches of His grace in His kindness toward us in Christ Jesus**. 8 For by grace you have been saved through faith, and that not of yourselves; it is the gift of God, 9 not of works, lest anyone should boast. 10 **For we are His workmanship**, created in Christ Jesus for good works, which God prepared beforehand that we should walk in them." (Eph 2:4-10)*

In the first chapter of Ephesians it says that we were chosen for the praise of the glory of His grace. Here in chapter 2, we see that we bring praise to the glory of His grace by being a demonstration of His grace and not as a result of our works, being *His workmanship*. In chapter 1, it says that we will be manifested as trophies of His grace *in the dispensation of the fullness of time.* In chapter 2, we see that this dispensation of the fullness of time will last *for the ages to come* before entering into eternity. Returning to chapter 1, we see that the ages will continue until all ~~things~~ have been gathered together in one in Christ. All will not be one in Christ until Christ has subjected all ~~things~~ unto Himself as we see in 1Corinthians 15:26-28:

*"The last enemy that will be destroyed is death. 27 For 'He has **put all ~~things~~ under His feet**.' But when He says 'all ~~things~~ **are put under Him**,' it is evident that He who put all ~~things~~ under Him is excepted. 28 Now **when all ~~things~~ are made subject to Him**, then the Son Himself will also be subject to Him who put all ~~things~~ under Him, **that God may be all in all**." (1Cor 15:26-28)*

Here, we see Paul saying the same thing, only with different words. He said in Ephesians that all that is in heaven and on earth will be reunited in Christ. Here, he expresses it by saying that *all will be made subject to Him*. However, here he reveals what will take place after that. He says that, when all ~~things~~ are made *subject* to Him, then He himself will be *subject* to the Father *that God may be all in all*. Paul here is describing the end of time – the end of the ages, when God becomes *all in all* in eternity. The reality of God being *all in all* does not leave room for an eternal hell after the end of the ages. The story of the ages ends by saying in essence: *"And they lived happily ever after, Amen!"*

The Manifestation of the Sons of God

"The Spirit Himself bears witness with our spirit that we are children of God, 17 and if children, then heirs — heirs of God and joint heirs with Christ, if indeed we suffer with Him, that we may also be glorified together. 18 For I consider that the sufferings of this present time are not worthy to be compared with **the glory which shall be revealed in us**. **19 For the earnest expectation of the creation eagerly waits for the revealing of the sons of God**. **20 For the creation was subjected to futility, not willingly, but because of Him who subjected it in hope**; **21 because the creation itself also will be delivered from the bondage of corruption into the glorious liberty of the children of God**. *22 For we know that* **the whole creation** *groans and labors with birth pangs together until now. 23 Not only that, but we also who have the firstfruits of the Spirit, even we ourselves groan within ourselves, eagerly waiting for the adoption, the redemption of our body." (Rom 8:16-24)*

Just as in Ephesians and 1Corinthians 15, here Paul also speaks of a universal restoration of *the whole creation*. However, in this passage he gives more details concerning this universal reconciliation. Here we see that the present time is for the preparation of the sons of God for the coming glory, when the co-heirs with Christ in His coming kingdom - the trophies of His grace, will be manifested to the rest of creation *(v.18)*. As we saw in James 1:18, we are only the firstfruits of the rest of creation which will be restored. It will be a total restoration of God's creation. No part of God's creation will remain in ruins forever. There is no such thing as an "eternal garbage dump" where God in eternity perpetually burns that which is useless. When God, who inhabits eternity, saw all that He had made, He said that it was *"very good." (Gen 1:31)*. We should keep in mind that the eternal God was viewing the whole panorama of the ages, and not just the beginning when He exclaimed: *"Indeed it is very good!"*

Since the beginning of time God had a plan which included the fall and also the restoration of all He was going to create. He had even preordained the futility to which the creation would be subjected: *"the creation was subjected to futility, not willingly, but*

because of Him *who subjected it in hope." (v. 20).* It was *because of Him* who works all things according to the council of His will, that creation was subjected to futility. None of us are sinners by our own choice; we were born in this condition. The only human being to whom we could place the blame for our condition is Adam and God gave to him and Eve a promise that one day Eve's seed – Jesus, would destroy the works of the enemy *(Gen 3:15).* If God promised restoration to the only man to whom we could possibly blame for our condition – the first Adam, how can it be possible that He will not ultimately restore all those in Adam through Christ – the last Adam? *(Rom 5:15-21; 1Cor 15:21,22).*

There is much discussion concerning the mystery of the existence of evil in God's creation. No matter how we may attempt to place the blame for its existence upon Satan, we all know that God created Lucifer, not only with the potential for conceiving evil, but also knowing beforehand that he was going to rebel and assume the role of our adversary. God is eternally omniscient and everything - absolutely everything, has always been working out according to His eternal plan for the ages, predetermined before creation. He *works all things according to the counsel of His will. (Eph 1:11).* "*Known to God from eternity are all His works." (Acts 15:18).*

What many are not aware of, or are unable to accept, is that God takes responsibility for the existence of evil. In Isaiah 45:6,7 God declares:

"That they may know from the rising of the sun, and from the west, that there is none beside me. I am the Lord, and there is none else. 7 **I form the light, and create darkness: I make peace, and create evil**: *I the Lord do all these things." (Isa 45:6-7 KJV)*

The Word "evil" is the Hebrew word *rá,* which usually expresses moral evil and is contrasted with peace. He accepts responsibility for the beginning of evil and also determines its end. It is irrational to think that the eternal plan of the all loving God would culminate in 90% ruin, with all except for a few elect burning in eternal flames or being exterminated. It is irreconcilable with His love, wisdom and foreknowledge to initiate a plan that would end so tragically.

How could a God of love, seeing the beginning and such a tragic ending for the vast majority, permit the existence of evil in His creation – much less create it? How could a God who is Love, see the final ruinous end of the work of His hands and say with great satisfaction: *"It is all very good."* Such a scenario is unthinkable! But if we could just see that the plan of God for the ages does not end in perpetual ruins, but rather with a total restoration that consummates with God being *all in all;* and if we can see that He Himself subjected creation to futility in hope of a glorious restoration of all, then it all begins to make sense.

God wouldn't have allowed the fall of Lucifer and He wouldn't have placed the tree of the knowledge of good and evil in Eden if He didn't also have a full restitution included in His plan. In the Law that God gave to Israel were included laws concerning restitution. These laws make each individual responsible for his actions. One of them says:

> *"And if a man shall open a pit, or if a man shall dig a pit, and not cover it, and an ox or an ass fall therein, the owner of the pit shall make it good...." (Ex 21:33 KJV)*

God placed the tree in the middle of Eden and permitted the serpent to tempt Eve. It is to be anticipated that God who gave us the law requiring the restitution of an ass falling into an uncovered pit, would also have a plan for the ages which also includes the restitution of all. And the one responsible for having left the pit uncovered is the one who must make restitution. The traditional view is comparable to making the ass responsible for having fallen in the pit and also ultimately the one responsible for his own restoration. But according to the psalmist, the One who placed the tree in the center of the garden is the one who will make restitution of all things.

> *"You turn man to destruction, and say, 'Return, O children of men." (Ps 90:3)*

The plan of God for the ages in the time between the creation and the restoration is to give us the opportunity of knowing the dimensions of His love, of His grace and His mercy. He created us in His image and likeness with the capacity to know Him as none other of His creatures possibly could. The plan of God is to prepare a people capable of an intimate relationship with Himself. Adam and Eve in their original state of innocence, before the fall, were flawless but not yet perfect or fully developed morally with God's positive holiness rather than mere innocence. In their innocent state they were incapable of knowing God intimately. In our humanity we can only be perfected or made complete through suffering *(Heb 5:8,9; James 1:2-4; 1Peter 4:13; Phil 1:29; 2Cor 4:10,11; 12:10, etc.)*. It was necessary to have the adversary, and to fall into disobedience and suffering in order to really know our redeeming God of love, grace and mercy. Even now, still in our fallen condition, we can praise God for His mercy and grace only because we have come to know those dimensions of His love through the fall.

Adam and Eve were not yet able to intimately know God fully, and they would have never been capable of such knowledge if it were not for the fall. Upon entering eternity all will be lovingly submitted to God and He will be *all in all (1Cor 15:28)*. Then we shall be capable of knowing Him even as we are known by Him: *"for now we see in a mirror, dimly, but then face to face. Now I know in part, but then I shall know just as I also am known." (1Cor 13:12)*.

Our election at the present time is in order to be the firstfruits. We are being prepared for the moment for which we all have awaited – indeed the whole creation awaits it – *the manifestation of the sons of God*. In the ages to come, we will display *the exceeding riches of His grace in His kindness toward us in Christ, to the praise of the glory of His grace (Eph 2:7; 1:6)*. Then all of creation will come to know Him and will *be delivered from the bondage of corruption into the glorious liberty of the sons of God (Rom 8:21)*. Then *every knee will bow, of those in heaven, and of those on earth, and of those under the earth, and every tongue will confess that Jesus Christ is Lord, to the glory of God the Father (Phil 2:10-11)*.

God does not forget our suffering. He has a book of remembrance and stores all our tears in His bottle. All suffering endured in this brief life will be richly compensated by God. Paul says:

> *"Therefore we do not lose heart. Even though our outward man is perishing, yet the inward man is being renewed day by day. 17 For our light affliction, which is but for a moment, is working for us a far more exceeding and eternal weight of glory, 18 while we do not look at the things which are seen, but at the things which are not seen. For the things which are seen are temporary, but the things which are not seen are eternal." (2Cor 4:16-18)*

Once we come to understand that God has a good purpose in permitting evil and suffering, it becomes much easier to embrace our pain and suffering as a treasure greater than silver or gold which perish, and we can begin to *grow* through our trials rather than simply *go* through them. Once we are able to see God's overall plan for the ages, from the creation to the restitution of all, we can only exclaim with Paul: *"Oh, the depth of the riches both of the wisdom and knowledge of God! How unsearchable are His judgments and His ways past finding out!" (Rom 11:33).*

The Universal Restoration

As I shared in the introduction, the text that the Lord used to remove the veil allowing me to see the contradictions with the traditional doctrine of eternal punishment was the message of Simon Peter on Solomon's Porch:

*"Repent therefore and be converted, that your sins may be blotted out, so that **times of refreshing** may come from the presence of the Lord, 20 and that He may send Jesus Christ, who was preached to you before, 21 whom heaven must receive **until the times of restoration of all things, which God has spoken by the mouth of all His holy prophets since the world began**." (Acts 3:19-22)*

As I meditated upon the meaning of this text, I realized that the early Church anticipated a *total* restoration of *all,* which was foreseen by the prophets since the beginning of the world. Also, I saw that the beginning of this restoration corresponds with *times of refreshing,* which will commence just prior to Christ's Second Coming. The traditional response, as usual, is to say that *"all"* does not mean *"all."* However, this time I was not willing to settle for this "explanation." I began to seek out the passages where the prophets had prophesied a total restoration. The first I found, as I already explained, was what Peter himself cited as an example in the same sermon:

*"You are sons of the prophets, and of the covenant which God made with our fathers, saying to Abraham, 'And **in your seed all the families of the earth shall be blessed**." (Acts 3:25)*

Reflecting upon this I observed two important implications: 1) If all the families of the earth are blessed by Jesus Christ, the seed of Abraham, then no individual is excluded. No family could be called blessed if any member of their family was eternally excluded without possibility of restoration. 2) In saying *"all the families will be blessed"* he was not making reference only to future families, but rather every family that has ever existed since the beginning. This is a promise of universal reach, just as was that of the promised seed of Eve that would come and destroy the enemy and bring restoration. It is a promise of universal restoration and in His due time, *all* the families of the earth will enjoy its fulfillment.

With my eyes now opened to the possibility of a universal restoration, I began to look in the Old Testament and was amazed to discover the abundance of references to a universal restoration. Here are some examples:

*"**All** the ends of the world shall remember and turn to the Lord, and **all** the families of the nations shall worship before You." (Ps 22:27)*

All the earth and all the families worshiping God together! How glorious! There comes a point at which it almost seems blasphemous to continue insisting that "all" doesn't mean *"all."* When it is necessary to repeat this qualification so often in order to limit the universal declarations of the Scriptures, it begins to look as though they are making God out to be a liar; like invalidating His Word in order to protect their traditions.

Some argue that, when we see *"all"* in these passages on universal restoration, it is just hyperbolic speech and shouldn't be taken literally. They cite examples of exaggerated speech such as: *"Then **all** the land of Judea, and those from Jerusalem, went out to him and were **all** baptized by him in the Jordan River, confessing their sins." (Mark 1:5).* However, common sense tells us when one is speaking literally or hyperbolically. If I were to say: *"**All** of Oakland came to the meeting,"* or *"the **whole** world knows that she is the best singer,"* we instantly know that it is exaggerated, hyperbolic speech used for greater impact. On the other hand, if the captain of a sinking ship were to say to those aboard: *"The ship is sinking, but don't worry, you will **all** be saved,"* could we still rationally say it is hyperbole? Will God someday reveal to us that His promises to save and restore *all* are deliberate exaggerations? Of course not! How could we even attribute such a deception to God?

The traditional doctrine of eternal punishment for the majority, can make us become like the scribes who *shut up the kingdom of heaven against men; neither entering themselves, nor allowing those who would enter to go in (Matt 23:13).* Continuing my search, I found many more universal passages:

*"Say to God, 'how awesome are Your works! Through the greatness of Your power **your enemies shall submit themselves to You**. 4 **All the earth shall worship You and sing praises to You**; they shall sing praises to Your name." (Ps 66:3-4)* [10]

What will happen to all the enemies of God? Someday, *every* knee (including His enemies) will bow in submission and worship God and they will *all* praise Him! So much for limiting the sovereignty of God by our "sovereign free-will!"

*"Yes, **all** kings shall fall down before Him; **all nations** shall serve Him." (Ps 72:11)*

*"**All** nations **whom You have made shall come and worship before You**, O Lord, and **shall glorify Your name**." (Ps 86:9)*

*"**All the kings of the earth shall praise You**, O Lord, when they hear the words of Your mouth." (Ps 138:4)*

In saying *"all the kings of the earth"* it is not to the exclusion of the rest of mankind. Kings are often singled out by the psalmist as examples to emphasize all of mankind, since kings, due to their exalted position, would be the last ones to hear the words of the Lord and bow the knee to Him in worship.

*"Jehovah is gracious, and merciful; slow to anger, and of great loving-kindness. 9 **Jehovah is good to all; and his tender mercies are over all his works**. 10 **All thy works shall give thanks unto thee**, O Jehovah; and thy saints shall bless thee." (Ps 145:8-10 ASV)*

Not only will every knee bow worshipping Him and sing praises to Him, but **all he has created** will give thanks to Him!

---

[10] The word for *"submit"* in this verse normally refers to a feigned submission. However, there are no words in Hebrew which express true, voluntary submission. Here it is the context itself which determines its meaning as true submission and adoration in spite of its normal meaning.

*"And in this mountain the Lord of hosts will make for **all** people, a feast of choice pieces, a feast of wines on the lees, of fat things full of marrow, of well-refined wines on the lees. 7 And He will destroy on this mountain, the surface of **the covering cast over all** people, and the veil that is spread over **all** nations. 8 **He will swallow up death forever**, and **the Lord God will wipe away tears from all faces**…" (Isa 25:6-8)*

God will wipe away tears from *all* faces and there will be no more death. He will destroy death forever. How is it possible to confess this, and at the same time maintain that the second death is eternal? The last enemy to be destroyed is death. Are we to believe that the second death will never come to an end nor be destroyed – that it will still exist in eternity when God will be all in all?

*"**Look to Me, and be saved, all you ends of the earth**! For I am God, and there is no other. 23 **I have sworn by Myself; The word has gone out of My mouth in righteousness, and shall not return, that to Me every knee shall bow, every tongue shall take an oath**. 24 He shall say, '**Surely in the Lord I have righteousness and strength**.' To Him men shall come, and all shall be ashamed who are incensed against Him." (Isa 45:22-24)*

The Lord God Almighty is not limited by our "free-will." When He says, *"look to Me and be saved,"* every knee shall bow, and every tongue will make an oath of loyalty to Him. Sooner or later all His enemies shall be ashamed for having been incensed against Him. Could it really be that this will eventually include *"all"* as stated or does it exclude people like Adolph Hitler?

*"No more shall every man teach his neighbor, and every man his brother, saying, 'Know the Lord,' for they **all shall know Me**, from the least of them to the greatest of them, says the Lord. For I will forgive their iniquity, and their sin I will remember no more." (Jer 31:34)*

*"However, **I will restore the fortunes of <u>Sodom</u> and her daughters and of <u>Samaria</u> and her daughters, and your fortunes along with them**, 54 so that you may bear your disgrace and be ashamed of all you have done in giving them comfort. 55 **And your sisters, <u>Sodom</u> with her daughters and <u>Samaria</u> with her daughters, will return to what they were***

> *before; and you and your daughters will return to what you were before....* Yet I will remember the covenant I made with you in the days of your youth, and I will establish an everlasting covenant with you. 61 Then you will remember your ways and be ashamed **when you receive your sisters, both those who are older than you and those who are younger.** I will give them to you as daughters, but not on the basis of my covenant with you." *(Ezek 16:53-55; 60,61 NIV)* [11]

How amazing! When the Lord says: *"Look to Me and be saved all you ends of the earth" (Isa 45:22)*, it means *"all,"* even including Sodom and Samaria, the younger and elder sisters of Judah! This was how the early Greek fathers understood this passage as we see expressed by Saint Jerome (AD 347 to AD 420): *"Israel and all heretics, because they had the works of Sodom and Gomorrah, are overthrown like Sodom and Gomorrah, that they may be set free like a brand snatched from the burning. And this is the meaning of the prophet's words, 'Sodom shall be restored as of old,' that he who by his vice is as an inhabitant of Sodom, after the works of Sodom have been burnt in him, may be restored to his ancient state."* [12]

> "Then to Him was given dominion and glory and a kingdom, **that all peoples, nations, and languages should serve Him**. His dominion is an everlasting dominion, which shall not pass away, and His kingdom the one which shall not be destroyed." (Dan 7:14)

Universal Reconciliation

> "For by (en) Him **all** ~~things~~ were created that are **in heaven** and that are **on earth**, **visible** and **invisible**, whether **thrones** or **dominions** or **principalities** or **powers**. All ~~things~~ were created through Him and for Him. 17 And He is before all ~~things~~, and in Him all ~~things~~ consist. 18 And He is the head of the body, the

---

[11] The King James Translators began verses 53 and 55 by adding "when" in order to imply an uncertain future fulfillment rather than translating it as it is: *"I will restore,"* which makes future fulfillment certain.

[12] J.W. HANSON, D. D. Universalism The Prevailing Doctrine Of The Christian Church During Its First Five Hundred   Years. http://www.tentmaker.org/books/

church, who is the beginning, the firstborn from the dead, that in all ~~things~~ He may have the preeminence. 19 For it pleased the Father that in Him all the fullness should dwell, 20 **and by Him to reconcile <u>all</u> ~~things~~ to Himself**, *by Him, whether ~~things~~* **on earth** *or ~~things~~* **in heaven**, *having made peace through the blood of His cross."* [13]

"21 And you, who once were alienated and enemies in your mind by wicked works, yet now He has reconciled." (Col 1:16-21)

Here we see that the Creator of *all* is also the One who reconciles *all*. It is very clear that the "all" in this passage is indeed "all" without any exclusion. It includes all that is in heaven and all that is on the earth; that which is visible and also that which is invisible; whether they be visible thrones or invisible thrones, visible dominions or invisible dominions, visible principalities or invisible principalities, visible powers or invisible powers – all here definitely means "all" and that's all *"all"* means. It leaves no bases uncovered. But the passage doesn't end with the creation of all. It ends with the reconciliation of that same "all" included in the creation; whether it be on earth or in heaven – *all* was reconciled through the blood of His cross. Paul says:

"Now **all** ~~things~~ *are of God, who has reconciled us to Himself through Jesus Christ, and* **has given us the ministry of reconciliation**, *19 that is, that God was in Christ* **reconciling the <u>world</u> to Himself, not imputing their trespasses to <u>them</u>, and has committed to <u>us</u> the word of reconciliation**. *20 Now then, we are ambassadors for Christ, as though God were pleading through us: we implore you on Christ's behalf, be reconciled to God. 21 For He made Him who knew no sin to be sin for us, that we might become the righteousness of God in Him." (2Cor 5:18-20)*

It is not possible for us to say, in the light of these passages, that God reconciled us, the elect, but not the rest. Paul seems to invert this reasoning when, after emphasizing with great detail that God

---

[13] Our English word *"things"* does not have an equivalent in Greek. Neither does the neuter form in Greek always indicate objects as in English. When the translators insert "things" in contexts that are evidently referring primarily to persons and not inanimate objects I take the liberty to cross it out in order to keep the focus where it belongs.

reconciled all of creation through the blood of the cross of Christ, afterwards says, almost as an afterthought: *"Oh, and you also He has reconciled" (Col 1:21)*. We have only been chosen to tell the good news of reconciliation to the rest. We have the privilege and the responsibility as the manifest sons of God, to reign with Christ until all have been reconciled and submitted unto Him. We were chosen to be His ambassadors of reconciliation to proclaim the message of reconciliation to all the captives, whether they be visible or invisible, in heaven or on earth, and yes, even those who are under the earth, will one day confess that Jesus Christ is Lord, to the glory of God *(Philippians 2:10)*. Upon arriving at the end of the ages, all will have become subject to Him and then God will be all in all. Praise His holy name!

The Destiny of Fallen Spirits

> *"**Look to Me, and be saved, all you ends of the earth**! For I am God, and there is no other. 23 **I have sworn by Myself; The word has gone out of My mouth in righteousness, and shall not return, that to Me every knee shall bow, every tongue shall take an oath**. 24 He shall say, '**Surely in the Lord I have righteousness and strength**.' To Him men shall come, and all shall be ashamed who are incensed against Him." (Isa 45:22-24)*

When I cited this passage earlier, I presented the question as to whether or not it would include Adolph Hitler. The answer should be obvious. If God swore by Himself that every knee will bow before Him and every tongue shall take an oath, this must include all - even Hitler. That is not to say that people like him will escape justice. God will mete out justice and only He knows how to do it. Again, we must confess with Paul: *"How unsearchable are His judgments and His ways past finding out! (Rom 11:33)*. However, we can rest assured that His judgments will be just and not eternal in duration.

The question we must resolve from the Scriptures is: What will become of Satan and the fallen angels? Will they continue for all eternity in outer darkness in opposition to God remaining with 90% of mankind? ¿Will there exist an eternal dualism - Satan in opposition to God, the kingdom of darkness against the kingdom of light, good against evil? Would that be a total victory for Christ?

Many who believe in a universal restoration and have written on the subject have avoided entirely any comments concerning the destiny of Satan and the fallen angels. I believe that some have not mentioned it because they do not believe that universal reconciliation could be so inclusive as to include even them. Others have preferred to not make declarations concerning the subject because they are not sure. But I believe that the majority do not bring up the subject of a restoration in the heavens because of the scandal that presenting this position could occasion among those who are so deeply rooted in the traditional doctrine of an eternal dualism that they are not even open to considering the Scriptural evidence.

I myself am fully convinced that this is precisely what the Bible presents, and therefore I feel the obligation to communicate what I consider to be the whole plan of God for the ages. Some, including myself, would prefer not to be controversial. However I, along with many of them, feel the need to communicate the Word of God as we have come to understand it regardless of the possible reactions of some, and I believe that we are doing the same that Paul said that he did: *"...I did not shrink from declaring to you the **whole** counsel of God." (Acts 20:27).*

Before the dualistic theology of Saint Augustine was popularized, several Greek fathers of the early Church did not hesitate to declare a universal restoration that included Lucifer and the fallen angels. Clement of Alexandria (AD 150 to AD 215) said: *"Therefore He indeed saves all universally; but some as converted by punishments, others by voluntary submission, thus obtaining the honor and dignity, that '**to Him every knee shall bow, of things in heaven, and things in earth, and things under the earth,' that is angels, and men**, and souls who departed this life before His coming into the world."* [14]

Origin, the successor of Clement, whose writings have been the most read of all the Church fathers with the exception of Saint Augustine, said: *"It is our conviction that the Word will prevail over **all the intelligent creation**."* [15] Commenting on Ephesians 1, Ambrose of Milan (AD 340 to AD 397), said: *"This seemed well to God...to manifest in Christ His will... specifically that He would be*

---

[14] Clement of Alexandria, *Comentary of 1John Adumbrat.* in Ep. I Johan., printed at the end of his Treatise, Quis dives salvetur, p.1009, Potter's Edit.

[15] Origin, *Against Selsum* 8.72.

merciful to **all who had been lost, whether it be in heaven or on earth**... **Every being**, then, in the heavens and on the earth are being restored as they were created until they come to know Christ." In his commentary on 1Corinthians 15:27 he says: *"When **every creature** learns that Christ is his head, and that the head of Christ is the Father, then God will be all in all; that is to say that **every creature** will believe in the same way, and that of one voice every tongue of the things **in heaven, on the earth and beneath the earth** will confess that there is one God of whom are all things."* [16]

Gregory of Nyssa (AD 330 to AD 394) wrote: *"Christ... not only delivers man from evil, but also **heals the very inventor of evil**."* [17] Jerome (AD 347 to AD 420) said: *"The cross of Christ has benefited **not only the earth but also heaven**... and **every creature** has been purified by the blood of his Lord. Therefore in the restoration of all things, when the true physician, Jesus Christ, has come to heal the body of the whole church, **every being**...will receive his due place...What I am saying is, the **fallen angels will become as they were created**, and humanity which has been expelled from paradise, will be once again restored to the place of caring for paradise. These things, then, will take place on **a universal level**."* [18] *"Most persons regard the story of Jonah as teaching the ultimate forgiveness of **all rational creatures, even the devil**."* [19] *"<u>**The apostate angels, and the prince of this world, and Lucifer**</u>, the morning star, though now ungovernable, licentiously wandering about, and plunging themselves into the depths of sin, **shall in the end, embrace the happy dominion of Christ and his saints**... No rational creature before God will perish forever."* [20]

Why is it that the early church fathers, especially those before the influence of Saint Augustine, taught this? I believe that they were simply affirming what the Scriptures teach without the influence of

---

[16] Allin, *Universalism Asserted*, p. 133.

[17] Gregory of Nissa, *Catechetical Oraciones*, Cap. 26.

[18] Allin, *Universalism Asserted*, p. 134.

[19] Jerome. In Ps. xcii. 9.22

[20] Jerome. In Ps. xcii. 9.22

traditional doctrine imposed by the Institutionalized Church in later centuries.

It is significant that the same prophet Isaiah, who mentions the fall of Lucifer in chapter 14, in chapter 45 verse 22 – 24, says that God has sworn that *all* of His enemies will be ashamed and take an oath of loyalty. Perhaps taken alone one might argue that it is only referring to men, but when we compare it with Paul's citation of the same passage, we see that it clearly refers to every rational being without any possibility of exceptions:

*"Therefore God also has highly exalted Him and given Him the name which is above every name, 10 that at the name of Jesus **every knee** should bow, of those **in heaven**, and of those **on earth**, and of those **under the earth**, 11 and that **every tongue** should confess that Jesus Christ is Lord, to the glory of God the Father." (Phil 2:9-11)*

So, we see that it is not just those on earth that will confess Jesus Christ as Lord, but also all that are in heaven and under the earth as well. Some argue that it will be an obligated confession. But comparing this text with its parallel in Isaiah, we see that it is not obligatory; all will return to Him and will be saved, making an oath of loyalty. Also, Paul says that it is for the glory of God the Father. What glory would the Almighty God get from obligating a confession? Maybe a tyrant with an authority complex would glory in seeing his enemies humiliated; prostrated in obligatory subjection, but Almighty God, who is Love, only receives glory in converting His enemies into loyal friends, to the praise of the glory of His grace:

*"Say to God, 'How awesome are Your works!' Through the greatness of Your power **your enemies shall submit themselves to You**. 4 **All the earth shall worship You and sing praises to You**; They shall sing praises to Your name." (Ps 66:3-4)* [21]

---

[21] The word for *"submit"* in this verse normally refers to a feigned submission. However, there are no words in Hebrew expressing true, voluntary submission. The context determines its meaning as true submission and adoration in spite of its normal meaning.

All His enemies will submit themselves to Him and worship Him. Does this sound like forced submission to you? [22]

---

[22] Paul also quotes from Isaiah 45 *("every knee shall bow....")* in Romans 14. Some, failing to see the context of the passage, have understood it as indicating that everyone will find themselves obligated to bow the knee at some general judgment at the end of time. However, upon examining the context, we see that Paul isn't even talking about the Great White Throne Judgment, as many think, but rather he is talking to brothers in Christ who were in disagreement with one another concerning the need to continue observing dietary restrictions and the Jewish Sabbath. In the context, he is telling the brethren to stop judging one another concerning these non-essentials, leaving all such judgment to God, before whom we all must ultimately bow in submission. He tells them:

*"But why do you judge **your brother**? Or why do you show contempt for **your brother**? For we shall all stand before the judgment seat of Christ. 11 For it is written: 'As I live, says the Lord, every knee shall bow to Me, and every tongue shall confess to God.' 12 So then each of us shall give account of himself to God. 13 Therefore let us not judge **one another** anymore, but rather resolve this, not to put a stumbling block or a cause to fall in **our brother's** way." (Rom 14:10-13)*

Those in view here are only believers – brothers in Christ. Paul makes it clear that those being addressed; no matter what side of the debate they were on, were already accepted by God in verse 3. The Judgment in view here is the Bema Seat Judgment, and not the Great White Throne Judgment, 1,000 years after His coming for His Church. The Bema Judgment is for reward or loss of reward *(1Cor 3:11-15),* and its purpose is that each and every one of His children might receive praise from Him. *(1Cor 4:5)* There is no condemnation for those who are in Christ Jesus. *(Rom 8:1; John 5:24,25)* We shall be resurrected and appear before Him in the resurrection unto life – not the resurrection unto condemnation 1,000 years later. *(John 5:28,29; Rev 20:4-6)*

The reference to Isaiah 45 by Paul in this passage, was in order to emphasize that all - even including us as believers, will eventually come into agreement with God and bend the knee to Christ, confessing Him as Lord. The word *"confess"* in Romans 14:11 is the same as in 1John 1:9: *"If we confess our sins He is faithful and just to forgive us and cleanse us from all unrighteousness,"* except that it is the strengthened form of the word *"confess."* In 1John 1:9 it is *homologeo,* which means "to confess or come into agreement." In this instance it is *exomologeo,* which means *"to fully agree with."* Everyone, including us as believers, and all who are in heaven, on earth and under the earth, will come into full agreement with God, but each one in his own order - not at the same time. Only when the last knee

In Colossians one, we see that there is reconciliation in the heavens. *(Col 1:16-18)* Among all those reconciled in heaven we see thrones, dominions, principalities and powers. What principalities exist in heaven that are in need of reconciliation? We see at least one in the book of Job:

"Now there was a day when the sons of God came to present themselves before the Lord, and Satan also came among them. 7 And the Lord said to Satan, 'From where do you come?" (Job 1:6-7)

It is Satan and the fallen angels under his command in heaven who are in need of reconciliation. There are no others in heaven in need of reconciliation except for them. Satan still accuses us before God just as he did with Job *(Rev 12:10)*. He, and the fallen angels under him, are the invisible thrones, dominions, principalities and powers which are in heaven and in rebellion against God, needing reconciliation. The angels of God who serve Him are not in need of reconciliation. We see the same groupings of fallen spirits mentioned in Ephesians 6:12:

*"For we do not wrestle against flesh and blood, but against **principalities**, against **powers**, against the **rulers of the darkness** of this age, against **spiritual hosts** of wickedness in the **heavenly places**." (Eph 6:12)*

Also, we see in Ephesians 3:10:

*"to the intent that now the manifold wisdom of God might be **made known by the church to the principalities and powers in the heavenly places**." (Eph 3:10)*

---

has bowed in subjection to Christ, will He then subject Himself to the Father, and then God will be all in all.

I don't see the fulfillment of Isaiah 45 as happening in a moment's time, such as at the Second Coming of Christ, or the White Throne Judgment, 1,000 years later. We, as believers, will come into full agreement with God when we stand before Him. Others will come into agreement with Him at the Great White Throne Judgment, but not all. Most will continue in defiance for ages, but God has sworn that eventually every knee will bow and every tongue in heaven; on earth and under the earth will confess Jesus as Lord.

We are already positionally and spiritually seated in the heavenly places with Christ:

*"and raised us up together, and **made us sit together in the heavenly places in Christ Jesus**, 7 **that in the ages to come He might show** the exceeding riches of His grace in His kindness toward us in Christ Jesus." (Eph 2:6-7)*

We see here that we are seated in the same heavenly sphere where they operate. It is there that God is going to demonstrate or *show* the glory of His grace through the Church, and those that are in heaven will also come to know His grace. God has made reconciliation also for them, having made peace through the blood of His cross, and we are His ministers of reconciliation; not only to those on earth but also - in the coming ages, to those who are under the earth and in the heavens.

If one were to argue that Satan and his angels will not be in heaven in the future, but under the earth, that doesn't exclude them either because *every knee* will bow, those that are *in heaven and in the earth and **under the earth**, and every tongue shall confess that Jesus Christ is Lord.* This confession will come from the Holy Spirit because no one can truly confess Jesus as Lord except by the Holy Spirit *(1Cor 12:3)*. No one in all of God's creation will be excluded. There is nowhere to hide from His Spirit and from His presence: *"If I ascend into heaven, You are there; If I make my bed in hell (sheol), behold, You are there." (Ps 139:8)*. When it says "all" in heaven, and on earth and below the earth; visible and invisible, it is all inclusive, it doesn't leave anything out in all of God's creation. Not even Lucifer is excluded. Although it is true that, at least for some, the lake of fire will last ~~forever and ever~~ (lit. "into the ages of the ages"), the Greek phrase *eis tous aionos ton aionon* does not refer to eternity but rather to a measure of time. Eternity is a reality that has always existed apart from time and therefore cannot be measured by hours, days, years, centuries and ages. We will see this in more detail in chapter five.

So far, we have clearly seen from the Scriptures that all God created through Christ He also reconciled to Him *by the blood of His cross (Col 1:20)*. There is a text that, taken by itself, *could* be interpreted as meaning that Satan and his angels are not included in the reconciliation that God provided in Christ: *"For indeed He does not give aid to angels, but He does give aid to the seed of Abraham."*

(Heb 2:16-17). How should we understand this text? Does it invalidate all we have seen so far? Let's look at the verse in its context:

> *"Inasmuch then as the children have partaken of flesh and blood, He Himself likewise shared in the same, that through death He might destroy him who had the power of death, that is, the devil, 15 and release those who through fear of death were all their lifetime subject to bondage. 16 For indeed* **He does not give aid to angels, but He does give aid to the seed of Abraham***. 17 Therefore, in all things He had to be made like His brethren, that He might be* **a merciful and faithful High Priest** *in things pertaining to God, to make propitiation for the sins of the people. 18 For in that He Himself has suffered, being tempted,* **He is able to aid those who are tempted***." (Heb 2:14-18)*

In the first place, it only mentions the *"seed of Abraham."* We know that Jesus Christ is the Savior of the whole world and not just the seed of Abraham. God's salvation also includes those who lived before Abraham and all the families who have ever been upon the earth among the nations. We also know from the Scriptures that all of creation will benefit from Christ's victory and not just mankind. Romans 8:20,21 says that *all creation* will be delivered in the time of the manifestation of the Sons of God, and that includes all things created in the heavens and things invisible. The invisible in heaven must be referring to Lucifer and the fallen angels because there are no others invisible in heaven that are in need of reconciliation except for them *(Col 1:18-20)*.

What then is the aid Christ came to give which didn't include the angels? He came to destroy *their* works – the works of the devil, and free the descendants of Abraham from *their* bondage to Satan, which began at the fall of Adam. He didn't come to give aid to the devil, nor to the angels that followed him in his rebellion against God. He came to give aid *from* them and not *for* them. He is the merciful and faithful High Priest who always lives to intercede for us *against* the accuser of the brethren, the devil. *He is able to aid those who are tempted* by the tempter – the devil. What this passage tells us is that His ministry, especially in this age, is to help us against *their* attacks. However, we have already seen that the reconciliation accomplished on the cross includes them, and before Christ submits Himself to the Father at the end of the ages, all of His enemies will have submitted themselves to Him *(Col 1:18-20; 1Cor 15:25-28),* making it a reality that God will be *all in all* in eternity. All, in heaven, on the earth and under the earth will have bowed the knee and every tongue will have confessed Him as Lord. To Him be the power and the glory, forever and forever; Amen!

> *"And **every creature which is in heaven and on the earth and under the earth** and such as are in the sea, and all that are in them, I heard saying: 'Blessing and honor and glory and power be to Him who sits on the throne, and to the Lamb, forever and ever!"* (Rev 5:13)

In this vision, John the Revelator saw a time when *every creature* - whether *in heaven* or *on the earth*, will give honor and glory to the Father and to the Lamb. What he foresaw was a vision of all of creation prepared to enter the eternal state, when all will have become subject to the Lamb and God will be all in all at the end of the ages.

So, to summarize, we have seen that the scope of the gospel is inclusive of all mankind and therefore brings great joy and peace to our hearts knowing that God has good-will towards us all. *"Then the angel said to them, 'Do not be afraid, for behold, I bring you good tidings of great joy which will be **to all people**... 14 'Glory to God in the highest, and on earth peace, **goodwill toward men**!" (Luke 2:10,14)*. Also we have seen that the gospel does not only include mankind but has a universal all-encompassing reach that includes all of God's creation, even including fallen angels and Satan himself. In the end of the ages, nothing in all of God's creation will be eternally in ruins, but rather all things will have been restored to Himself. *"For of Him and through Him and **to** Him are all things." (Rom 11:36)*. All that has its beginning in Him will end up in Him again when all is said and done.

In chapters four and five we will examine what the Scriptures have to say about the purpose, nature and duration of hell. But we have already seen that the abundant testimony of Scriptures confirms a universal restoration.

Chapter two
Christ the Last Adam

> *"But the free gift is not like the offense. For if by the one man's offense many died, **much more** the grace of God and the gift by the grace of the one Man, Jesus Christ, abounded (periseuo – "super-abound") to many… 18 Therefore, as through one man's offense judgment came **to <u>all men</u>**, resulting in condemnation, even so through one Man's righteous act the free gift came **to <u>all men</u>**, resulting in justification of life. 19 For as by one man's disobedience **many** were made sinners, so also by one Man's obedience **many** will be made righteous. 20 Moreover the law entered that the offense might abound. But where sin abounded, grace abounded **much more**." (Rom 5:15,18-20)*

> *"For as in Adam all die, even so in Christ **all shall be made alive**. 23 But each one in his own order…" (1Cor 15:22,23)*

Christ, being the promised seed of Eve since the fall of Adam, came and undid all that Satan, in the form of the serpent, managed to do in the fall *(Gen 3:15)*. Through Adam's fall came sin, condemnation and death, and it passed to all of us as his descendants. But then Jesus Christ, as the last Adam and head of the new creation, restored all that was lost in Adam and much, much more. Where sin abounded in Adam, in Christ *grace abounds **much more***.

> *"But the free gift is not like the offense. For if by the one man's offense **many** died**, <u>much more</u>** the grace of God and the gift by the grace of the one Man, Jesus Christ, abounded (periseuo – "super-abound") to **many**." (Rom 5:15)*

God, in His infinite wisdom, put in motion His plan for the ages. He had predestined the fall of Adam as well as the redemption that was to come through Christ, the last Adam. We see in Scripture that Christ, the last Adam was predestined from before the foundation of the world to redeem us *(1Peter 1:18-21; Rev 13:8)*. If the end result wasn't going to be *"very good indeed" (Gen 1:31),* God would not have created us in the first place. If God saw that the final result was going to be a great tragedy for the majority, He would not have commenced creation. Even if the final result was going to be equal to the beginning, He would not have initiated His eternal plan. In God's plan the end result must be better than the beginning; otherwise He wouldn't have set it in motion. What He begins He perfects. What we now have in the last Adam is much more glorious than what we would have had in the first Adam, even if he hadn't fallen. The fall didn't result in redemption as plan "B." The fall of man and the Lamb slain from the foundation of the world was part of His plan from the very beginning.

Those who hold to the doctrine of eternal torment for the majority, whether they be Calvinists or Arminians, have to limit the word *"all"* in these verses to just a few chosen from the human race when *all* is used to refer to those who benefit from the work of Christ, while at the same time insisting that *all* means *"all without exception"* when referring to those condemned in Adam. They must demonstrate that *all* doesn't mean *"all"* when referring to salvation. Is that starting to sound familiar? What they must do with these verses is the following:

What Adam did	**What Christ did**
1) Condemned ***all***	1) Justified ~~all~~ ***a few***
2) Made many ***(all)*** sinners	2) Made ~~many~~ ***a few*** righteous
3) In Adam ***all*** die.	3) In Christ ~~all~~ ***a few*** will be made alive

This doesn't sound like *much more abounding grace!* Their reinterpretation would also make it necessary to invert Paul's words in Romans 5:15 to say: "If the grace of God and the gift of grace of the one Man Jesus Christ abounded to many, much more abounded one man's offense and resulting death." But the verse says: *"But the free gift is not like the offense. For if by the one man's offense many died,* ***much more*** *the grace of God and the gift by the grace of the one Man, Jesus Christ,* ***abounded*** *to many." (Rom 5:15).* Jesus said:

> *"And I, if I am lifted up from the earth, will draw* ***all*** ~~peoples~~ *to Myself." (John 12:32)* [23]

---

[23] The word *"peoples"* is not in the Greek text but was added by the translators, allowing Calvinists to say it only refers to *"all peoples"* or *"people groups"* rather than everyone.

Would it not be much better to accept the meaning of the text as written?

What Adam did	**What Christ did**
1) Condemned **all**	1) Justified **all**
2) Made many **(all)** sinners	2) Made many **(all)** righteous
3) In Adam **all** die.	3) In Christ **all** will be made alive

Paul, in Romans 5:12, already established that by the one man *all* have sinned and *all* die:

*"Therefore, just as through one man sin entered the world, and death through sin, and thus death spread to all men, because **all sinned**." (Rom 5:12. cf. 3:23; 6:23)*

He also establishes in the first three chapters of Romans that in Adam *all* are condemned and under the judgment of God *(Rom 3:19)*. In each of the three parallels that Paul makes, if *all* is *"all"* in Adam than it follows that in Christ *all* also must mean *"all."* It must be the same *all* and not another *all* – otherwise the parallel doesn't correspond – it wouldn't be a comparison.

Take for example Romans 5:18:

*"Therefore, __as__ through one man's offense judgment came to **all men**, resulting in condemnation, __even so__ through one Man's righteous act the free gift came to **all men**, resulting in justification of life."*

If the *"all"* of the second group is not the same *"all"* in the first group, then it wouldn't make sense to use the parallel comparison *"as...even so..."* For the sake of illustration, let us imagine that someone was to rob $100,000 from you and it was all you had to your name. Then upon catching the thief you were to say to him: *"**As** you took **all** I had, **even so** I want you to give it **all** back."* What would you be demanding of him? A tithe? No. The expression *"**even so**"* following *"**as**"* means the last must be equal to the first.

Some attempt to limit the second phrase to those presently in Christ. In reply to this argument we see, in the first place, that Romans 5:18 does not say, "all in Christ" but rather simply, *"all men."* Also, in 1Corinthians 15:22 it says, *"in Christ all"* and not, "all in

Christ." The order of the words is important. "All in Christ" *could* give the impression that the *all* is restricted to those who are already in Christ. It would be like saying, "As in Adam all die, even so *all who are now in Christ* will be made alive." But this example still wouldn't be grammatically correct since the phrase *"as…even so…"* would not be parallel, because the *"all"* in Adam would not be the same, quantitatively, as the *"all"* in Christ. But it says, *"in Christ all* will be made alive" and not, "all in Christ." In the commentary *Barne's Notes*, he, although not himself a Universalist, agrees:

> *"1Corinthians 15:22*
> *If this passage means, that in Adam, or by him, all people became sinners, then the correspondent declaration 'all shall be made alive' must mean that all people shall become righteous, or that all shall be saved. This would be the natural and obvious interpretation; since the words 'be made alive' must have reference to the words 'all die,' and must affirm the co-relative and opposite fact. If the phrase 'all die' there means all become sinners, then the phrase 'all be made alive' must mean all shall be made holy, or be recovered from their spiritual death; and thus an obvious argument is furnished for the doctrine of universal salvation, which it is difficult, if not impossible, to meet. It is not a sufficient answer to this to say, that the word 'all,' in the latter part of the sentence, means all the elect, or all the righteous; for its most natural and obvious meaning is, that it is co-extensive with the word 'all' in the former part of the verse."* [24]

Some point out that in Romans 5:19 it says *"many"* and not *all* shall be made righteous in Christ. However, when Paul uses the word "many" in place of all, it is not speaking of something less than "all." When he says *"all sinned" (Rom 5:12),* he is not contradicting himself by saying later *"many were made sinners" (Rom 5:19).* He is just emphasizing that *the one* individual – Adam, made *the many* sinners, but the other *one* individual – Christ, made the same *many* righteous. The contrast is between *the one* and *the many*. The definite article is used in both cases making it say, *"**the** many."* The same *many* that were made sinners by *the one* – Adam, are also *the many* made righteous by *the one* - Christ.

---

[24] from Barnes' Notes on 1Corinthians 15:22

Some see Romans 5:17 as limiting those in the Last Adam to those who personally and actively receive Christ:

*"For if by the one man's offense death reigned through the one, much more **those who receive** abundance of grace and of the gift of righteousness will reign in life through the One, Jesus Christ." (Rom 5:17)*

However, as we see throughout this entire passage, the contrast is between that which *all men receive* in Adam and that which *all men receive* in Christ the Last Adam. The word *"receive"* is the Greek word *lambano,* which has two distinct usages: 1) *to actively take or receive*, or 2) *to receive as a passive recipient.* The context must determine whether the receiving is passive or active. For example, in several New Testament passages we see that the recipient must receive something he did not even desire to receive, such as a *just reward for his disobedience (Heb 2:2),* or a *greater judgment (Luke 20:47).* In other instances, the recipient receives that which he was not even anticipating. For example, everyone in Cornelius' house was surprised when the Gentiles suddenly *received* the Holy Spirit *(Acts 10:47).* In these examples it is obvious that the recipient is passive.

The highly esteemed Greek scholar Marvin Vincent correctly applies the passive meaning also to Romans 5:17. He says: *"They which receive (hoi lambanontes). Not 'believingly accept,' but simply 'the recipients."* [25] Although he does not go into further detail, his rendering of *lambano* in the passive sense is necessitated by the context. The contrast throughout is between what *all men receive* in Adam as opposed to what *all men receive* in Christ, the Last Adam. **As** all men passively *receive* death, condemnation, and bondage to sin through the one man's disobedience, **even so** all *receive* life, justification, and dominion restored, through the one man, Christ.

However, that being said, just as not every man *experientially* entered into Adam's death, condemnation and bondage to sin at the moment Adam sinned, even so not everyone *experientially* received life, justification or dominion at the moment when Christ, the Last Adam, died and rose from the dead. Even as man must be born into Adam to *experience* the death, condemnation and bondage to sin he

---

[25] Vincent's Word Studies in the New Testament, Romans 5:17

brought upon us all, so also must every man be made alive or born again before *experientially* entering into that justification and dominion which every man received when Christ the Last Adam died and rose again. Of the Last Adam's death and resurrection, it is written, *"The first man Adam became a living being.* **The last Adam became a life-giving spirit.***" (1Cor 15:45).* And again, *"as in Adam all die,* **even so** *in Christ* **all shall be made alive.***" (1Cor 15:22).*

While it is true that no one personally and experientially receives the benefits of justification, sanctification or being made alive in Christ until they have believed in Him for salvation, what we see is that *all*, in due time, will come to faith in Christ and will submit to Him. Every tongue will eventually confess that Jesus Christ is Lord to the glory of God. In Christ *all* will eventually be made alive. At present only those who receive Him are born again and justified and are being sanctified to be received unto Him at His coming. But in due time *all* will be in Christ – justified, sanctified and subjected to Him as Lord.

In 1Corinthians 15:22,23[a] we saw that all will be made alive but not at the same time. In the following verses Paul makes it clear that not all will be made alive at Christ's Second Coming. There are ages to come which will culminate in the destruction of the last enemy, which is death, once and for all:

"For as in Adam all die, even so in Christ all shall be made alive. 23 But **each one in his own order***: Christ the firstfruits, afterward* **those who are Christ's at His coming***. 24* **Then comes the end***..." (1Cor 15:22-24[a])*

Some only see the resurrection and glorification of the saints at the Second Coming of Christ in these verses; *"those that are Christ's at His coming."* But the saying, *"each one in his own order"* requires that others follow those being made alive or immortalized at Christ's coming. Also, we know that there will be at least one other resurrection a thousand years after the first resurrection. Hades will deliver up the dead that are still there and they will all appear before the White Throne Judgment. John the revelator was shown two resurrections:

"...Then I saw the souls of those who had been beheaded for their witness to Jesus and for the word of God, who had not worshiped the beast or his image, and had not received his mark on their

foreheads or on their hands. **And they lived and reigned with Christ for a thousand years.** *5* **But the rest of the dead did not live again until the thousand years were finished. This is the first resurrection***. 6 Blessed and holy is he who has part in the* **first resurrection***. Over such the* **second death** *has no power, but they shall be priests of God and of Christ and shall reign with Him a thousand years." (Rev 20:4-6)*

"Then I saw a great white throne and Him who sat on it, from whose face the earth and the heaven fled away. And there was found no place for them. 12 And I saw the dead, small and great, standing before God, and books were opened. And another book was opened, which is the Book of Life. And the dead were judged according to their works, by the things which were written in the books. 13 The sea gave up the dead who were in it, and Death and Hades delivered up the dead who were in them. And they were judged, each one according to his works. 14 Then Death and Hades were cast into the lake of fire. **This is the second death***. 15 And* **anyone not found written in the Book of Life was cast into the lake of fire***." (Rev 20:11-15)*

Revelation 20:4-6 speaks of those who are Christ's at His Second Coming being made alive. They are the first in the order of those who will be made alive unto immortality. The word *"make alive"* in 1Corinthians 15:22 is *zoopoiéo*. There are two other Greek words used to express resurrection, *(egeiro* and *anastasis)* but they are often used to refer to a strictly temporal and physical resurrection, as in the case of Lazarus and others who were raised to life but died afterwards. In contrast, *zoopoiéo* is always used in reference to resurrection and glorification. It is used to refer to the receiving of a perpetual life in an immortal body that all will receive, but *each in his own order*.

Here in Revelation 20 we see the first stage or order; *"those who are Christ's in His coming."* Also, we see another resurrection at the end of the thousand years. The second resurrection isn't the resurrection to life immortal, but to judgment *(Jn 5:29)*. Those who are not found written in the book of life at that time will then be cast into the lake of fire which is the second death. It follows that those who are found written in the book of life will not be hurt by the second death but will at that time be glorified. So, many will be made alive or glorified at this time. I will say more about the second death further along. I would just like to point out for the time being that although the second death will last for ages and ages (at least for some) it is not eternal. In 1Corinthians 15:26 it says that Christ will reign until all His enemies have been subdued, and the last enemy to be destroyed is death. In eternity there will be no more death *(Rev 21:4)*. If Christ only destroys the first death, then it couldn't be said that the last enemy has been destroyed and it couldn't be said of eternity that there will be no more death. It will not be until all death (first and last) has been swallowed up in victory *(1Cor 15:54)*, that we can truly say that the last enemy has been destroyed. It is not possible to say that death has been destroyed and swallowed up in victory as long as there is even one individual in a state of death.

So, we have already seen that there are at least two stages in the order of those made alive in Christ; 1) Those who are His at His coming and 2) Those that are found written in the book of life in the judgment of the Great White Throne a thousand years after the first resurrection. Then the end comes when the last individual will have become subject to Christ:

> ***"Then comes the end**, when He delivers the kingdom to God the Father, when He puts an end to all rule and all authority and power. 25 For He must reign till He has put all enemies under His feet. 26 The last enemy that will be destroyed is death. 27 For 'He has put (subjected 'Gr. hupotaso') all things under His feet.' But when He says 'all things are put (hupotaso) under Him,' it is evident that He who put (hupotaso) all things under Him is excepted. 28 Now when all things are made subject (hupotaso) to Him, then the Son Himself will also be subject (hupotaso) to Him who put all things under Him, that God may be all in all." (1Cor 15:24-28)*

Paul, speaking about the order, first mentions those who are Christ's at His coming. Then he says, *"Then comes the end."* The word translated end is *telos* which means: *end, conclusion, fulfillment or final result*. I think that perhaps the best way to understand *"the end," telos* in this context is, *"then comes the fulfillment."* In other words, it speaks of the fulfillment of the declaration that *all* will be made alive in Christ, and not just *those that are Christ's at His coming*. This is verified by looking at the verses that follow, declaring that Christ will continue reigning until every enemy has been destroyed (Gr. *katalúo* "render null or void"), and all have become subject to Him. It says that the last enemy to be destroyed will be death. That cannot happen until *all* have been made alive in Christ.

That the subjection of all to Christ is voluntary is evident, seeing that it is the same word *hupotaso* that is used of Christ when it says that He Himself will also be *subject* (hupotaso) to the Father. No one would question the fact that Christ's subjection to the Father will be voluntary. It will be a voluntary subjection in the case of all others as well, but *"each in his own order."*

The saying *"each in his own order"* could be understood as meaning that, after the glorification of those who are Christ's in His coming, and those made alive in the second resurrection - thereafter it will be *each in his own order.* In other words, each individual will be *made alive when it is his time.* The Scriptures say very little about the order of resurrections beyond the Second Coming of Christ. It doesn't even give details concerning those whose names are written in the book of life in the Great White Throne Judgment at the second resurrection.

The statement *"each in his own order"* to me implies that, beyond the second resurrection, each person will be made alive individually and not collectively. That would be in agreement with what we see in Revelation concerning the entrance of the individuals of the nations into the New Jerusalem whose gates are continually open. (see chapter nine: Her Gates are Always Open). Also, in Hebrews we see that the subjection of all to Christ is progressive and individual:

> *"Thou hast **put all** things **in subjection** (hupotaso) under his feet. For in that he put **all** in subjection (hupotaso) under him, he left nothing that is not put under him. But now we see **not yet all** things put under him (hupotaso). 9 But we see Jesus, who was made a little lower than the angels for the suffering of death, crowned with glory and honor; that he by the grace of God should taste death for **every man**." (Heb 2:8-9 KJV)* [26]

Here in Hebrews 2 we see that *all* have been put in subjection to Christ. Although we do not yet see it, every knee will bow, and every tongue will confess Jesus as Lord, to the glory of God the Father, but not yet. It will be *each in his own order,* until all have finally become

---

[26] Our English word *"things"* does not have an equivalent in Greek. Neither does the neuter form in Greek always indicate objects as in English. When the translators insert "things" in contexts that are evidently referring primarily to persons and not inanimate objects I take the liberty to cross it out in order to keep the focus where it belongs.

subjected to Him. We can see the same truth expressed in 1Timothy 2:6:

*"who gave Himself a ransom for **all**, to be testified **in due time**." (1Tim 2:6)*

Paul here says once again that Jesus is the Savior of *all,* and *in due time (kairos) all* will benefit from His redemption. In chapter 4 verse 10 he says: *"who is the **Savior of all men, especially of those who believe**."* Someday all will have come to know Jesus as Savior. Blessed are those who choose Him now, but one day every knee will have bowed to Him and every tongue will have confessed Him as Lord.

Therefore, we can see that the order is, first those who are Christ's at His coming, and then the second resurrection followed by the *end or fulfillment*, when all will have been finally made alive in Christ. The New Revised Standard Version, recognizing this, left a footnote after *"then comes the end"* in 1Corinthians 15:23 to clarify the sense of the word *"end" (telos)* in the context. The footnote says: "or *'then come the rest.'"*

We, the Church and Bride of Christ, will celebrate the wedding feast at the Second Coming, and nevertheless we are only the firstfruits *(Jas 1:18).* In *the dispensation of the fullness of the times* the Church will be manifested to the rest of creation. We are only the first of many to follow: *"that **we who first trusted in Christ** should be to the praise of His glory… in the ages to come." (Eph 1:12; 2:7).*

Chapter three
Does God Get What He Wants?

> *"For this is good and acceptable in the sight of God our Savior, 4 who **desires all men to be saved** and to come to the knowledge of the truth. 5 For there is one God and one Mediator between God and men, the Man Christ Jesus, 6 who **gave Himself a ransom for all**, to be testified **in due time**." (1 Timothy 2:3-6)*

This passage clearly tells us that God *desires* the salvation of *all* men, and also that, with that end in mind, Christ Jesus gave Himself a ransom for *all*. This harmonizes perfectly with Universalism which affirms that God will indeed save *all in due time*. But with the traditionalists who believe that the majority will never be saved, it is necessary to change the obvious sense of this passage. The Arminians and the Calvinists have two very distinct ways of explaining why this text doesn't mean what it appears to mean.

Two Traditional Opinions

The Arminians

The Arminians are in agreement with the text in the sense that Christ Jesus paid the ransom for the whole human race – that He *gave Himself a ransom for all*. Nevertheless, according to them, the majority will never be saved, due to their belief that the will of God for man is frustrated by man's own free-will. In order to maintain some semblance of sovereignty for God, they must argue that the word *"desire" (thelo),* in this instance, does not mean something that He will achieve, but rather it is merely a wish or aspiration. Barnes, in his commentary on 1Timothy 2:4 is representative of the explanation given by the Arminians:

> *"[Who will have all men to be saved] That is, it is in accordance with his nature, his feelings, his desires. **The word 'will' cannot be taken here in the absolute sense**, denoting a decree like that by which he willed the creation of the world, **for if that were so then all men would be saved**. But the word is often used to denote a desire, wish, or what is in accordance with the nature of anyone. Thus it may be said of God that he 'wills' that his creatures may be happy because it is in accordance with his*

*nature, and because he has made abundant provision for their happiness though it is not true that he wills it in the sense that he exerts his absolute power to make them happy. God wills that sickness should be relieved, and sorrow mitigated, and that the oppressed should go free, because it is agreeable to his nature; though it is not true that he wills it in the sense that he exerts his absolute power to produce it. A parent wills the welfare of his child. It is in accordance with his nature, his feelings, his desires; and he makes every needful arrangement for it. If the child is not virtuous and happy, it is his own fault. So God wills that all people should be saved. It would be in accordance with his benevolent nature. He has made ample provision for it. He uses all proper means to secure their salvation. He uses no positive means to prevent it, and **if they are not saved it will be their own fault**. For places in the New Testament where the word here translated 'will' thelo, means to desire or wish, see Luke 8:20; 23:8; John 16:19; Gal.4:20; Mark 17:24; 1Cor. 7:7; 11:3; 14:5; Matt. 15:28."* [27]

It is not without importance to note that none of the passages he cites here to show that *thelo* at times expresses a simple *desire* or *wish* have reference to the will of God. The will of man can be frustrated by circumstances beyond his control. That's why James said that our determinations should be conditioned by, *"if God wills (thelo)...we will do this or that." (James 4:13-15).* We can make a determination to do something and not be able to do it because it ultimately depends upon the determinative will of God. James continues saying, *"all such boasting is evil." (v. 16).* Nevertheless, according to Arminianism, what God desires for us is subordinate to the "free-will" of man to such a degree that they, in essence, invert the words of James to say, "if man wills God will do," instead of saying "if God wills man will do." Such boasting is not good, according to James. It is the essence of humanism, putting the will of man above the will of God.

There is an abundance of Scriptures that clearly indicate that the will of God, when all is said and done, cannot be frustrated by the will of man:

---

[27] Barnes Notes, *Commentary on 1Timothy 2*.

*"**Whatever the Lord pleases (thelo) he does**, in heaven and on earth." (Ps 135:6)*

In this passage the same Greek word *thelo,* is used in the LXX. Some say that the other words expressing "desire" *(boule, bouléo, boúlomai)* express more strongly the idea of *deliberation* than *thelo*. [28] *Thelo* is said to express *determination* in contrast with *boule*. Marvin Vincent, commenting on *thelo* as used in 1Timothy 2:4 says: *"He desires the salvation of all. Thelo (to desire) indicates a **determined** purpose."* [29] Be that as it may, we find that both words are used to express the will of God concerning our salvation. Peter uses the word *boúlomai* to express that God is not *willing (boúlomai)* that any of us should perish.

*"The Lord is not slack concerning His promise, as some count slackness, but is longsuffering toward us, **not willing (boúlomai) that any should perish but that <u>all</u> should come to repentance**." (2Peter 3:9)* [30]

Even taking into account whatever distinction of meaning between *thelo* and *boule,* we see in the Scriptures that neither His *thelo* nor His *boule* can ultimately be frustrated by man:

*"The Lord of hosts has sworn, saying, 'surely, as I have thought, so it shall come to pass, and **as I have purposed (bouléo), so it shall stand**." (Isa 14:24)*

*"Declaring the end from the beginning, and from ancient times things that are not yet done, saying, '**My counsel shall stand,***

---

[28] Vines Expository Dictionary of the New Testament on *boúlomai*.

[29] Marvin Vincent, *Vincent´s Word Studies of the New Testament* on 1Timoteo 2:4.

[30] In this passage we see God's determinative will exercised in the salvation of all His elect, the Church of the firstfruits, before the day of the Lord commences at the Second Coming. The limiting expressions *"beloved"* and *"toward us"* show clearly that he is here specifically referring to the elect and not the rest of the world who will believe through us in the coming times of the restoration of all. The Lord will not return until the *"fullness of the Gentiles"* has come into the Church and all of us as His *"firstfruits"* have been harvested.

and I will do <u>all</u> My pleasure (bouléo),' 11 *Calling a bird of prey from the east, the man who executes My counsel, from a far country.* **Indeed I have spoken it; I will also bring it to pass**. *I have purposed it; I will also do it." (Isa 46:10-11)*

But if there should still remain doubt as to whether or not He exercises His will in a determinative way for the salvation of all mankind, let us look again at what He declares in Isaiah 45:

"Tell and bring forth your case; yes, let them take counsel together. **Who has declared this from ancient time**? *Who has told it from that time?* **Have not I, the Lord**? *And there is no other God besides Me, a just God and a Savior; there is none besides Me.* 22 **Look to Me, and be saved, all you ends of the earth**! *For I am God, and there is no other.* 23 **<u>I have sworn</u> by Myself; the word has gone out of My mouth in righteousness, and shall not return, <u>that to Me every knee shall bow, every tongue shall take an oath</u>**. 24 *He shall say, 'Surely in the Lord I have righteousness and strength.' To Him men shall come, and all shall be ashamed who are incensed against Him." (Isa 45:21-24)*

Here we see that it is not simply a passive desire or an aspiration of God that all be saved, but rather that He himself has sworn that all shall be saved – that every knee shall bow, and every tongue shall take an oath of loyalty to Him.

This contradicts what Barnes and other Arminians affirm when he says: *"The word 'will', cannot be taken here in the absolute sense, denoting a decree…"* And why do they insist so much that it cannot be understood in an absolute sense? Barnes explains their reasoning: *"for if that were so then **all men would be saved**."* However, the salvation of *all* is precisely what Paul affirms in 1Timothy. After saying in 2:4 that God desires *all* men to be saved and that Christ gave Himself as a ransom *for all;* in 4:10 he goes on to say that He is *"the Savior of **all** men, **especially of those who believe**."* According to Paul, Christ gave Himself as a ransom for *all* and His mission will not be frustrated by the free-will of man. Even those who have not yet believed will believe in His due time. Those who believe in universal salvation can take these passages in their plain and obvious sense. But when these texts are approached with the presupposition of eternal punishment, combined with the exaltation of the free-will of man against the free-will of God to save, it then becomes necessary for them to change the obvious meaning of Scripture in order to maintain their traditions.

That is not to say that God never lets man make decisions independently on his own. God allows us to make our own decisions in order that we may learn from our mistakes and mature. What these texts do say is that God has the last word. What God desires He does, in heaven and on earth, and what he desires is the ultimate salvation of *all* mankind, and in His own time it shall be accomplished.

God, as Creator and Father of all, permits us to exercise our will within certain parameters the same as any father who wants his son to mature and learn to make wise decisions. But what would we say of a father who never intervenes even when his son's decisions could cause irreparable harm or death? Love promotes the exercise of free-will decisions in our children for the development of their personalities. However, at the same time, we exercise influence to guide them, and if necessary, deny the free expression of their will in certain circumstances until they learn to make more mature decisions. No good father would give his son's will free reign without parental intervention when necessary. That would be parental negligence and indifference – not love. And much less would one of us let our son commit suicide without restraining intervention. How can we attribute to our Father God something infinitely worse?

Barnes, as cited above, unwittingly presents God as if He were the worst, most indifferent and negligent Father of all. He said, referring to man's salvation: *"(God) has made ample provision for it. He uses all proper means to secure their salvation. He uses no positive means to prevent it, and **if they are not saved it will be their own fault**."* [31] This is an example of how much the traditional doctrine of eternal punishment can harden our hearts. The attitude of God that Barnes presents here is as if a father were to say concerning his son: "Well, I provided for my son all that he needs to live a happy life. I'm not going to tie him to the railroad tracks, but if he decides to take his life it will be his own fault." However, what they attribute to God is much worse than this illustration depicts. They sing hymns affirming that the mercy of God endures forever, but at the same time teach that if one does not accept His provision of

---

[31] Barnes Notes, *Commentary on 1Timothy 2*.

salvation in time, God himself will cast them into an eternal lake of fire without any hope of ever being saved for all eternity.

According to them, God has so much respect for man's free-will that He wouldn't even intervene to prevent His children from going to an eternal hell, even knowing that they are headed there because they are blinded by inherited sin. Nevertheless, at the judgment, when they finally come to themselves and bow the knee to Him, confessing Him as Lord, they will be cast into the lake of fire, without mercy and against their free-will that He is said to honor so much, forever and ever.

Continuing with the example of the father and son, it would be as if the father; seeing that his wayward son did not gratefully receive his provision promptly, were to tie his son on his knees to the train rails, without showing mercy to his son's confession that he had acted shamefully, and turning a deaf ear to his promises to be an obedient son, given another opportunity, until finally the train runs over him. Of course, this illustration falls short because the train passes, but according to them, hell never ends.

This parable is very different from the one Jesus used to illustrate Father God's heart toward his prodigal son, but it is nevertheless descriptive of the father of the Arminians towards a wayward, ungrateful son in the far country. They would allow that the Father is as presented in Jesus' parable as long as the son's heart continues beating, but does the Father's love and mercy end in a heartbeat or are His love and mercy eternal even as the Bible declares?

The Calvinists

The Calvinists, in contrast to the Arminians, believe that, according to the Scriptures, God is absolutely sovereign and cannot be frustrated by the free-will of man. A Calvinist, John Gill, says the following concerning the same passage in 1Timothy 2:4:

*"The salvation which God wills **that all men should enjoy**, is **not a mere possibility of salvation**, or a mere putting them into a salvable state; or an offer of salvation to them; or a proposal of sufficient means of it to all in his word; but **a real, certain, and actual salvation, which he has determined they shall have**... wherefore the will of God, that all men should be saved, is not a conditional will, or what depends on the will of man, or on anything*

*to be performed by him... but it **is an absolute and unconditional will respecting their salvation, and which infallibly secures it**...but the will of God concerning man's salvation is entirely one, invariable, unalterable, and unchangeable... but it is his ordaining, purposing, and determining will, which is never resisted, so as to be frustrated, but is always accomplished: the will of God, the sovereign and unfrustratable will of God, has the governing sway and influence in the salvation of men."* [32]

So far Gill gives us the impression that he is eloquently arguing in favor of Universalism - that God wills all men to be saved and nothing nor anyone can frustrate His desire. However, since Calvinists do not believe that God wills to save all, they have to argue that *all* here does not mean *"all."* After declaring that *all* men will be saved, he "clarifies" that *all men* does not mean *"all men":*

*"nor are any saved, but whom he wills they should be saved: **hence by all men...cannot be meant every individual of mankind, since it is not his will that all men, in this large sense, should be saved**, unless there are two contrary wills in God; for **there are some who were before ordained by him unto condemnation**, and are vessels of wrath fitted for destruction; and **it is his will concerning some, that they should believe a lie, that they all might be damned**; nor is it fact that all are saved, as they would be, if it was his will they should; for who hath resisted his will? But there is a world of ungodly men that will be condemned, and who will go into everlasting punishment."* [33]

Here we see a representation of the Calvinistic position that says that God always gets what He wants but He simply doesn't want to save all. On the contrary, some (the majority according to them) were predestined by God to an eternal hell and He wants them to believe the lie, in order that they might be damned. That doesn't resonate with me as being the good news for *all people* that the angel announced to the shepherds *(Lu 2:10).*

---

[32] John Gill, *New John Gill Exposition of the Entire Bible.* Commentary on 1Timothy 2:4

[33] John Gill, *New John Gill Exposition of the Entire Bible.* Commentary on 1Timothy 2:4

Based on this position they must argue that *"all men"* does not refer to *all without exception* but rather to *all without distinction*. In other words, a *few,* representative of every nation, race, social rank, age and sex. Nevertheless, they say that *"all men"* refers to everyone without exception when Paul says that *"all have sinned." (Rom 5:12)* But how can we possibly say that Christ's victory was much greater than Adam's defeat if in Adam *all without exception* are lost but in Christ only "*all without distinction*" are saved? *(cf. Rom 5:15-17).*

To illustrate how illogical this explanation is to limit "all" - saying it doesn't mean all without exception but only "all without distinction," let us imagine that an embassy with 3,000 people inside is taken by terrorists and all 3,000 are held as hostages. Then the Special Forces storm the embassy in an attempt to save them. After a great conflict, only 30 of the 3,000 are saved alive. The rest are killed by the terrorists. What would be the reaction of the families of the victims and the rest of the public if they were informed that the rescue operation was a total success – the Special Forces were able to save "*all without distinction*"? Would it be possible to consider that a total victory just because the survivors were composed of representatives of every nation, sex and age group? Such distinctions cause us to attribute to God that which is absurd and unacceptable even on a human level.

The Common Denominator between Arminians and Calvinists

There is a common denominator that the Arminians and Calvinists hold in common against the Universalists. The common denominator is not the Gospel. Christian Universalists also believe the same gospel that salvation only comes through Christ's redemptive work on the cross. Biblical Universalists also believe in the inspiration and authority of the Scriptures. So, what is the presupposition that they hold in common against the Universalists? The common denominator is that both camps assume that not all will be saved. Gill the Calvinist says that *all* cannot mean *"all,"* "*since it is not his will that all men, in this large sense, should be saved."* Barnes, as an Arminian, on the other hand argues that it is his will that all men be saved but it is not a determinative will, *"for if that were so then all men would be saved."* The point of reference for both sides is the presupposition that not all will be saved. Both sides, because of their traditional doctrine of eternal punishment for the majority of mankind, must argue that the text doesn't mean what it seems to mean; namely that God has made provision for the salvation of all and has determined that all will be saved. The Arminians get around having to say that God will save all by subordinating God's sovereignty to the "free-will" of man and the Calvinist gets around saying God will save all by saying that *all* doesn't mean *"all."* In contrast, the Universalist can say that God is sovereign and will indeed save *all* without violating man's free-will. God in His sovereignty has sworn that every knee will bow before Him and every tongue will confess Him as Lord under oath. And that includes *all* in heaven, on the earth and under the earth *(Isa 45:21,22; Phil 2:10,11).*

Free-Will?

While the tendency among the Arminians is to limit the sovereignty of God to protect the free-will of man, the Calvinist tends to minimize or even deny the free-will of man in order to protect the sovereignty of God. It is true that there are many limitations to what we call "free-will." None of us were able to choose the environment in which we were born. We didn't choose to be born with a bent to sin. We didn't choose our parents. We couldn't choose whether to be born in a Christian home or an atheist or Muslim home. We couldn't choose between being born in the United States or Iran, and for the majority, their free-will is of little or no avail for changing their social status or nationality. All these things and many more, limit or influence our "free-will." It is more likely that one born into a loving Christian home in a time of spiritual revival will exercise their "free-will" to accept Christ than an Indian in the heart of the jungle who has never seen civilization; much less heard the gospel. Certainly, at best our "free-will" is limited by the hand of cards that life has dealt to us. If the eternal destiny of every person were to depend upon a decision for Christ with the limitations of their "free-will" during the brief span of their lifetime, then there would be much inequity in the world which would be very difficult to reconcile with the love and justice of God. But if we understand that Christ is the Savior of all mankind without exception, including those who have not believed as of yet *(1Ti 4:10),* then it becomes possible to trust that God, in His time, will bring justice, grace and mercy to all.

I believe that what we find in the Scriptures is that God's sovereignty is always absolute. His council will stand and all that He desires will be done *(Isa 46:10),* and what He desires is the salvation of all. Also, the victory of Christ on the cross reconciled the whole world to Himself and obtained the salvation of all. But at the same time, no one benefits from that salvation against his own will. God has reconciled the world to Himself in Christ, but we do not enjoy that reconciliation until we have been reconciled to God in our minds *(2Cor. 5:19,20; Col. 1:21)*. Christ is the Savior of the whole World, but we do not *experience* this salvation until we put our faith in the Savior. The problem with the traditional position is their insistence that the only opportunity that God gives us is in this life, and obviously not all are reconciled to God, accepting His salvation in this life. In fact, the vast majority never even heard the good news of salvation in their lifetime.

The disparity between the sovereignty of God and the free-will of man does not exist with the Universalist. The debate between Arminianism and Calvinism is rooted in the presupposition of the traditionalists that say that it is necessary to be saved within the nanosecond of our earthly existence. As it is obvious that not all are saved in this life, they must justify this reality. The Calvinists put the blame on God saying that He doesn't want to save all. The Arminians put the blame on man's free-will saying that man doesn't want to be saved. The Universalist, however, can say with the Scriptures that God wants all to turn to Him and be saved, and He has sworn that, sooner or later, every knee shall indeed bow, and every tongue shall confess Jesus as Lord of their own free-will *(Isa. 45:21-24; Phil. 2:10,11)*.

God does not have to violate one's free-will in order to cause them to turn to Him. His patience and His power of influence are infinite, and He is capable of bringing them voluntarily to their knees, confessing Him as Lord, instead of sending them to an eternal hell against their "free-will" as soon as their heart stops beating. God working in us to desire and to do His good will is what will finally result in all voluntarily submitting themselves to Him.

> *"That at the name of Jesus every knee should bow, of those in heaven, and of those on earth, and of those under the earth, 11 and that every tongue should confess that Jesus Christ is Lord, to the glory of God the Father... 13 for it is God who works in you both to will and to do for His good pleasure." (Phil 2:10,11,13)*

It was God working in the life and circumstances of Jonah in the storm and the great fish; and in the life of Paul on the road to Damascus, that caused them to will and to do His good pleasure.

God changed their "free-will" to align it with His and didn't wait for them to choose His will on their own – something they would have never done. They would have never chosen the good will of God by their independent free-will until God produced the desire in them, and the same is true of you and me and everyone else who has ever bowed the knee and confessed Jesus Christ as Lord *(Rom. 3:11,12)."No one can say that Jesus is Lord except by the Holy Spirit (1Cor 12:3).* God accomplishes what He desires and what He desires is that *all* be saved, and so shall it be done according to His predetermined will.

Chapter four
God's Nature and Hell

God's Holiness and His Love

In order to have a proper understanding of the purpose and nature of hell, we must first have a clear understanding of God's nature and His purpose for the ages. Since Augustine, the Church has begun with the presupposition of unending torments for the majority of mankind, and based upon that understanding, have sought to determine the nature and purposes of God accordingly. However, any proper understanding of hell, or any other doctrine for that matter, must begin with a true understanding of the revelation of God's nature and His purposes for the ages. Only then can we hope to understand the true nature of hell and God's purpose in creating it.

The Bible says that God is love *(1Jn 4:8,16)*. It doesn't simply say that God loves, but that He himself ***is*** love. God loves because He is love, and His love is infinite and immutable. He can never act in an unloving way because love is the essence of His being. Even when He is angry and disciplines, it is because He is love. He loved us and saved us, even being His enemies, and not only us but the whole world.

> *"For **whom the Lord loves He chastens**, and scourges every son whom He receives." (Heb 12:6)*
>
> *"But God demonstrates His own **love toward us**, in that **while we were still sinners**, Christ died for us." (Rom 5:8)*
>
> *"For God so **loved the <u>world</u>** that He **gave His only begotten Son**, that whoever believes in Him should not perish but have everlasting life." (Jn 3:16)*
>
> *"God was in Christ **reconciling the <u>world</u> to Himself**, not imputing their trespasses to them…" (2Cor 5:19)*

It is impossible that God should stop loving someone from one moment to the next, just because their heart stops beating before having heard or believed in the good news. It isn't even possible for God to stop loving someone for refusing to submit to Him during his lifetime because God is love and His love never ends *(1Cor 13:8)*. His mercy is forever. The unconditional love of God cannot say: "I love you with a love that never ends, but if you don't respond to my love now, I will hate you for all eternity." Would we consider it true love if a man were to propose marriage to his girlfriend saying to her: "I love you with all my heart, and if you accept my proposal for marriage, you will live happily as my wife, but if you say no, I will cut you into a thousand pieces and throw you to the crocodiles?" Would that be considered true unconditional love? Of course not! Why do many think God would do something infinitely crueler and more selfish? Just because tradition says that's the way it is? Is that really the good news of great joy announced by the angel to the shepherds? No! A thousand times no! God is love and all he does - even His punitive and correctional actions, are based on His love and have a restorative purpose.

The traditional response to this is: *"Yes, God is love, but you must also understand that He is more than love. The Bible also says that God is **holy** (Lev 20:26; 1Peter 1:16). In fact, His holiness is His dominant attribute, because; due to his holiness, He cannot love that which is evil. And since God is infinite in His holiness, His just punishment also must be infinite, even if it's just one sin. Sin is sin before a Holy God, whether it be showing anger or murder, all sin is equal with God."*

I am familiar with this argument because it was my customary response to thoughtful and sensitive individuals who dared to question the doctrine of eternal punishment. I always hoped they would be more satisfied with that answer than I, but their look usually showed puzzlement. Sometimes they would say: *"But what about those who never had the opportunity to hear the gospel?"* I would respond by telling them that they have enough revelation from created things to leave them without excuse for not believing in God and seeking Him *(Rom 1:19,20)*. I assured them that if they were to truly seek God as revealed in creation then God would do everything necessary to get the gospel message to them.

However, I began to see the fallacies in this traditional response. In the first place, it presents His holiness as if it were an attribute separate from, and contrary to His love. In the second place, it doesn't take into account the universal provision which God himself made by the blood of the cross, and in the third place it goes against all sense of justice and even the very law of God itself, giving an eternal life sentence for finite offenses.

A Divided God?

To present God as being restricted in the free exercise of His love by His holiness is to present a divided God, as though His love and His holiness were opposite poles. Also, it presents His holiness as immutable and infinite, but His love as mutable and finite, subordinated to His holiness. It is not the unconditional love as seen in 1Corinthians 13 - a love that doesn't take into account a wrong suffered and never ends.

The law was given to reveal loving holiness. Something that the scribes and Pharisees did not comprehend was that true holiness is not an attribute separated from love, but rather that it is love in action. Holiness, divorced from love, is not holiness at all, but only a caricature of it. True holiness finds its greatest expression in love.

> *"Owe no one anything except to love one another, for **he who loves another has fulfilled the law**. 9 For the commandments, 'You shall not commit adultery,' 'You shall not murder,' 'You shall not steal,' 'You shall not bear false witness,' 'You shall not covet,' and if there is any other commandment, are all summed up in this saying, namely, 'You shall love your neighbor as yourself.' 10 Love does no harm to a neighbor; therefore **love is the fulfillment of the law**." (Rom 13:8-10)*

> *"Jesus said to him, '**You shall love the Lord your God** with all your heart, with all your soul, and with all your mind.' 38 This is the first and great commandment. 39 And the second is like it: '**You shall love your neighbor as yourself**.' 40 **On these two commandments hang all the Law and the Prophets**." (Matt 22:37-40)*

Here we see that holiness and the love of God are indivisible. We cannot really be holy without love and we cannot love apart from holiness. Love is holiness and holiness is love. The holiness void of the love of God is the good side of the tree of the knowledge of good and evil, and religion separated from the God of love. It is the essence of spiritual death. Those who partake of the evil side of the tree, like prostitutes and tax collectors, are not the only ones lacking in the presence of God/Love. Those most lacking in love in history have not been so much the "sinners" as the "saints" who separate holiness from love.

That is why Jesus said to the religious Pharisees of His time: *"Assuredly, I say to you that tax collectors and harlots enter the kingdom of God **before you**." (Matt 21:31).* The sect of the Pharisees, which introduced the doctrine of eternal torments into Judaism, was born out of the concept of a legal holiness without love, designed to isolate themselves from the moral degradation prevalent during the Intertestamental period. The very title *Pharisee* meant *"separate, separatist or holy one"* but they had only a caricature of holiness – a legal holiness void of love and mercy. That is why Jesus said to them when they censured Him for befriending sinners: *"But go and learn what this means: '**I desire mercy and not sacrifice**.' For I did not come to call the righteous, but sinners, to repentance." (Matt 9:13).* He reproached them for maintaining the appearance of holiness while overlooking its essence - love and justice:

> *"But woe to you Pharisees! For you tithe mint and rue and all manner of herbs, and **pass by justice and the love of God**. These you ought to have done, without leaving the others undone." (Luke 11:42-43)*

Sadly, the leaven of the Pharisees has persisted in the traditional dogmas of many churches even to this day, making even justice appear to be a negative attribute. Nevertheless, Jesus, in His Sermon on the Mount, explains that true divine holiness and perfection are inseparable from unconditional love:

> *"You have heard that it was said, 'You shall love your neighbor and hate your enemy.' 44 But I say to you, love your enemies, bless those who curse you, do good to those who hate you, and pray for those who spitefully use you and persecute you, 45 **that you may be sons of your Father in heaven**; for He makes His sun rise on the evil and on the good, and sends rain on the just and on the unjust…. 48 **Therefore you shall be perfect, just as your Father in heaven is perfect**." (Matt 5:43-45,48)*

We see from Scriptures that God is holy or set apart from all other gods or men. But it is His love and mercy which sets Him apart – not His wrath. Wrath without love is common not only to the Pharisees but to all fallen men and all false gods. Only God can be said to be love in all He does, including His judgments, and we become saints or set apart ones only by being created anew in His own image. Although there be many gods in this world, known for their severity and implacable wrath, there is only one Holy God who is both just and a Savior *(Isa 45:21)*. Through the prophet Hosea God explains in what way He is different or set apart:

> *"How can I give you up, Ephraim? How can I hand you over, Israel? How can I make you like Admah? How can I set you like Zeboiim?* **My heart churns within Me; my sympathy is stirred. 9 I will not execute the fierceness of My anger;** *I will not again destroy Ephraim.* **<u>For I am God, and not man</u>, <u>the Holy One</u>** *in your midst; and* **I will not come with terror.***" (Hos 11:8-9)*

In what way is God holy or set apart from all the rest? It is His goodness which sets Him apart. It is because He is love that He is compassionate and relents from punishment when His children repent of evil. In His wrath He remembers mercy because He is love *(Hab 3:2)*.

Therefore, any true interpretation of the Scriptures must be one which reconciles the love of God with His holiness. It is inconceivable that there should be an eternal contrast and tension between the two, as would be the case with an eternal hell which has no restorative purpose. Love, while it exists, will always find a way to be reconciled with the object of its affection without compromising holiness, which is love itself in action. And that is exactly what God did in Christ on the cross.

When Righteousness and Peace Kissed each other

> *"Mercy and truth have met together; Righteousness and peace have kissed." (Ps 85:10)*

Since before the foundation of the world, God had a plan, eternally conceived in His wisdom, omniscience and love. It included the fall, reconciliation, redemption the and restoration of all. At great cost to Himself He obtained our redemption and reconciliation. He couldn't simply pass over His justice, justifying the ungodly, while at the same time maintaining His holiness. Therefore, He himself, in the person of the Son, by His immense love, took our place as our substitute and thereby became the propitiation, not for our sins only but for the sins of the whole world *(1Jn 2:2)*. Because of this He can be just and at the same time justify the unjust. On the cross justice and peace kissed each other.

> *"For He made Him who knew no sin to be sin for us, that we might become the righteousness of God in Him." (2Cor 5:21)*

> *"being justified freely by His grace through the redemption that is in Christ Jesus, 25* **whom God set forth as a propitiation by His blood, through faith, to demonstrate His righteousness, because in His forbearance God had passed over the sins that were previously committed**, *26 to demonstrate at the present time His righteousness,* **that He might be just and the justifier** *of the one who has faith in Jesus." (Rom 3:24-26)*

> *"Therefore, as through one man's offense judgment came to all men, resulting in condemnation, even so* **through one Man's righteous act the free gift came to all men, resulting in justification of life***." (Rom 5:18)*

God has always had a plan to have a people of His own, an intimate companion who knows first-hand the depths of His love. Christ the Lamb of God was slain from the foundation of the world. He didn't come only to save some but all. All will know him, and all will know that the Lord most holy is love.

Righteous Justice is a Just Measure

> *"Shall not the Judge of all the earth do right?" (Gen 18:25)*

The argument for eternal punishment, as we have seen, is that: since God is infinite in His holiness the punishment must also be infinite. But as we have already seen, this logic isn't found in the Scriptures. The traditionalist argument that says that *infinite holiness requires infinite punishment*, wasn't even known prior to the end of the eleventh century when the philosopher and Archbishop of Canterbury, Anselm, first presented it to justify an eternal hell.

True justice would be a necessary and just discipline which corresponds with the offense. An infinite sentence for a finite offense would not be just judgment. Even justice without mercy would be *an eye for an eye, tooth for tooth, hand for hand… (Ex 21:23-25)*. Anything beyond that would be unjust punishment according to the law of God and also according to human law. God placed the limit of punishment for an offense to 40 lashes in Deuteronomy 25:1-3:

> *"If there is a dispute between men, and they come to court, that the judges may judge them, and they justify the righteous and condemn the wicked, 2 then it shall be, if the wicked man deserves to be beaten, that the judge will cause him to lie down and be beaten in his presence, **according to his guilt, with a certain number of blows**. 3 **Forty blows he may give him and no more**, lest he should exceed this and beat him with many blows above these, and your brother be humiliated in your sight." (Deut 25:1-3)*

The system of justice that God established in the law is righteous judgment, according to the offense and not according to the eminence of the person offended. Would God have a system of justice distinct from that which He prescribed in the law – one that administers infinite punishment just because it was committed against Him?

God has always meted out righteous judgment, according to the offense. It is not in His nature to give an eternal flogging without mercy. *"I know, O Lord, that Your judgments are right, and that in faithfulness You have afflicted me." (Ps 119:75).* Here we see that the judgments of God are not unjust, they are in proportion to the offense, and also we see here that He punishes us out of faithfulness, just as any good father would do. He does not delight in afflicting the sons of men.

God's Hatred

The Church of the Dark Ages, with the exception of a few dissenters, lost sight of the Scriptural revelation of God as a God of Love. The fear of a vindictive, hateful god ruled the day. The masses were fed a steady diet of sermons picturing God as an angry vengeful god who must be placated by sacrifices and offerings to the Church. Graphic paintings and dramatizations of Dante's hell served the Church well to fill the coffers and maintain the masses in fearful subjection.

Martin Luther, the great reformer, as a young man, was tormented by fear of a hateful vindictive God and the torments of hell. While riding horseback he was almost struck by lightning and understanding it to be a manifestation of the wrath of God, he swore he would become a monk. However, in spite of all his sacrifices and disciplined life, he always felt unworthy and fearful of God and an eternal flaming hell.

His transforming revelation came while, as a monk, he was doing penances, going up the steps to a cathedral on his knees. As he was engaged in the exercise of this penance, the truth of Romans 1:17 was enlightened to his understanding: *"The just shall live by faith."* He, at that moment, discovered the truth of justification by grace through faith in the vicarious sacrifice of Jesus Christ. This revelation would set in motion what we know today as the Reformation Movement.

However, in spite of the fact that he had discovered God's love and forgiveness, he still, in many ways remained fettered by the Augustinian Dark Ages concept of God. Although he had experienced the transforming power of the love of God in his own life; because of his remaining roots in the traditional doctrines of the Church, he still maintained that God hated the majority of mankind. We can observe this in his writings:

"The love and hate of God towards men are immutable and eternal, existing, not merely before there was any merit or work of 'free-will,' but before the world was made; [so] all things take place in us of necessity, according as He has from eternity loved or not loved.... Faith and unbelief come to us by no work of our own, but through the love and hatred of God" [34]

According to Luther, and even some Christians to this very day, God, from eternity and unto all eternity has hatred towards the majority of mankind. And what's worse, they say that He will never get over it – it is immutable. He will forever hate. Sadly, many Christians are uncompromising in their insistence that God is eternal hate and eternal wrath. They choose to compromise and contradict the love of God in order to protect their image of a hateful, angry God. However, as we have already seen, it is God's love that never ceases and not His hatred and wrath:

"Love never ends…" (1Cor 13:8 ESV)

---

[34] *Martin Luther: The Bondage of the Will*, pp. 226, 228-229.

> *"For I will not contend forever, **nor will I always be angry**; **For the spirit would fail** before Me, and **the souls which I have made**." (Isa 57:16)*

> *"For the Lord **will not cast off forever**. 32 Though He causes grief, yet **He will show compassion** according to the multitude of His mercies. 33 For **He does not afflict willingly**, nor grieve **the children of men**." (Lam 3:31-33)*

God is love. Love never ceases. Love does not willingly cause grief, as hatred does. It is compassionate and only afflicts for the purpose of correction – for removing the evil which is the object of holy paternal hatred. The Lord will not cast off forever as would be the case if His hatred were eternal and directed against the individual and not against the sin.

God is love and therefore *does not afflict willingly, nor grieve the children of men.* Because He is love He will not always be angry but will bring about reconciliation for all. Note that *the children of men* and *the souls which I have made,* refers to all mankind and not just the elect. The Calvinists would say that He will eternally torment the children of men whom He has created, not only willingly, but *for His own pleasure.* The Westminster Confession of Faith states:

> *"Neither are any other redeemed by Christ, effectually called, justified, adopted, sanctified, and saved, but the elect only… The rest of mankind **God was pleased**, according to the unsearchable counsel of His own will, whereby He extendeth or withholdeth mercy, **as He pleaseth, for the glory of His Sovereign power over His creatures**, to pass by; and to ordain them to dishonour and wrath for their sin, **to the praise of His glorious justice** (emphasis mine)."* [35]

According to them, God who is love, chose to redeem the elect only. This contradiction of divine character defies imagination. That is why they call it *"the **unsearchable** counsel of His own will."* For the rest (90%), *God was pleased* to withhold mercy, reserving them for eternal torture for His own pleasure, and that is said to result in *"the praise of His glorious justice."*? This outdoes all the pagan gods

---

[35] The Westminster Confession of Faith, *Chap. 3 — Articles 6 and 7.*

such as Zeus, Dagon or Molech. At least they didn't claim that their gods were love.

I believe, based upon the overall testimony of Scripture, that God is love and therefore does not willingly afflict the children of men. I also firmly believe that we can say, based upon the Scriptures, that *God loves the sinner while hating the sin*. However, there are those who insist that God does indeed hate the sinner and they also have texts which seem to back up their affirmation. There are three passages which refer to God's hatred towards certain individuals. They are the following:

"The Lord tests the righteous, but **the wicked** *and the one who loves violence* **His soul hates**.*" (Ps 11:5)*

"These **six things the Lord hates**, *yes, seven are an abomination to Him: 17 A proud look, a lying tongue, hands that shed innocent blood, 18 a heart that devises wicked plans, feet that are swift in running to evil, 19 a false witness who speaks lies, and one who sows discord among brethren." (Prov 6:16-19)*

"As it is written, 'Jacob I have loved, but Esau **I have hated**.*" (Rom 9:13, cf. Mal 1:2,3)*

How are we to understand these statements in the light of God's nature as revealed throughout the Scriptures? Here we see clearly declared God's hatred towards sinners. Hatred, in its strongest sense would be antonymous with love. The two are mutually exclusive. Does God really hate the sinner as we understand hatred? No. We can clearly see in numerous passages that God also loves the sinner. That is what redemption is all about. Paul makes it clear that God loves us even when we are sinners:

"But God demonstrates His own love toward us, in that while we were still sinners, Christ died for us." (Rom 5:8)

For God so loved the world that He gave His Son so that through Him we might have life eternal. To say that God hated us, as we understand hatred, would make it impossible for Him to love us and send His only begotten Son to reconcile us to Himself.

Furthermore, Jesus tells us that we are like our Father in heaven when we love our enemies, instead of hating them:

*"You have heard that it was said, 'You shall love your neighbor and **hate your enemy**.' 44 But I say to you, **love your enemies**, bless those who curse you, do good to those who hate you, and pray for those who spitefully use you and persecute you, 45 **that you may be sons of your Father in heaven**; for He makes His sun rise on the evil and on the good, and sends rain on the just and on the unjust." (Matt 5:43-45)*

How are we to reconcile these three passages declaring that God hates the sinner with the abundance of Scriptures that clearly declare God's love for all? There are two considerations which harmonize the two seemingly antonymous statements: 1) The meaning of the word *hate* in the original text and 2) The temporary nature of His hatred.

Hate Defined

The Hebrew word for hatred in the Old Testament passages is *sané*. *Vines Expository Dictionary of Old Testament Words,* reveals that there are two different senses in which the word is employed:

"Sané represents an emotion ranging from intense 'hatred' to the much weaker 'set against' and is used of persons and things (including ideas, words, inanimate objects)." [36]

God's hatred towards sinners is obviously in the milder sense of being "set against" an individual because of his sin and rebelliousness. Understanding it in this sense we can readily identify with this emotion even towards our own children when they defy us or misbehave.

With this understanding in mind, let us personalize this *hatred,* expressing it towards our own children when they are disobedient. Applying the seven things the Lord hates in Proverbs 6 we could say: *"I set myself against my child and do not tolerate it when he misbehaves. I will not tolerate it when he looks at me with defiance, when he lies, when he bullies his little brothers and sisters or causes them to fight among themselves, etc."*

---

[36] Vine's Expository Dictionary of Biblical Words, Copyright © 1985, Thomas Nelson Publishers.

If they were children of a stranger, we would actually be less likely to personally intervene in such a way, since they are not our responsibility. Understanding the Hebrew word *sané* in this sense, we see that it is actually an intervention of love towards another and not pure hatred, which would of itself exclude love. It is the act of setting oneself against someone, opposing them in order to correct their behavior. This is God's purpose in all of His corrective punishments – He opposes us, setting Himself against us in order to separate us from evil:

"For whom the Lord loves He chastens, and scourges every son whom He receives." (Heb 12:6)

In response to the statement: *"God loves the sinner while hating the sin,"* traditionalists would say that one cannot separate the sin from the sinner. However. that is precisely what God does in discipline:

*"The word of the Lord came to me, saying, 18 'Son of man, **the house of Israel** has **become dross to Me**; they are all bronze, tin, iron, and lead, in the midst of a furnace; they have become dross from silver. 19 Therefore thus says the Lord God: 'Because you have all become dross, therefore behold, I will gather you into the midst of Jerusalem. 20 **As men gather silver, bronze, iron, lead, and tin into the midst of a furnace, to blow fire on it**, to melt it; so **I will gather you in My anger and in My fury, and I will leave you there and melt you**. 21 Yes, I will gather you and blow on you with the fire of My wrath, and you shall be melted in its midst. 22 As silver is melted in the midst of a furnace, so shall you be melted in its midst; then you shall know that I, the Lord, have poured out My fury on you... Therefore I have poured out My indignation on them; I have consumed them with **the fire of My wrath**; and **I have recompensed their deeds** on their own heads,' says the Lord God." (Ezek 22:17-23,31)*

Here we see that God's *hatred* and even His *wrath* against His beloved Israel is in the form of the purifying fires of affliction. God sets Himself against His people and throws them into the fire as silver, bronze or lead. But the furnace of fire is in order to separate the dross or scum from their lives. The end result is that they come forth from the furnace pure and separate from sin. Just as is the case with a loving father disciplining his son, His *hatred* is actually His love acting against the sin in their lives. The end result is the peaceable fruit of righteousness, as we can see further along in Ezekiel 36:

> *"For I will take you from among the nations, gather you out of all countries, and bring you into your own land. 25 Then I will sprinkle clean water on you, and you shall be clean; I will cleanse you from all your filthiness and from all your idols. 26 I will give you a new heart and put a new spirit within you; I will take the heart of stone out of your flesh and give you a heart of flesh." (Ezek 36:24-26)*

The end result of God's opposition towards Israel is that they become cleansed of all their filthiness and are given a new heart. The same could be said concerning his affliction of any of the children of men whom He has created. He does not willingly afflict nor grieve them. What He does, He does only for their own benefit. Therefore, we can see that God's *hatred,* correctly defined, refers to God's dealing with His wayward, rebellious children, and is in no way incompatible with love.

We have also seen from God's dealings with Israel that it is indeed possible to separate the sinner from the sin. That is the precise purpose for the furnace of fire. Hell is not a place designed for meaningless torment, for God's *pleasure* and *the praise of His glorious justice*, as the traditionalists claim, but is rather a purifying furnace. In His time, His corrective *opposition* will have done its work in each individual, and the lake of fire, having served its purpose, will cease to exist along with the last enemy, the second death.

This brings us to the second consideration, which reveals that God's hatred, rightly understood, is not incompatible with His loving nature.

The Temporal Nature of God's Hatred

It is God's love that never ceases. We have seen that His anger, wrath and even His abandonment, are temporal and for our correction. He *will not cast off forever. (Lam 3:31-33)* All death – even the second death – the last enemy will finally be done away with, having served its purpose.

The *hatred* of God will also cease when sin is finally and eternally separated from the last sinner – when every knee will have bowed, and all will have become subject to Him. There is no such thing as an eternal dualism in the plan of God for the ages. He will not always be angry, eternally lashing 90% of His creatures in an eternal torture chamber, which He was *pleased* to create for *the praise of the glory of His justice*. That is an invention of Greek mythology and a hangover from the Dark Ages that has been read into Christian theology, having been inspired by demons.

We can see from Scriptures that God will overcome those He *hates* by the power of His infinite love. Rather than eternally tormenting His enemies, He reconciles them to himself by the blood of His cross:

*"Say to God, 'how awesome are Your works! Through the greatness of Your power **your enemies shall submit themselves to You**. 4 **All the earth shall worship You and sing praises to You**; they shall sing praises to Your name'." (Ps 66:3-4)* [37]

"and by Him to reconcile all things *to Himself, by Him, whether* things *on earth or* things *in heaven, having made peace through the blood of His cross." (Col 1:20)*

"Now when all things *are made subject to Him, then the Son Himself will also be subject to Him who put all* things *under Him, that God may be **all in all**." (1Cor 15:28)*

Therefore, when all, having been reconciled to God through His own blood shed upon the cross, become subjected to Christ, Christ will then subject Himself to the Father and from that point on God shall eternally be *all in all*. All His anger, hatred and wrath, which were His holy loving nature acting against sin, will no longer have an environment in which to manifest. We, however, will retain the knowledge of His hatred of evil – something that Adam and Eve had no comprehension of.

---

[37] The word for *"submit"* in this verse normally refers to a feigned submission. However, there are no words in Hebrew which express true, voluntary submission. Here it is the context itself which determines its meaning as true submission and adoration in spite of its normal meaning, since feigned submission would never result in His enemies worshipping and praising Him.

Also, His grace, mercy, compassion and longsuffering will cease to manifest, since the only environment in which they could become evident was in the context of man's fall and his sinful condition. Our comprehension of good and evil with its awful consequences, followed by God's grace and mercy, made freely available by His sacrifice of love on the cross, will be retained in our hearts as an invaluable and eternal treasure of the experiential knowledge of God's love – something Adam and Eve in their primitive state of innocence had no way of imagining.

Entering into the eternal state, when God shall be all in all, we will finally understand the manifold wisdom of God in creation. We will understand why He created Satan, why he set before man the Tree of the Knowledge of Good and Evil, knowing beforehand that they would fall. We will also see before us the Lamb of God, slain from before the foundation of the world for the reconciliation of all creation; the calling out of an elect people to be a first fruits of His new creation in Christ - the preordained Last Adam. We will also see how we, the Church, the assembly of the elect, were chosen as ambassadors of reconciliation for the rest of creation. We will finally see the last knee bow in humble loving submission to Christ, at which time Christ will deliver all to the Father and then, for all eternity, God will be all in all.

All found their origin in Him *(Col 1:16 lit. "in Him"),* they exist by Him, and they will finally return to Him and He will then be all in all. *"For of (ek) Him and through (dia) Him and to (eis) Him are all things, to whom be glory forever. Amen." (Rom 11:36).*

The Relative Nature of Godly Hatred

We further see that the hatred we are told by Jesus we must have in order to be His disciples, is not absolute in the sense that we as sinners often manifest hatred towards God and our fellow man. The people Jesus commands us to hate are the very ones we are elsewhere commanded to love:

> *"If anyone comes to Me and does not* **hate his father** *and* **mother, wife and children, brothers and sisters***, yes, and* **his own life** *also, he cannot be My disciple." (Luke 14:26)*

We are commanded to love and honor our parents *(Matt 19:19; Eph 6:2). We* are to love our wives even as Christ loves the Church *(Eph 5:25).* We are to exercise brotherly love, loving our neighbors as ourselves *(Rom 12:10)*. If we were to understand *hate* in its absolute sense, as do our traditional brethren, then we would be confronted with a blatant contradiction.

However, Matthew's account interprets what Jesus meant when He told us we must *hate* others in order to be His disciples:

> *"He who loves father or mother **more than Me** is not worthy of Me. And he who loves son or daughter **more than Me** is not worthy of Me." (Matt 10:37)*

Matthew's rendering of Jesus' words should make it very clear what He meant by hate. When we love someone with all our hearts, our lives revolve around that person, and all we want to do is please him. It is good and right that we should love our parents, our mates, our children and brothers. It is even right that we should love ourselves in the way that God loves us. However, our first love is to be reserved for God as we also see commanded by Jesus:

> *"And you shall love the Lord your God with all your heart, with all your soul, with all your mind, and with all your strength. This is the first commandment. 31 And the second, like it, is this: You shall love your neighbor as yourself. There is no other commandment greater than these." (Mark 12:30-31)*

Here we see that our love for our fellow man is commanded, but it must be subordinate to our first love – our love for God. Therefore, when someone we love would have us do something against the One we love the most, we must set ourselves against that individual, even though we love them as well, in order to do the will of God - our first love. Here again we see the word *hate* used in the sense of *"setting oneself against"* the individual who would impose his will upon us in opposition to the will of God.

We also see the same idea expressed concerning God's hatred towards Esau:

> *"As it is written, 'Jacob I have loved, but Esau **I have hated**." (Rom 9:13, cf. Mal 1:2,3)*

Paul explains that God's hatred was not based upon something Esau had done during his lifetime, but rather was solely based upon His sovereign election *(Rom 9:11)*. He chose Jacob over Esau before they had even been born in order that they both might fulfill a specific purpose. Just as He hardened Pharaoh in order to fulfill a specific temporal purpose in His plan for Israel, God chose Jacob over Esau.

However, as we have already seen, election is not to the eternal exclusion of the non-elect, but rather they are chosen to be light for the reconciliation of the rest of creation. Paul, in response to those who would question the Lord's justice in choosing some and passing over others, says that God, in the outworking of His own purposes, *has mercy on whom He wills, and whom He wills He hardens (Rom 9:18)*. However, we see that, in the overall plan of God for the ages, He has determined to finally have mercy on all without exception:

*"For God has committed ~~them~~ [38] all to disobedience, that He might have **mercy on all**... 36 For of Him and through Him and to Him are all ~~things~~, to whom be glory forever. Amen." (Rom 11:32,36)* [39]

We can also see that the *hatred* that the Lord showed to Esau, preferring Isaac, is not different in nature from the hatred Jesus said we must have towards those we are also commanded to love. It is evident that Esau was also loved and favored, even though, temporally speaking, not to the degree Jacob was. We see God's favor and love for Esau demonstrated when the time came for Israel, Jacobs's descendants, to enter the land of Canaan:

*"And the Lord spoke to me, saying: 3 'You have skirted this mountain long enough; turn northward. 4 And command the people, saying, 'You are about to pass through the territory of your brethren, the descendants of Esau, who live in Seir; and they will be afraid of you. Therefore **watch yourselves carefully**. 5 **Do not meddle with them**, for I will not give you any of their land, no, not so much as one footstep, **because I have given Mount Seir to Esau** as a possession." (Deut 2:2-5)*

---

[38] *"them"* is not in the original Greek text, but was added by the translators.

[39] Our English word *"things"* does not have an equivalent in Greek. Neither does the neuter form in Greek always indicate objects as in English. When the translators insert "things" in contexts that are evidently referring primarily to persons and not inanimate objects I take the liberty to cross it out in order to keep the focus where it belongs.

Obviously, if God had hated Esau in a sinful way as mankind often does, He wouldn't have given him any possession as an inheritance. Therefore, God's hatred must be understood in the light of His eternal nature. God is love. Therefore, all that He does is ultimately rooted and grounded in His love. His hatred, anger, wrath and even rejection are His loving response against all evil within us, disciplining us and even casting some in the lake of fire, in order that all may ultimately partake of the peaceable fruit of righteousness. God does not hate any individual in the sense in which many of us as sinners hate those who have sinned against us. His hatred is His opposition to our sinful actions and becomes favor as soon as the sin has been separated from the object of His love.

Becoming Rooted and Grounded in the Knowledge of God's Love

In order for our lives to be transformed by the indwelling Christ, we must be firmly rooted and grounded in the love of God. The flesh profits nothing. We must be filled with all the fullness of God in order to be transformed into His image. If we are rooted in fear instead of the knowledge of the love of God, we do not have the confidence necessary in order to draw near to God and receive freely of His fullness. That is why Paul prayed that we would all receive a revelation of the Love of God:

> *"For this reason I bow my knees to the Father of our Lord Jesus Christ... 17 that Christ may dwell in your hearts through faith; that you, being rooted and grounded in love, 18 may be able to comprehend with all the saints what is the width and length and depth and height — 19 to know the love of Christ which passes knowledge; that you may be filled with all the fullness of God." (Eph 3:14,17-19)*

The early Church, although persecuted by the authorities, was rooted and grounded in the love of God. Being filled with His fullness, they experienced the transformation that comes by grace, through the indwelling Christ. Having been born again by the Spirit, they enjoyed a righteousness of life which comes through communion in relationship with the indwelling Christ. They served God *in the newness of the Spirit and not in the oldness of the letter (Rom 7:6)*. Being rooted and grounded in the love of God, they had no difficulty believing in the ultimate reconciliation and restoration of all of God's creation.

However, in AD 313 the Roman Emperor Constantine, after declaring himself to be a Christian, enacted the Edict of Milan, legalizing Christianity. Special privileges were then granted to those uniting with the Church and positions were granted, not based upon spiritual stature but often solely as political favors. By the time Saint Augustine converted to Christ in AD 387 the churches were full of professing Christians, many of whom had never experienced the transforming power of the love of God through the new birth.

In order to bring order into a mixed multitude within Christianity, some of the Church fathers, while still believing in universal restoration, began to practice *reserve* - only teaching the full gospel of a universal reconciliation to the regenerate and spiritually mature, and keeping it concealed from the masses.

Augustine, however, being heavily influenced in his youth by Manichaeism and later by Greek Neo-Platonian philosophy, becoming alarmed by the increasing ungodliness and corruption evident within the Christian Church, began to change the face of God, introducing a fear-based religion in order to control the growing tide of ungodliness creeping into the church.

The God of love, taught in Scriptures and known by the early Church, was redefined by the dualism of the Manicheans, and hell began to be presented as being unending, and purely vindictive torment, inflicted upon all but the elect by a capricious god, much like the vindictive Greek gods, instead of presenting hell as an *age-during* correction by a loving Father and Creator, as taught in Scriptures and understood by the early Church.

Since the new theology of Augustine served the purposes of the now *institutionalized secular church*, which had by that time become primarily an instrument of the state, it was soon imposed upon all and became an integral part of Church doctrine, introducing the Church into the Dark Ages. The public was deprived of the Scriptures, teaching instead their Augustinian doctrines and Church traditions, in order to control the primarily unregenerate masses within the church.

It wasn't until a thousand years later, with the invention of the printing press, that the Scriptures became available to the masses. The rediscovery of the Scriptures started the Reformation, with the revelation of justification by faith by Martin Luther. However, Church tradition, which had held sway practically uncontested for more than a thousand years, is not quickly uprooted.

Most of us today are shocked when we read some of the dualistic and often barbaric ways in which God's character and hell are misrepresented by many early post-reformation preachers. However, we must put ourselves in their place and realize how difficult it is even for us, hundreds of years later, to abandon our traditions for the truth as revealed in the Scriptures.

In order for us to rediscover the pure and true doctrine, once and for all delivered unto the saints of the first centuries before the Dark Ages, we must be transformed by the renewing of our minds, and not fettered by the doctrines and traditions of men. We must become firmly rooted and grounded in the unfathomable love of God which casts out all fear, freeing us to draw near to the only One who can transform us into His own image.

Below are a few examples to show how much tradition had limited the ability of early post-reformation preachers to comprehend the true nature of God and His purposes in punishments. We should honor them for the advances they courageously made, while at the same time being thankful that the reformation did not end with them. The reformation will not end until the Church once again draws near enough to God to know Him as He is. At that moment the Church will have been perfected in love and prepared as the Bride to Meet with Christ in the air.

Preachers' Depictions of Eternal Punishment

Some, still fettered by traditions and doctrines of men and demons, have presented God as one comparable to a sadistic child torturing a spider by holding it over the fire. Some have preached using graphic details of torture, to which the lost will be eternally subjected. The following are some examples:

Jonathan Edwards

> *"The God that holds you over the pit of hell, much as one holds a spider, or some loathsome insect over the fire, abhors you, and is dreadfully provoked: his wrath towards you burns like fire; he looks upon you as worthy of nothing else, but to be cast into the fire; he is of purer eyes than to bear to have you in his sight; you are ten thousand times more abominable in his eyes, than the most hateful venomous serpent is in ours…and when you shall be in this state of suffering, the glorious inhabitants of heaven shall go forth and look on the awful spectacle, that they may see what the wrath and fierceness of the Almighty is; and when they have seen it, they will fall down and adore that great power and majesty…"* [40]

Jesus said that by loving our enemies and blessing those who curse us we become like our Father in heaven *(Matt 5:44,45)*. Tradition has distorted the character of God to the degree that we think God finds pleasure in torturing His enemies and that it is His will that we should also delight in seeing Him do it.

> *"The view of the misery of the damned will double the ardor of the love and gratitude of the saints of heaven."* The sight of hell torments will exalt the happiness of the saints forever. Can the believing father in Heaven be happy with his unbelieving children in Hell? I tell you, yea! Such will be his sense of justice that it will increase rather than diminish his bliss." [41]

What a perverse sense of justice, void of love that we see presented in these famous sermons! The newspapers in Jonathan Edward's time reported suicides resulting from the sense of despair produced in the hearts of some who heard them. Both he and Charles Finney said that one hadn't preached effectively on hell

---

[40] http://www.tentmaker.org/articles/sinners_in_the_hands_of_an_angry_god_edwards.html

[41] http://www.tentmaker.org/Quotes/hellfire.htm ["The Eternity of Hell Torments" (Sermon), April 1739 & Discourses on Various Important Subjects, 1738]

unless some went insane as a result. Though both were mightily used of God, I do not find this spirit present in the Bible and believe that they were influenced by tradition and not the Word of God in this respect.

How incredibly has the doctrine of an eternal hell of unimaginable torments perverted our concept of the justice of God into a diabolic sadism that would actually find pleasure in burning and dismembering its victims for all eternity! What a perverse concept to imagine that seeing the torments of the damned would produce greater happiness in the saints of God! What kind of love could be redoubled seeing one's parents, sons, brothers and sisters and friends held by God over the eternal flames? Is this the love that never ceases? No! Of course not! God's love is a love that does not take into account a wrong suffered and is full of mercy and compassion.

Pedro Lombardo

> "Therefore the elect shall go forth…to see the torments of the impious, seeing which they will not be grieved, but will be satiated with joy at the sight of the unutterable calamity of the impious." [42]

How can one possibly love his neighbor as himself and be satiated with joy at the sight of their calamity?

Gerhard

> "…the Blessed will see their friends and relations among the damned as often as they like but without the least of compassion." [43]

Could it be that the saints of God in their perfect state will be without natural affection?

---

[42] Thomas Allin, *Christ Triumphant*

[43] Thomas Allin, *Christ Triumphant*

Samuel Hopkins

> "This display of the divine character will be most entertaining to all who love God, will give them the highest and most ineffable pleasure. Should the fire of this eternal punishment cease, it would in a great measure obscure the light of heaven, and put an end to a great part of the happiness and glory of the blessed." [44]

And we censure the Romans for having entertained themselves by watching the killings in the arena! And worse yet, this sort of depiction of hell was also used to frighten children into obedience. The following is from a story for children, intended to promote good behavior:

Sermon by Father John Furniss

> "The fifth dungeon is the red hot oven. The little child is in the red hot oven. Hear how it screams to come out; see how it turns and twists itself about in the fire. It beats its head against the roof of the oven. It stamps its little feet on the floor." [45]

If after this sermon the Sunday school teacher was to lead the children in the song "Jesus loves me" would they really believe it after hearing that horror story about what He would do to them if they weren't good?

In 1Corinthians 13 it is *agape* love that endures forever, but this doctrine of eternal punishment presents true *agape* love as ending and being transformed into a perverse sadistic "love" that delights in seeing one's neighbor being tormented. In contrast, we see that the Scriptures present God differently:

> "For **the Lord will not cast off forever**. 32 Though He causes grief, yet He will show compassion according to the multitude of His mercies. 33 For **He does not afflict willingly**, nor grieve the children of men." (Lam 3:31-33)

---

[44] Thomas Allin, *Christ Triumphant*

[45] Thomas Allin, *Christ Triumphant*

"Who is a God like You, pardoning iniquity and passing over the transgression of the remnant of His heritage? **He does not retain His anger forever, because He delights in mercy.***" (Mic 7:18)*

Also, God, with the blood of Christ at great cost to Himself, obtained the right to show mercy. In Romans 9 Paul says that *God has mercy on whom He wills (v.18)*. Later in 11:32 He says that He wills to have mercy on all: *"For God has committed* ~~them~~ [46] **all** *to disobedience, that He might have* **mercy on all**.*"* And it is the same *"all"* that he has referred to since chapter three where he said, *"they are **all under sin**...**all have sinned** and come short of the glory of God." (3:9; 3:23)*. Also it is the same *all* of 5:18: *"Therefore, as through one man's offense* **judgment came to all men***, resulting in condemnation, even so through one Man's righteous act the* **free gift came to all men***, resulting in justification of life."*

So, we have seen that God is perfect both in holiness and love. Both are the essence of His being and are not in conflict one with the other. God in Jesus Christ is the satisfactory propitiation of His own righteous requirements, in order that He may be merciful to all according to His will, without compromising His holiness.

The Fatherhood of God

When we receive Christ, we are born again as children of God, born of the Spirit of God as John says:

"But as many as received Him, to them He gave the right to become children of God, to those who believe in His name: 13 **who were born***, not of blood, nor of the will of the flesh, nor of the will of man, but* **of God***." (John 1:12-13)*

This new birth is the rebirth of our spirit which was dead in sins: *"even when we were dead in trespasses, made us alive together with Christ (by grace you have been saved)" (Eph 2:5)*. Christ explained to Nicodemus that it is the spirit of man that is born again: *"That which is born of the flesh is flesh, and that which is born of the Spirit is spirit." (John 3:6)*. Without this new birth, we cannot see; much less enter, the kingdom of God *(Jn 3:3-5)*. Physically speaking, we are sons of God before the new birth. But *flesh and blood cannot inherit*

---

[46] *"them"* is not in the original Greek text, but was added by the translators.

the kingdom of God (1Cor 15:50). Nevertheless, Christ came to give us new life, and in due time, *all* will be made spiritually alive and will put on immortality:

> *"And so it is written, 'The first man Adam became a living being.' The last Adam became a **life-giving spirit**." (1Cor 15:45)*

> *"…in Christ **all shall be made alive**. 23 But each one in his own order." (1Cor 15:22-23)*

The majority of the Partialists (those who do not believe in the salvation of all) would say that God doesn't consider us to be His sons until we have been born again - that men are creatures of God but that He isn't our Father until we are born again, becoming part of the new creation. This, according to them, absolves God of all responsibility as a Father to mankind. But this is not what we find in the Scriptures. The Prodigal son never ceased to be a son to his father, even in the far country. When he returned, it was like being born again but he never stopped being considered a son by his father. The father in the parable is an expression of Father God's heart towards all His lost children. Even though they rebel against Him and are in the far country, wasting the Father's hard-earned inheritance, His love for them never diminishes. What did the father say to the elder son when his lost son returned? *"It was right that we should make merry and be glad, for your brother was dead and is alive again, and was lost (apólumi) and is found." (Luke 15:32)*. God considers all to be His sons and not just those who have already been made alive or born again. The Scriptures affirm the fatherhood of God and His loving care for *all* of His children:

> *"Men of Athens… God, who made the world and everything in it… gives to all life, breath, and all things. 26 And He has made from one blood every nation of men to dwell on all the face of the earth… 28 for **in Him we live and move and have our being**, as also some of your own poets have said, 'For **we are also His offspring**.' 29 **Therefore, since we are the offspring of God**, we ought not to think that the Divine Nature is like gold or silver or stone, something shaped by art and man's devising." (Acts 17:22-29)*

Here, Paul affirms the fatherly care of God towards all mankind, including the unbelieving men of Athens, saying that *all are His offspring*. I believe Paul would have been reproved in many traditional church circles today for stating that God was the Father even of unbelievers. This is not the only instance in which Paul states that God is the Father of all:

*"one God and **Father of all**, who is over all and through all and in all." (Eph 4:6 NIV)*

Here, we see God's universal Fatherhood stated. Some Greek manuscripts end this verse with the personal pronoun *"us"* and others with *"you."* However, they were most likely added by traditional scribes who couldn't accept that God is actually present in all His creation, including His lost sons, and therefore added the pronouns to give the impression that God is *only* in believers. While it is true that Christ only comes to dwell in our hearts when we receive Him, there is also a very real sense in which God is in all: *"In Him we live and move and have being." (Acts 17:28)*. Whatever the correct reading of the last phrase of the verse is, we can be certain that God is the Father of all, as Paul already stated some ten verses earlier:

*"For this reason I bow my knees to **the Father**…from whom **the whole family in heaven and earth is named**." (Eph 3:14,15)*

Here, Paul includes both those who are in heaven and on earth as part of God's family. Jesus also spoke to the multitudes, affirming that God was their Father:

*"Then Jesus spoke to the **multitudes** and to His disciples, saying…**One is your Father**, He who is in heaven." (Matt 23:1,9)*

Some would argue that God cannot be the Father of all because Jesus told the Pharisees that the devil was their father:

*"You are of **your father the devil**, and the desires of your father you want to do." (John 8:44)*

*"In this the **children of God** and the **children of the devil** are manifest: Whoever does not practice righteousness is not of God, nor is he who does not love his brother." (1John 3:10)*

Nevertheless, it is obvious that it is not referring to their *origin*, but rather to their *character*. They originated from God, as do all, and not the devil. One's conduct cannot change one's origin. If an individual were to be separated from his father in infancy and imitated his adoptive father, would that make him less a child of his true father? No. However, those who have been born again normally act like God, whereas others may act like the devil. What these verses emphasize is that we cannot convincingly claim to be sons of God if we act like the devil.

However, in the sense of origin, even Satan and his angels are called *sons of God (Gen 6:2,4; Job 1:6; 2:1)*. Jesus and John were referring to their conduct and not their origins. We express this idea as: *"Like father, like son."* In this sense, even the Gentiles who believe like Abraham, are called *"sons of Abraham." (Gal 3:6,7)*. However, all of us - without exception - are sons of God in virtue of the creation:

"Have we not all one Father? *Has not one God* **created us**?" *(Mal 2:10)*

To say that God is our Creator, but denies being our Father, is contrary to God's faithfulness. We consider it unacceptable when a man procreates a son and doesn't accept responsibility for him as a father, and yet some would say that God is absolved of all paternal obligations towards His creation. They say that, even though He created us, He doesn't regard us as being sons until we are born again. Thomas Allin in his book *Christ Triumphant* comments:

"We are told God is not the Father of all men; He is only their Creator! What a total misapprehension these words imply of all that is involved in creating man in the likeness of God, in the image of God... For what do we mean by paternity and the obligations it brings? The idea rests essentially on the communication of life to the child by the parent. Now paternity is for us largely blind and instinctive; but Creation is Love acting freely, divinely; knowing all the consequences, assuming all the responsibility, involved in the very act of creating a reasonable immortal spirit... It seems, then, very strange to seek to escape the consequences of the lesser obligation, by admitting one still greater; to seek, in a word, to evade the results of a divine universal fatherhood, by pleading that God is only the Creator of all. Hence a good Creator, freely creating for a doom of endless sin, freely introducing a dualism, is a profound moral contradiction. Can we even imagine a Good Being of His own freewill calling into existence creatures to hate Him forever, or

certainly creating those who will, as He knows, hate Him forever, and sin forever!" [47]

Paul says that one who does not provide for his family is worse than an unbeliever *(1Ti 5:8)*. How could we arrive at the point of thinking that God would not accept responsibility for all His children that were created by Him in His own image and likeness? The genealogy of Luke 3 ends in verse 38 saying: *"the son of Enosh, the son of Seth, the son of **Adam, the son of God**.* If God has not denied that Adam, the originator of sin to the human race is His son, how is it possible that He would deny the sonship of Adam's descendants who are victims of the sin nature inherited from him? As Father God has said: *"Behold, all souls are Mine..." (Ezek 18:4)*. Thomas Allin also says:

"The essence of Christianity perishes in the virtual denial of any true Fatherhood of our race on God's part. Follow out this thought, for it is of primary importance. We lose sight of the value of the individual soul, when dealing with the countless millions who have peopled this earth and passed away. What is one among so many? we are tempted to say, forgetting that the value of each human being is not in the least thereby altered. Each soul is of infinite value, as if it stood alone, in the eyes of God, its Father. And more than this, we are altogether apt to forget another vital point, to forget whose the loss is, if any one soul perishes... It is God's loss: it is the Father Who loses His child. The straying sheep of the parable is the Great Shepherd's loss: the missing coin is the Owner's loss. In this very fact lies the pledge that He will seek on and on till He find it. For only think of the value He sets on each soul. He has stamped each in His own image... and you must see how impossible it becomes to credit that unworthy theology, which tells you that such a Father can ever permit the work of His own fingers, His own offspring, to perish finally." [48]

---

[47] Thomas Allin, *Christ Triumphant*

[48] Thomas Allin, *Christ Triumphant*

Created Out of Nothing or Out of God?

How did we come into existence? Were we created out of nothing or out of God? Since Augustine, traditional Christianity has argued for a creation by God *ex nihilo* or *"out of nothing."* For many years, that reasoning was acceptable to me, since I believe in a special six-day creation as related in Genesis. And as opposed to evolution from the *ex magnus crepitus* (big bang), it seemed the most logical option of the two.

It is more logical to believe that the eternal God, *"the Uncaused Cause,"* created everything *out of nothing* than to believe that *nothing* caused *everything* as the atheistic evolutionists do. Intelligent design and beauty are better explained by the existence of the Intelligent and Loving Designer than to argue that *nothing* somehow exploded in a "big bang," producing the astronomically complex and precise order and the glorious creative beauty all around us.

However, upon discovering God's marvelous plan for the ages from the creation to the consummation, I realized that God's creation is much more personal and intimate than can be adequately expressed by the Latin term *ex nihilo*. If creation was from nothing, then that raises another question: Where does *nothing* come from if God is omnipresent and there is nowhere that God isn't? Does nothing come out of *nowhere*? But if God is *everywhere,* then there is no *nowhere* for *nothing* to have come from. As creationists, we insist that there must be a Creator – a self-existent uncaused first cause, who is the source of all things. To the atheistic evolutionist we respond: *ex nihilo nihil fit, "out of nothing, nothing comes."* They say we were formed out of a primitive mass. If that were so, then we would be back where we started: Where did the mass originate - from nothing or from God? If everything is the result of a "big bang," what exploded?

Nevertheless, we as creationists should realize that the saying *"out of nothing, nothing comes"* also rules out the belief in creation *ex nihilo*. Since it is true that *"out of nothing, nothing comes,"* then we must have come out of God as to source, just as the Scriptures declare. Some Christians would argue that *nothing* refers to the invisible world and that *out of nothing* means to make something invisible appear, much like a rabbit out of a hat. In support of this idea, they cite Hebrews:

> *"By faith we understand that **the worlds** (aionas) were framed by the word of God, so that **the things which are seen were not made of things which are visible**." (Heb 11:3)*

However, the word translated *"worlds"* here is *aionas* in the Greek which means *eons*. Eons are, by their very nature invisible; a measure of time, and ages or eons are only visible in the sense that time-markers, such as the stars, the sun and the moon used to measure them are visible. The invisible realities such as the eons, sound waves, spirits, etc., are just as much a part of creation as that which we can see. In reality, according to science, the objects that are visible and tangible to us, are nothing more than different concentrations of invisible energy contained in atoms. The invisible world was created along with the visible tangible world, which can be seen by us. However, the eons or ages, although invisible, are not *nothing*. It is incorrect to say that *nothing* refers to the invisible, because the invisible world is also a part of the creation of God, as we see in Colossians:

> *"For by (en "in") Him **all things were created** that are in heaven and that are on earth, **visible and invisible**, whether thrones or dominions or principalities or powers. All things were created through Him and for Him." (Col 1:16)*

God Himself is Spirit and therefore is also invisible to us. Therefore, invisibility cannot be synonymous with *nothingness*.

While philosophers and theologians go in unending circles of reasoning concerning our origins, I believe that the Bible is simple, clear and at the same time profound in its revelation concerning our origins:

> *"Now **all ~~things~~ are of God** (ek theos), who has reconciled us to Himself through Jesus Christ, and has given us the ministry of reconciliation." (2Cor 5:18)* [49]

---

[49] Our English word *"things"* does not have an equivalent in Greek. Neither does the neuter form in Greek always indicate objects as in English. When the translators insert "things" in contexts that are evidently referring primarily to persons and not inanimate objects I take the liberty to cross it out in order to keep the focus where it belongs.

This text tells us that all are *"ex Deo"* or "out of God" *(Gr. ek Theos)*. It further states that, as firstfruits of the New Creation *(v.17)*, we who have already been reconciled to God have been given the ministry of reconciliation for the benefit of the rest of creation.

In all of God's Book, the term *ex nihilo* or "out of nothing" never appears. What we do see clearly stated more than once is that all things are *"ex Deo"* or "out of God." There is a world of difference between saying that we were created *"by God out of nothing"* and *"by God and out of God Himself."* The first is impersonal and by nature independent of God. The second is very personal and implies a connectedness and dependence.

I remember a tale about a kind farmer who cared well for all of his farm animals and they all loved him. When he fell on hard times the mother hen wanted to do something for him as an expression of love and gratitude. She got together with mister pig, who she knew was also very grateful to the kind farmer, to see what they could do for him. When mother hen suggested preparing a ham and egg breakfast for the farmer, mister pig replied: *"That's easy for you to say. For you it would just be a contribution but for me that would be a personal commitment."*

While the illustration falls short, it does demonstrate the difference in personal value placed upon something existing external to oneself as opposed to the value placed upon something which is actually a part of oneself. What would you be most likely to care for and maintain, your foot or the shoe you made for it? The answer should be obvious. We may throw away anything that we made out of nothing and for our own benefit like the shoe, for example. But we would do everything in our power, and even beyond, in order to save our foot because it is a part of us.

Traditionalists would have us think that we are something external to God, created out of nothing, only to serve His purposes. If He decides that we no longer serve His purposes well, it is no loss to Himself if He throws us into the fire, much as we would do with anything that is no longer useful to us.

That is why annihilationists see no problem with God exterminating 90% of His creation. They would say *ex nihilo ad nihilo,* "from nothing to nothing." Our word "annihilate" is from the same Latin words *ad nihilo (to nothing).* As we would say: *"Easy come, easy go."* They would emphatically deny that the God of love is as detached from His creation as their belief in *ex nihilo ad nihilo* implies. However, in reality, according to their belief, human life as with the rest of creation, is just as disposable to God as an old shoe.

Having been raised under the annihilationist doctrine, I know first-hand the low sense of self-worth that that doctrine instills in an individual before God on a heart level. Though they present God as a God of love, I didn't feel less hope or self-worth during my brief time as an atheist than I did as a child, believing in the annihilation of all but the strongest and the best.

When I had my saving encounter with God at 18 years of age, His love was shed abroad in my heart by the Holy Spirit. I didn't know anything about theology; I just knew from the very depths of my being and without any room for doubt that God loved me and that I was valued by Him more than I could fathom. It wasn't until I began studying theology that I began to have fears and doubts once again concerning His love for me and my worth in His eyes.

Within a few years' time, without even realizing it, I went from the *selective ex nihilo ad nihilo (from nothing to nothing)* belief of the annihilationists, to the *absolute ex nihilo ad nihilo* fatalism of the atheist, then finally entering into the infinite sea of God's love, only to come out on the other side through the influence of the traditional fear-based doctrine of eternal punishment for the majority.

If it were not for my personal encounter with the love of God at 18 years of age, which served as an anchor for my soul, I would have been worse off than when I still believed in the annihilation of the lost. At least at that time, when I felt low self-worth and feared rejection by God, I could console myself with the thought that I would be incinerated and eventually go out of existence. But once I was taught to believe that the unworthy "throw-aways" were burned in hell forever, the knowledge of the unconditional Love of God began to be challenged by a continuous tug-of-war conflict with a fear of an eternal hell.

All of us, if we are honest, experience failure and sin, and fall prey to the accuser of our souls. If we are not rooted and grounded in the love of God, we begin to struggle with low self-worth. That leads us to have fear and doubts concerning our standing with a god, whom we are told is unending love, but at the same time eternal hate and if we don't die on good terms with him, he will hate us and burn us in the flames of hell forever and ever.

Little by little, I came out of the first-love encounter with the Lord where I felt safe in His love, into a dualistic traditional doctrine of God in which I went from saying: *"He loves me!"* to *"He loves me, He loves me not, He loves me, He loves me not."* My sense of self-worth before God began to be based upon my performance rather than upon His unconditional love for me.

When I was in the Arminian church, I was told that God loved me *unconditionally,* but unless I persevered to the end, He would send me to an eternal hell. The Calvinists told me that if I was one of the elect, I didn't need to worry. But if I didn't persevere to the end, then that meant I was never elect in the first place. Both positions led to the same sense of insecurity. Calvinism is called "eternal security," but in reality, neither position offers the hopeful sinner any real sense of security.

In my opinion, to say that we come out of nothing, *ex nihilo*, as do the traditionalists, tremendously devalues us as God's creatures. It is an expression which inadvertently depersonalizes God's creation, converting us into throw-away items like an old shoe. What we see presented in the Scriptures is that all things came out of God *ex Deo,* and since we came out of God, we also exist by Him, somewhat as our foot exists due to the fact that it is part of us. Even though man fell, and nature was subjected to vanity, all things still originated in Him, are sustained by Him and will eventually return to Him. What we discover in the Scriptures is not *"ex nihilo et nihilo ad nihilo" (out of nothing, for nothing, into nothing)* but rather the glorious truth: *"ex Deo per Deo ad Deo" (out of God, through God and into God):*

"For of (ek) Him and through (dia) Him and to (eis) Him are all things, to whom be glory forever. Amen." (Rom 11:36)

In this passage alone, we can see God's wonderful plan for all of His creation summed up. All that which had its beginning in Him is sustained by Him and will return to Him. There are no throw-aways in all of God's creation. We are not objects *ex nihilo* to be thrown away as worthless trash, but rather created out of God Himself, and of infinite worth in His eyes. That is why He will ultimately restore all to Himself:

*"Now **all things are of God** (ek theos), **who has reconciled us to Himself** through Jesus Christ, and **has given us the ministry of reconciliation**." (2Cor 5:18)*

Here we see that all creation originated in God, and although we fell, He has also reconciled us to Himself and given us, as His elect, the ministry of reconciliation for the rest of creation. In Colossians 1:15-19, we see that the reconciliation is of all creation, both visible and invisible. In Romans 8:18-23, we see that, in the time of the manifestation of the sons of God, *all creation* will be set free. There are no throw-aways, no eternal garbage dump. In eternity, *all* will have been reconciled and God will then be *all in all*.

The truth that we are created out of God rather than out of nothing, is not to be confused with pantheism which teaches that all *is* God. Although creation began *in Christ (Gr. "en auto" Col 1:16), and came out of* Him, it is nonetheless distinct from Him. The triune personal God eternally self-exists. In the beginning, before creation, God, being eternal, already was:

"In the beginning God created *the heavens and the earth." (Gen 1:1)*

*"For by Him (lit. "in Him") all things were created that are in heaven and that are on earth, visible and invisible, whether thrones or dominions or principalities or powers. All things were created through Him and for Him. 17 And **He is before all things**, and in Him all things consist." (Col 1:16,17)*

God is eternal, without beginning. Creation, on the other hand, had a beginning. Yet it did not begin out of nothing *ex nihilo*, but rather out of God *ex Deo*. We are *of God*, much in the same way as Eve was *out of Adam:*

*"For as woman came **from (ek) man**, even so man also comes through (dia) woman; but all things are **from (ek) God**." (1Cor 11:12)*

Having come out of Him, there is still distinction just as there is distinction between Adam and Eve, even though she came out of him. However, having come out of Adam they were *one flesh*. There is union in distinction, in the same way mankind came out of God, and while there will always be distinction of persons, all of us live and move and have our being in Him. Although many, as the men of Athens to whom Paul preached, are yet blinded to this reality because of sin, and alienated in their minds, we all live by Him. None of us are self-existent. We may be, for a time, spiritually separated from God, but it is impossible that there should be spatial separation from Him because in *Him all things consist:*

> *"so that they should seek the Lord, in the hope that they might grope for Him and find Him, though **He is not far from each one of us**; 28 for **in Him we live and move and have our being**, as also some of your own poets have said, 'For we are also His offspring.' 29 Therefore, since we are the offspring of God, we ought not to think that the Divine Nature is like gold or silver or stone, something shaped by art and man's devising." (Acts 17:27-29)*

Paul is referring here to those who were at that time as yet unregenerate. Many of them even scoffed at him. Yet he included them in his declaration that each one of us; as His offspring, live and move and have our being in Him. While we are each individuals, we all came out of Him, exist by Him and shall also all return to Him. The end result is that He will be *all in all*.

Does God show Favoritism?

A phrase we see repeated several times in the Scriptures is, *"God shows no partiality." (Deut 10:17; 2Chron 19:7; Acts 10:34; 1Peter 1:17; Gal 2:6; Ro 2:11; Eph 6:9; Col 3:25)*. By this we understand that He treats all with equity. First, we see God's impartiality in the sense that all will be judged without exception:

> *"And if you call on the Father, who **without partiality judges** according to each one's work, conduct yourselves throughout the time of your stay here in fear." (1Peter 1:17)*

All will be judged according each man's works. Although Jesus said that those who believe will not be judged in a judicial manner *(John 3:18)*, in some sense, all without exception, will have to give an account for what we have done in this life, whether good or bad. Speaking of Christians Paul said the following:

"each one's work will become clear; for the Day will declare it, because it will be revealed by fire; and the fire will test each one's work, of what sort it is." (1Cor 3:13)

"For we must all appear before the judgment seat of Christ, that each one may receive the things done in the body, according to what he has done, whether good or bad." (2Cor 5:10)

Although many are in agreement that God is impartial in judgment, the traditionalists have to present God as being partial in showing mercy. The Calvinists say that only the elect will receive mercy, while the rest receive eternal wrath without mercy in hell. The Arminians say that only those who hear the gospel and believe before they die will receive mercy. In both scenarios it is impossible to say that God isn't partial as long as some will be tormented forever in hell, either because they were not among the elect, or because they missed the opportunity of hearing the gospel before dying. But is God presented in the Scriptures as being partial in His mercy? In the Bible we find that God, sooner or later, will be merciful to all:

*"The Lord is **good to all**, and **His tender mercies are over all** His works." (Ps 145:9)*

*"Therefore, as through one man's offense judgment came to all men (without partiality), resulting in condemnation, even so through one Man's righteous act **the free gift came to all men** (without partiality), resulting in justification of life." (Rom 5:18 parenthesis added)*

Also, we see repeated multiple times in the Scriptures that His mercy endures forever and not just for the brief time we are alive on this earth. The biblical Universalists are in agreement with the traditionalists in that one receives God's mercy when he repents and puts his faith in Christ. The difference between them and the traditionalists is that the Universalist does not find support from the Scriptures for the belief that the opportunity to receive God's mercy ends with physical death. God is not partial to anyone. All will have equal opportunity, not only to hear the gospel, but also to comprehend it and believe in Him, and that includes those who didn't hear the good news in this life.

Some would say that God actually is partial to certain people based upon Romans 9:18 where Paul says: *Therefore, He has mercy on whom He wills, and whom He wills He hardens."* However, if we follow the logic of Paul through to chapter 11, we see that although God, in order to accomplish His purposes in the ages, hardens some for a time while having mercy on others, in the end He is merciful to all:

*"For God has committed ~~them~~ [50] **all** to disobedience, that He might have mercy on **all**." (Rom 11:32)*

Many think of the election of grace as meaning that God chooses some *in preference to* others, and to the eternal exclusion of the rest, but what we see in the Scriptures is that election is in order to fulfill a specific purpose in a given time. Israel was chosen to be light to the nations and the Church of the firstborn (prototypes) - the firstfruits, have been chosen to manifest the glory of God's grace in the coming ages to the rest of God's creation. The elect of this age are the weakest and therefore the first to recognize their need of grace *(1Cor 1:26-29)*. However, the time will come when not only the present elect, but all of God's creation will have been restored and God will be all in all.

If we were to limit our perspective to this life, it is obvious that there exists much inequity and we would be forced to say that the Bible contradicts itself and that God in reality is partial to some. However, if we understand that the mercy of God is forever and that all in the end, in His due time, will receive mercy, it all begins to make sense. The Universalist can understand these Scriptures in their obvious sense, knowing that God does not have a time limit in which He must accomplish His purposes in our lives. In His time, He will make all things new. In the end all in heaven and on the earth will be reunited in Christ in the dispensation of the fullness of the times *(Eph 1:10)*.

As we have already seen, God is the Father of all: **"Have we not all one Father?** *Has not one God* **created us?***" (Mal 2:10)* Jesus also affirmed the fatherhood of God; not only to the disciples but also to the multitudes: *"Then Jesus spoke* **to the multitudes** *and to His disciples, 2 saying…***One is your Father***, He who is in heaven." (Matt 23:1,9)*. If God is the Father of all, how can He love some to the exclusion of others?

---

[50] *"them"* is not in the original Greek text but was added by the translators.

Even though we as fathers are evil compared to our heavenly Father, we love our sons equally without exception. If a father of four children, were to awaken in the night and discover his house was in flames, he would risk his own life in order to rescue each of his four sons. He couldn't endure the thought of losing even one of his children in spite of their defects and differences in character. How can we attribute to God a partiality much more heartless; that of choosing a few of His children and then personally throwing the rest into eternal flames? One cannot escape the presence of God, even in Hades *(Ps 139:8)*. Is it possible that God, who is love, could be enjoying the company of His few elect children at the same time that He is hearing throughout eternity the screams and cries for mercy from the vast majority of His children in hell, without being moved to compassion for them?

As parents we understand the need to correct and punish our children when they are disobedient, but it would be unthinkable to torture or kill them, no matter how rebellious they may become. On the contrary we are compassionate towards them and are quick to show them mercy, no matter what it is they may have done. And as soon as we see that our correction has accomplished its purpose, we take them in our arms and confirm our affection for them. We understand that our Father does not reject his children forever, nor does He torture them – much less for all eternity, but rather He punishes them and corrects them for their own good:

*"For **the Lord will not cast off forever**. 32 **Though He causes grief, yet He will show compassion according to the multitude of His mercies**. 33 For **He does not afflict willingly**, nor grieve the children of men." (Lam 3:31-33)*

In conclusion, to my way of thinking, only those who believe in a universal restoration can say with Peter, without any need for clarification or exceptions: *"In truth I perceive that God shows no partiality." (Acts 10:34)*

The Inclusion of Children and the Mentally Handicapped

According to Augustinian tradition, the only ones saved are those who have heard the gospel and put their faith in Christ during the course of their earthly life. Since we are all born into sin and under condemnation because of Adam's original sin, the only way of being saved is to receive Christ as Savior and, for the traditionalist, it is necessary to do so before physical death.

This presents a moral dilemma for the traditionalists since the great majority of humanity has not even had the opportunity to hear the gospel in the brief course of their lifetime. If, in order to be saved, all must make a decision for Christ in this lifetime, then what about infants, children and those with mental handicaps who are not even able to distinguish their right hand from their left?

In the past the Church took the position of Saint Augustine concerning this subject which offers little or no hope of salvation for these unfortunate individuals. According to tradition, the same destiny of eternal torment awaits them just as with the rest who die without having put faith in Christ. Until recent years this was the official belief of the Church. The following are some examples of this barbaric belief:

Jonathan Edwards

> "Reprobate **_infants_ are vipers of vengeance**, which Jehovah will hold over hell, in the tongs of his wrath, till they turn and spit venom in his face!" [51]

Jeremy Taylor

> "Husbands shall see their wives; parents **shall see their children tormented before their eyes**...the bodies of the damned shall be crowded together in hell like grapes in a winepress, which press on one another till they burst..." [52]

Reverend J. Furniss

> "**Little child**, if you go to hell there will be a devil at your side to strike you. He will go on striking you every minute for ever and ever without stopping. The first stroke will make your body as bad as the body of Job, covered, from head to foot, with sores and

---

[51] http://what-the-hell-is-hell.com/AncientHell.htm

[52] http://what-the-hell-is-hell.com/AncientHell.htm

*ulcers. The second stroke will make your body twice as bad as the body of job. The third stroke will make your body three times as bad as the body of Job. The fourth stroke will make your body four times as bad as the body of Job. How, then, will your body be after the devil has been striking it every moment for a hundred million years without stopping? Perhaps at this moment, seven o'clock in the evening, **a child** is just now going into hell. Tomorrow evening, at seven o'clock, go and knock at the gates of hell and ask what the child is doing. The devils will go and look. They will come back again and say, **the child is burning**. Go in week and ask what the child is doing; you will get the same answer - it is burning; Go in a year and ask and the same answer comes—it is burning. Go in a million of years and ask the same question, the answer is just the same--it is burning. So, if you go for ever and ever, you will always get the same answer--it is burning in the fire."* [53]

In these examples we can see how blind followers of tradition arrive at such extremes that they consider infants to be vipers of vengeance and worthy of eternal flames. Also, those with mental handicaps were called "idiots" and said to have become that way as a consequence of the sins of their fathers, and therefore were damned. As recently as 1990 Gerstner wrote the following in his book, *Repent or Perish: "Infants are not innocent, but are born with guilt and sin. Therefore, until they are born again, they are in imminent danger of eternal condemnation and should be informed of their danger as soon as possible."* [54]

Nevertheless, in more recent times, the majority of traditionalists find the eternal torment of little children and the mentally handicapped incompatible with the love and justice of God and have sought means to justify their inclusion in the kingdom of God without requiring a decision of faith on their part. Many Churches in the last couple of centuries have presented exception clauses in their creeds. Some say an infant will be saved if it is baptized before death. Others say that only children of baptized Christian parents will

---

[53] http://what-the-hell-is-hell.com/AncientHell.htm

[54] Gerstner, *Repent or Perish, Ligonier,* Soli Deo Gloria Publicaciones, 1990

be saved. Many Calvinists like Jonathan Edwards believe that only elect children will be saved, while the rest will go to eternal hellfire.

The position adopted by the majority of the evangelical church at present is that all children will be saved without the need of having made a personal decision of faith until they reach "the age of accountability." The majority put twelve years of age as the age of accountability. Certainly, this doctrine is preferable to the original position of the institutionalized Church. The main problem, however, with this position is that it doesn't have Scriptural support. One text used to justify this doctrine is in Deuteronomy where children are allowed to enter the Promised Land whereas their parents were doomed to die in the wilderness for their unbelief:

> **"your little ones and your children**, who you say will be victims, **who today have no knowledge of good and evil, they shall go in there**; to them I will give it, and they shall possess it. 40 But as for you, turn and take your journey into the wilderness by the Way of the Red Sea." (Deut 1:39-40)

Here we see that their little ones and children who did not yet know to distinguish between good and evil were permitted entrance into the Promised Land. According to them there is a pattern set here which would apply for the salvation of children and the mentally handicapped who are not able to distinguish between good or evil. However, in the example given of the children of Israel the "age of accountability" was twenty years of age and not twelve:

> "The carcasses of you who have complained against Me shall fall in this wilderness, all of you who were numbered, according to your entire number, **from twenty years old and above**. 30 Except for Caleb the son of Jephunneh and Joshua the son of Nun, you shall by no means enter the land which I swore I would make you dwell in. 31 But your little ones, whom you said would be victims, I will bring in, and they shall know the land which you have despised. 32 But as for you, your carcasses shall fall in this wilderness." (Num 14:29-32)

It is not possible to establish from Scriptures that there is an "age of accountability." One Scripture utilized to establish the inclusion of children in the kingdom is Mathew 19:14 *"But Jesus said, 'Let the little children come to Me, and do not forbid them; for of such is the kingdom of heaven'."* However, this verse doesn't establish an age at which one becomes accountable. One final verse is presented from 2 Samuel. When David committed adultery with Bathsheba, Uriah's wife, she became pregnant and gave birth to a son. As a judgment against David for his sin with Bathsheba, and for having Uriah killed in battle to cover up his sin of adultery, the baby died. When David knew that his son had died, he said: *"I shall go to him, but he shall not return to me." (2 Sam 12:23b)*. While this doesn't establish an age of responsibility it clearly indicates that children enter the kingdom of heaven at death. However, this is also in harmony with Universalism which teaches that all will eventually enter the kingdom of heaven, even those who have not yet believed *(1Ti 4:10)*. David did not anticipate that his baby son nor he himself, for that matter, would go to an eternal hell. In fact, the Old Testament doesn't even mention punishment after death. In spite of the fact that David knew his son had died because of his own sin of adultery and murder, he was confident that he would be with him in paradise and that he *would go to him* upon dying.

The belief that a child goes to heaven upon dying without accepting Christ until he turns twelve but goes to hell if he dies after turning twelve, not only lacks Scriptural support but also goes against logic and all sense of justice. If this were true, someone who knew about it could accept Christ one day before his birthday, whereas another who doesn't know about the "age of accountability" could die the day after and go to hell for having passed the "age of accountability" by one day without making a decision. If it were true, then abortion would be the best way to guarantee that your child would be in heaven. There has been more than one incident in which parents have killed their children before reaching the age of accountability for fear they would end up in hell if they continued living. We could say that such a parent would be mentally unstable, but we cannot contradict their logic, given their belief that their son or daughter could end up in hell if they were to live beyond the age of responsibility.

Andrea Yates, in 2001, drowned her five children in a bathtub. She was emotionally unstable, but much of her instability was due to the emphasis on hellfire in the church she and her husband attended. She became convinced that she was unable to raise her children in a way that would result in them being saved and decided that the only way to save them from an eternal hell was to kill them before they turned twelve. According to her belief, her act was motivated by a love for her children; not wanting them to end up in hell forever.

And the truth is that her reasoning would be sound and her act justifiable if the traditional doctrine of eternal punishment after the age of accountability were true.

Many, although they are not Universalists, admit to the possibility of salvation after death. Martin Luther expressed his belief in the possibility of post-mortem salvation when he said: *"God forbid that I should limit the time of acquiring faith to the present life. In the depth of the Divine mercy there may be opportunity to win it in the future."* [55]

C.S. Lewis was a man who had great influence upon Christian thought in the twentieth century and his influence continues to the present. His mentor, George MacDonald, was a prominent Universalist. C.S. Lewis, however, was not a declared Universalist. He sustained the possibility that some *could* spend eternity in hell, but not because it is God's will but rather the will of the individual himself to remain there. As he said: *"The doors of hell are locked from within,"* implying that no one must remain there, obligated against their free-will.

This interpretation of hell is being adopted by many in the Church at the present time. This perspective takes into account the passages that indicate the possibility of responding to the gospel after death *(1Peter 3:18-20; 4:6; 1Tim 4:10; Eph 4:8-10; Ps 68:18)*. Nevertheless, they do not give sufficient weight to the passages that emphasize the restoration of all and a universal reconciliation, with every creature ultimately being subjected to Christ, culminating in the eternal state in which God shall be all in all. It is my opinion that many who publicly present this point of view, in reality are Universalists by conviction, but they have opted not to declare it openly, fearing that they would lose opportunities for ministry. As one evangelical leader who defends Universalism without committing himself to it said: *"Today it would be ministerial suicide to express openly the hope of a universal salvation."*

---

[55] Martín Lutero, *Carta a Von Hansen Rechenberg en 1522*

Chapter five
The Duration of Punishment

In the majority of the translations of the Bible there exists a great contradiction between the Scriptures we have seen up to this point concerning universal restoration and the translator's renditions of the words *olam* in Hebrew and *aión* and *aiónios* in the Greek of the New Testament. The Bible speaks of *"olam* shame," *"aionios* fire," *aionios* punishment" and "*aionios* perdition." Also, it speaks of the lake of fire which will last "for the *eons* of the *eons."* If it can be demonstrated that these words express eternity or duration without end, then a universal restoration of all, which many Scriptures indicate, would not be possible. A restoration of all is not possible if the great majority of God's creatures are being tormented in the lake of fire forever. Both cannot be true simultaneously.

If these words always express the idea of eternity, then those who affirm that hell is eternal – without end, have a strong argument in their favor, unless we were to say that eternity is a hyperbolic expression. Actually, hyperbole was very common with the Hebrews - especially in the Scriptures. Even today it is common to use expressions like: "It took forever to get home in the traffic" or "he took forever but he finally did it" or "I thought I had lost you forever." These hyperboles are exaggerations which are common to us and we know not to take them literally.

Nevertheless, the words translated, "eternal" "eternity" and "forever," as we shall see, could not possibly mean "eternal"; at least not in the majority of the contexts in which they are employed. Even the traditional translators recognize this. *Olam*, which is used 438 times in the Old Testament is translated in the King James Version as *"always, ancient, anymore, continuance, eternal, forever, everlasting, for ever more, of old, lasting, long time, perpetual, at any time, world."* *Aión* appears 120 times in the New Testament and is translated as: *"age, course, eternal, forever, ever, evermore, world."* *Aionios* appears 73 times and is translated: *"eternal, forever, everlasting, and world"* [56] Examining all of these texts it becomes

---

[56] New Exhaustive Strong's Numbers and Concordance with Expanded Greek-Hebrew Dictionary.

very obvious that these words cannot possibly mean *"eternal"* in the majority of the contexts in which they appear. As we will see, the translators rendered these words erroneously. More recent translations have corrected some of these errors and also several literal translations have come out which consistently correct all of them. The most popular one is Young's Literal Translation published in 1898 by Robert Young who also compiled Young's Analytical Concordance.

OLAM

The Hebrew word *olam* is derived from the word *alam* which means, *"hidden or out of sight."* The same idea is expressed in the word *olam* as with its derivative *alam*. Strong's Concordance translates it in the following manner: "derived from *alam*; properly, *concealed,* i.e. *the vanishing point*; generally, *time out of mind (past or future)...*" If he would have stopped there, he would have adequately expressed the real sense of the word, but he continues, saying: *"i.e. practically eternity..."* [57] The *Encyclopedia of the Bible,* Ediciones Garriga S.A. defines *olam* as follows:

> *"Olam in the line of duration, indicates times undetermined, remote, obscure, whether it be past or future, the duration of the life of a man or a long extension which comes to designate* **indefinite duration... It does not express the platonic and modern concept of eternity."** [58]

According to this encyclopedia and many other authorities on the subject, the concept of eternity as we understand it now, wasn't even conceived of until it was put forth by the philosopher Plato in the third century before Christ. The words *olam, aión* and *aionios,* often translated as referring to eternity, simply mean *"a time of indefinite duration."* Although eternity has always been a reality, in ancient times no words existed in their vocabulary to express that concept. The Bible is not dedicated to describing eternity. The primary focus of the Scriptures is the plan of God in time – His plan for the ages. The Old Testament only uses the word *olam* which expresses the

---

[57] New Exhaustive Strong's Numbers and Concordance with Expanded Greek-Hebrew Dictionary.

[58] La Enciclopedia de la Biblia de Ediciones Garriga S.A.

idea of time of unknown duration beyond the horizon. It can have reference to indefinite past time, *"from olam";* indefinite future time, *"to olam,"* or simply unknown time *"olam."* Just a few examples will be enough to illustrate that *olam* does not mean forever:

1. Indefinite Past Time:

> "There were giants on the earth in those days, and also afterward, when the sons of God came in to the daughters of men and they bore children to them. Those were the mighty men who were **of old** (olam), men of renown." (Gen 6:4)

> "And Joshua said to all the people, 'Thus says the Lord God of Israel: 'Your fathers, including Terah, the father of Abraham and the father of Nahor, dwelt on the other side of the River **in old times** (olam); and they served other gods." (Josh 24:2-3)

> "And David and his men went up and raided the Geshurites, the Girzites, and the Amalekites. For those nations were the inhabitants of the land **from of old** (olam), as you go to Shur, even as far as the land of Egypt." (1 Sam 27:8-9)

> "In the days of her affliction and roaming, Jerusalem remembers all her pleasant things that she had in **the days of old** (olam)." (Lam 1:7)

> "So Joshua burned Ai and made it a heap **forever** (olam), a desolation **to this day**." (Josh 8:28)

> "I (Jonah) went down to the moorings of the mountains; the earth with its bars closed behind me **forever** (olam); **yet You have brought up my life from the pit**, o Lord, my God." (Jonah 2:6)

In these examples it is very clear that eternity is not in view. *Olam*, in these verses, only has reference to past time with an undefined point of beginning. In each case the time is limited; the shortest span of time being the time during which Jonah was in the belly of the great fish.

2. Indefinite Future Time:

> *"But Hannah went not up; for she said unto her husband, (I will not go up) until the child be weaned; and then I will bring him, that he may appear before Jehovah, and there abide **forever** (olam)." (1 Sam 1:22)*
>
>> *"But this time Hannah did not go. She told her husband, 'As soon as the child is weaned, I will take him to the house of the Lord, where he will stay **all his life** (olam)." (1 Sam 1:22 TEV)*
>
> *"Then his master shall bring him to the judges. He shall also bring him to the door, or to the doorpost, and his master shall pierce his ear with an awl; and he shall serve him **forever** (olam)." (Ex 21:6)*
>
>> *"Then his master shall take him to the place of worship. There he is to make him stand against the door or the doorpost and put a hole through his ear. Then he will be his slave **for life** (olam)." (Ex 21:6 TEV)*
>
> *"But the Lord shall endure **forever** (olam); he has prepared His throne for judgment." (Ps 9:7)*

All of these texts express indefinite future time – time beyond the horizon. In the case of the first two examples the duration is for the life of Samuel and the bond-slave. In the last text it is referring to God's existence, and although we know He is eternal, the word *olam* doesn't communicate this reality. It simply says that He will endure throughout time. As He himself is the Creator of time with its ages (Heb 1:2 "He made the ~~worlds~~ ages"), we know that He is eternal and exists independently of time. In order for God to have made the ages, He must have an existence independently of them.

3. *Indefinite Past and Indefinite Future Time combined when referring to God:*

> *"Before the mountains were brought forth, or ever You had formed the earth and the world, even **from everlasting to everlasting** (from olam to olam), **You <u>are</u>** God." (Ps 90:2)*

Since the Hebrew language didn't have a word in their vocabulary to express the eternity of God, they formed phrases to express it. The phrase *"from olam to olam you ARE (present tense) God"* says in so many words what we can now express by simply saying *"eternal God"* – i.e. God always IS.

When Moses asked God: *"when I come to the children of Israel and say to them, 'The God of your fathers has sent me to you,' and they say to me, 'What is His name?' what shall I say to them?" (Ex 3:13),* God responded saying that He is the eternal God but in words that seem strange to us since we now have "eternal" in our vocabulary and we don't need to use so many words to express His eternity: *"And God said to Moses, 'I AM WHO I AM.' And He said, 'Thus you shall say to the children of Israel, I AM has sent me to you." (v. 14).* In our vocabulary today we would simply say "I AM the Eternal One – He who always IS." His name Jehovah means: *"He who exists"* or *"The eternal one."*

Examples of where Olam was mistranslated.

> *"And God said: 'This is the sign of the covenant which I make between Me and you, and every living creature that is with you, for **perpetual** (olam) **generations**." (Gen 9:12, cf. 9:16)*

Neither the sign of the rainbow nor generations are perpetual. In the resurrection we will be like the angels – we will no longer engender children. Therefore, there will not be generations perpetually.

> *"…Up to the utmost bound of the **everlasting** (olam) hills. They shall be on the head of Joseph, and on the crown of the head of him who was separate from his brothers." (Gen 49:26)*

The hills are not eternal but rather were created and someday will be leveled and burned. *(Isa 40:4; 2Peter 3:10)*

> *"So this day shall be to you a memorial; and you shall keep it as a feast to the Lord **throughout your generations**. You shall keep it as a feast by an **everlasting** (olam) ordinance." (Ex 12:14)*

The duration of *olam* here is limited by the phrase *"throughout your generations,"* unless we are to understand that the Israelites will be perpetually generating throughout all eternity. This phrase is used with *olam* more than 20 times in the Old Testament.

> *"And you shall gird them with sashes, Aaron and his sons, and put the hats on them. The priesthood shall be theirs for a **perpetual** (olam) statute. So you shall consecrate Aaron and his sons." (Ex 29:9)*

The Aaronic priesthood ceased to have relevance when Christ, our Passover, was sacrificed for us and He became a priest after the order of Melchizedek *(Heb 7)*.

> *"The sons of Aaron, the priests, shall blow the trumpets; and these shall be to you as an ordinance **forever** (olam) throughout your generations." (Num 10:8)*

God ceased requiring the blowing of the trumpets and observing other rituals of the Old Testament such as Sabbath observance and sacrificial offerings when Christ initiated the New Covenant and the temple was destroyed *(Heb 8:8-13)*.

> *"then you shall take an awl and thrust it through his ear to the door, and he shall be your servant **forever** (olam)." (Deut 15:17)*

> *"An Ammonite or Moabite shall not enter the assembly of the Lord; **even to the tenth generation**. None of his descendants shall enter the assembly of the Lord **forever** (olam)." (Deut 23:3)*

Here we see that *olam* was limited to ten generations.

> *"Then you shall answer them that the waters of the Jordan were cut off before the ark of the covenant of the Lord; when it crossed over the Jordan, the waters of the Jordan were cut off. And these stones shall be for a memorial to the children of Israel **forever** (olam)." (Josh 4:7)*

Where is the monument of stones today?

> *"But Hannah did not go up, for she said to her husband, 'Not until the child is weaned; then I will take him, that he may appear before the Lord and remain there **forever** (olam)." (1 Sam 1:22)*

Hannah didn't mean to say by this that Samuel would remain in the tabernacle for all eternity but rather during his lifetime or indefinitely.

> "And the Lord said to him: 'I have heard your prayer and your supplication that you have made before Me; I have consecrated this house which you have built to put My name there **forever** (olam), and My eyes and My heart will be there perpetually." (1 Kings 9:3)

God promised to inhabit the temple of Salomon until *olam*. Salomon's temple lasted only 400 years. During much of that time it was defiled by idolatry and the glory of God had already departed from it years before its destruction.

> "Therefore the leprosy of Naaman shall cling to you and your descendants **forever** (olam). And he went out from his presence leprous, as white as snow." (2 Kings 5:27)

Naaman's leprosy clung to Gehazi forever *(olam)* but only until his death.

> "... and Aaron was set apart, he and his sons **forever** (olam), that he should sanctify the most holy things, to burn incense before the Lord, to minister to Him, and to give the blessing in His name **forever** (olam)." (1Chron 23:13)

The Aaronic priesthood came to an end with the New Covenant initiated by the shedding of the blood of Christ once and for all.

> "You who laid the foundations of the earth, so that it should not be moved **forever** (olam)." (Ps 104:5)

The earth will remain until *olam* but not forever. "You, Lord, in the beginning laid the foundation of the earth, and the heavens are the work of Your hands. 11 **They will perish**, but You remain; and they will all grow old like a garment; 12 Like a cloak You will fold them up, and they will be changed. But You are the same, and Your years will not fail." (Heb 1:10-12 cf. Mt 24:35; Rev 21:1).

> "And you shall prepare a grain offering with it every morning, a sixth of an ephah, and a third of a hin of oil to moisten the fine

*flour. This grain offering is a **perpetual** (olam) ordinance, to be made regularly to the Lord." (Ezek 46:14)*

*"I (Jonah) went down to the moorings of the mountains; the earth with its bars closed behind me **forever** (olam); Yet You have brought up my life from the pit, o Lord, my God." (Jonah 2:6)*

Here in Jonah's case, *olam* only lasted for the three days and three nights that he was in the belly of the great fish.

The examples here presented should suffice to demonstrate that *olam* does not mean "eternal" or "forever." Although it often refers to a long time, it can also have reference to a very short time, such as the three days during which Jonah was in the belly of the great fish.

Olam and Beyond

There are a few instances in which the writer wished to communicate the idea of an infinite future. In these cases we see the use of *olam* followed by *a-ad*. The word *a-ad* is translated in the Greek LXX translation of the Old Testament with the word *eti*, which, according to Strong's means: *"yet, still (of time or degree): - after that...."* The Hebrew to Greek translation is called the LXX or 70 because it was translated by 70 Jewish scholars in the second century before Christ. They were all Hebrews who spoke the Koine Greek of the time, and for that reason their rendering of the Hebrew to Greek helps us to determine the meanings of the Hebrew words in their epoch. According to them, the idea expressed in *a-ad* is equivalent to *eti* in the Greek language. *Olam*, followed by *a-ad*, therefore, expresses the idea of "for *olam* and beyond," which is the closest that they could come to expressing "forever" in their language. One example is Exodus 15:18: *"The Lord shall reign **forever and ever** (olam a-ad)* or "for *olam* and beyond."

The Shame and self-Contempt is for olam and No More.

It is interesting to see how the phrase *olam a-ad* is used in Daniel 12:2,3:

*"And many of those who sleep in the dust of the earth shall awake, some to **everlasting (olam) life**, some to shame and **everlasting***

*(olam) contempt. 3 Those who are wise shall shine like the brightness of the firmament, and those who turn many to righteousness like the stars **forever and ever (olam a-ad "for olam and beyond")**." (Dan 12:2-3)*

This passage is very significant in relationship to the subject of eternal punishment and universal restoration which we have been considering, given that it is the only text in the Old Testament that speaks of the state of the unjust after being resurrected for judgment. In verse two it says that their contempt (lit. shame or self-contempt) will last for *olam* (an indefinite period of time). It also says of the just that they will be resurrected to life *olam*. However, in verse three it clarifies that the life unto which the just will be resurrected is everlasting, *(olam a-ad "olam and beyond")*, and not just *olam* as is the case with those who will suffer shame and self-contempt.

This is very similar to what Jesus said in Matthew 25:46: *"And these will go away into everlasting (aionios) punishment, but the righteous into eternal (aionios) life."* We see that Jesus was probably referring back to Daniel 12:2: *"some to everlasting (olam) life, some to shame and everlasting (olam) contempt."* In both instances they make reference to two groups of people; in Daniel it speaks of those resurrected, whereas in Matthew it appears to be limited to those of the nations which are alive upon the earth when Christ returns and separates the sheep from the goats.

Many have argued that if the punishment in Matthew 25:46 isn't eternal, then neither is the life eternal. However, we have seen in the parallel passage in Daniel 12 that the life of the just isn't simply for *olam*, as is the case with the shame and self-contempt of the unjust, but rather "for *olam* and beyond." Also, in Matthew 25:46, as we will see in more detail later, the word translated "punishment" *(Greek kolasis)* does not refer to torture but to *correction*. Correction has a positive purpose and therefore must end when its purpose has been accomplished. If it were not so, then it would not be correction. The traditional model presents the punishment administered by God as if it were motivated by a rage which can never be placated. It presents God as a father who eternally flogs his children just for the satisfaction of His implacable wrath. But such conduct would not be consistent with the God of love presented to us in the Scriptures who is just and merciful without exception of persons. Jesus refers to us as being evil fathers in comparison to our Father God. Who of us as fathers – however angry we may be with our rebellious child, would whip him for a whole day? Yet God is infinitely more compassionate, just and good than the best father on earth.

AIÓN, AIONIOS

When *olam* was translated into Greek in the LXX, they always translated it *aión* o *aionios*. The concept of eternity was conceived and first taught by the Greek philosopher Plato (427 to 347 B.C.). By then the Old Testament had already been completed. Plato borrowed the word *aionios* to express the philosophical concept of "eternity" in contrast with the word *chronos,* referring to the concept of "time." Nevertheless, in the mind of the Hebrews and in the Bible, *aión* and its adjective *aionios* continued to convey the same idea as *olam* – that of time beyond the horizon and therefore indefinite but not eternal.

The concept of eternity existing independently from time was popularized among the Jews by Philo, a Jewish contemporary of Jesus (20 BC to AD 50), who was schooled in the philosophy of Plato. Nevertheless, the philosophical concept of eternity wasn't articulated by the Church fathers until Saint Augustine, (AD 354 to AD 430), who, adopting many of the concepts of Plato, introduced them into the theology of the Church.

Coinciding with this philosophical definition of *aionios* by Plato, the Greeks also believed in eternal torment. Although the Old Testament does not speak of the torment of the unjust after death beyond the single allusion to shame and self-contempt lasting for *olam (Dan 12:2)*, many of the Pharisees in Jesus's time believed in eternal punishment through the combined influences of the Egyptians and the Greeks. Nevertheless, continuing in the influence of the Scriptures, they did not normally use *aionios* in reference to eternity as did the Greek philosophers. When they wished to communicate eternity, they normally used the word *aidíos* instead of *aionios*. [59]

Some Church fathers, even before Saint Augustine, following the doctrines of the Pharisees and Philo, expressed a belief in eternal punishment. Nevertheless, seeing how *aión* and *aionios* are used in the New Testament, it is evident that the writers of the New

---

[59] http://www.tentmaker.org/books/prevailing/upd3.html

Testament retained the meaning of *olam* of the Old Testament as having reference to time and not eternity when using *aión* or *aionios*. This is especially evident in Romans 16:25-27:

> *"Now to Him who is able to establish you according to my gospel and the preaching of Jesus Christ, according to the revelation of the mystery* **kept secret since** ~~the world began~~ *(cronois aioniois* **"times of the ages"***) 26* **but now made manifest***, and by the prophetic Scriptures made known to all nations, according to the commandment of the everlasting God, for obedience to the faith — 27 to God, alone wise, be glory through Jesus Christ forever. Amen." (Rom 16:25-27)*

Here, the New King James Version "translates" the plural of both *chronos* and *aionios*, which actually means *"times of the ages"* for *"since the world began."* Most traditionalists insist that *aionios* always means eternal but the translators of the King James, realized that they couldn't translate the text *"times eternal"* because eternity doesn't have "times." The American Standard Version does translate it *"times eternal"* but *"times eternal"* is still an anomaly since eternity exists apart from time. Also, one cannot say that something which is *now made manifest* is an *eternal secret*, since an *"eternal secret"* would never be revealed. This text should have been translated literally *"hidden since the times of the ages,"* as we see in the literal translations:

> *"Now to Him Who is able to establish you in accord with my evangel, and the heralding of Christ Jesus in accord with the revelation of a secret hushed in* **times eonian***, yet manifested now..." (Concordant Literal Version)*

> *"And to Him who is able to establish you, according to my good news, and the preaching of Jesus Christ, according to the revelation of the secret, in the* **times of the ages** *having been kept silent, and now having been made manifest..." (Young's Literal Translation)*

Plato used *chronos* to refer to time and *aión* and *aionios* in reference to eternity. Here we see both *chronos* and *aionios* used together in reference to time which demonstrates that the New Testament did not use *aión* or *aionios* in the Platonic sense of eternal. The traditionalists who translated the King James Version recognized that it was often impossible to translate *aión* and its adjective *aionios* to mean "eternal." Nevertheless, because of their Augustinian/Platonic influence, they insisted on imposing the definition "eternal" as often as possible, and when it wasn't possible, instead of rendering *aión* or *aionios* to express time they often concealed it by rendering it "world" or "worlds" which have no relationship whatsoever to its real meaning *(cf. Luke 1:70; John 9:32; Acts 3:21; Rom 16:25; Heb 1:2; 11:3).*

Some justify the rendition *"worlds"* in Hebrews 11:3, saying that *aión* cannot have reference to ages since *aión* is referred to as that which is seen, and time is not something which can be seen:

> *"By faith we understand that **the worlds** ("ages," aionas, pl.) were framed by the word of God, so that the **things which are seen** were not made of things which are visible." (Heb 11:3)*

However, this verse only affirms what many of us often overlook – that time is an essential part of the material creation and is intrinsically dependent upon it. Without the heavenly bodies there would be no way of measuring time. Even history is defined by physical events such as "before Christ," "after Christ," "iron age," "industrial age," etc. Without these material markers there would be no reference points for time, time with its days and ages would essentially be nonexistent. Time began with the physical creation. We measure time through the material universe. Nevertheless, *aión* and *aionios* continue being time words and therefore cannot be correctly translated as referring to the material "world" or "worlds."

Aión

An examination of the contexts in which *aión* is used will make it clear that, in the majority of its occurrences, "eternal" would make no sense. The following are a few examples of passages in which *aión* would make no sense translated "eternity":

> *"...whosoever shall speak against the Holy Spirit, it shall not be forgiven him, neither in **this eternity, nor the eternity to come**." (Matt 12:32)*

> *"...and **the cares of this eternity** and the deceitfulness of riches choke the word, and he becomes unfruitful." (Matt 13:22)*

"...the harvest is **the end of the eternity**, and the reapers are the angels. 40 Therefore as the tares are gathered and burned in the fire, so it will be at **the end of this eternity**." (Matt 13:39,40)

"...Tell us, when will these things be? And what will be the sign of Your coming, and of **the end of the eternity**?" (Matt 24:3)

"Jesus answered and said to them, '**The sons of this eternity** marry and are given in marriage'." (Luke 20:34)

"...whose minds **the god of this eternity** has blinded, who do not believe, lest the light of the gospel of the glory of Christ, who is the image of God, should shine on them." (2Cor 4:4)

"...Now all these things happened to them as examples, and they were written for our admonition, upon whom **the ends of the eternities** have come." (1Cor 10:11)

"...**that in the eternities to come** He might show the exceeding riches of His grace in His kindness toward us in Christ Jesus." (Eph 2:7)

"...to Him be glory in the church by Christ Jesus to all generations, **for the eternity of the eternities**. Amen." (Eph 3:21)

"for Demas has forsaken me, having loved **this present eternity**..." (2Tim 4:10)

"...And the smoke of their torment ascends **for the eternities of the eternities**." (Rev 14:11)

"...but **now**, once **at the end of the eternities**, He has appeared to put away sin by the sacrifice of Himself." (Heb 9:26)

In these examples we see the absurdities and anomalies that result when we take a word that refers to time and impose upon it consistently the idea of eternity. How is it possible to add a day to eternity; much less add eternities to eternities or speak of the eternity of the eternities? How is it possible to be living in time and love this present eternity? How can we speak of coming eternities or the ends of the eternities? Is Satan the god of eternity? Were the disciples asking Jesus for signs of the end of eternity? Is it possible to speak of the present eternity and the coming eternity?

Understanding that eternity has an existence independent of time, how can we use *aión,* which is a measurement of time, in reference to eternity? Although time came into existence alongside of eternity, time is a creation of God *(Heb 1:2 lit. "made the ages"),* time is measurable and finite. On the other hand, eternity always is - it is infinite and cannot be measured. Seconds, minutes, days, years, centuries and ages, are segments of time and cannot be used to refer to eternity. The only words that express "eternity" are the names of God, I AM and Jehovah. All the rest have a beginning and an end. There are other words to express "forever" which refer to an infinite future or future without end such as *"cannot die" (Luke 20:36), "immortal" (Gr. atanasia)* and *"incorruptible" (aftharsía) (1Cor 15:53),* but these words are only applied to God and His glorified saints. They, are never used in reference to the punishment of the unjust that are in Hades or Gehenna (hell). Therefore, there are no words used in the New Testament that are applied to the unjust which would imply their continuance in hell beyond the end of the ages when God shall be all in all.

Those who believe on Jesus have eternal life and will live **forever**, but they are *not eternal.* We can say that we will live forever, referring to the future, and that we will be incorruptible and immortal, but we cannot say that we are eternal. From the moment we are baptized into Christ, He becomes our life *(Col 3:3,4; 1Jn 5:11,12).* We continue living in time as the rest, but at the same time, we now have Eternity dwelling in us because we have been made partakers of His divine nature *(2Peter 1:4).* However, we are not in and of ourselves eternal.

If *aión* is translated with the words, "epoch," "eon," or "era" as we find in the literal translations of the New Testament, the anomalies we have seen cease to exist and we avoid misinterpreting the Scriptures. These words all express a long but usually indefinite period of time. The English word *eon* and its adjective *eonian* are derived from the Greek *aión* and *aionios* and today still carry the same meaning: "a vast amount of time, the longest unit of time."

Aionios

As we have already seen, *aionios* is the adjective of *aión.* An adjective is restricted in its meaning to that of its noun. The adjective of "hour" is "hourly" of "day" it is "daily" of "year" it is "yearly" of "century" it is "centennial" and the adjective of "eon" is "eonian." To define *aionios* - the adjective of *aión (age)*, as "eternal" is like saying that "heavenly" is the adjective of "earth" – there is no correspondence. In the same way, *aionios* must agree or correspond with the noun *aión*. In English we would not say that "eternal" is the adjective of "epoch" or of "era." The adjective must always agree in meaning with its noun. However, "eternal" not only doesn't agree with "eon"; it is antithetical with it – one is "time" and the other is "timelessness" – one is finite and the other is infinite. In English there are some fourteen literal translations of the New Testament and all I have seen consistently translate *aionios* as corresponding to a long measure of time; either "age during," "eonian," or "epochal."

What the Linguists Say

One of the most distinguished Greek scholars of recent times, Marvin Vincent, D.D. in His Greek commentary, *Vincent's New Testament Word Studies,* explains the following about *aión* and *aionios:*

> *"Aión transliterated 'aeon,' is a period of time of longer or shorter duration, having a beginning and an end, and complete in itself. Aristotle (peri ouranou, i. 9, 15) says: 'The period which includes the whole time of each one's life is called the aeon of each one.' Hence, it often means the life of a man, as in Homer, where one's life aión is said to leave him or to consume away (Iliad, v. 685; Oddysey, v. 160). It is not, however, limited to human life; it signifies any period in the course of events, as the period or age before Christ; the period of the millennium; the mythological period before the beginnings of history. The word has not 'a stationary and mechanical value' (DeQuincey). It does not mean a period of a fixed length for all cases. There are as many aeons as entities, the respective durations of which are fixed by the normal conditions of the several entities. There is one aeon of a human life, another of the life of a nation, another of a crow's life, another of an oak's life. The length of the aeon depends on the subject to which it is attached...* **The word always carries the notion of time, and not of eternity**. *It always means a period of time. Otherwise it would be impossible to account for the plural, or for such qualifying expressions as this age, or the age to come. It does not mean something endless or everlasting..."*
>
> *"The adjective aionios in like manner carries the idea of time. Neither the noun nor the adjective, in themselves, carry the sense of 'endless or everlasting.' They may acquire that sense by their*

connotation, as, on the other hand, aidíos, which means 'everlasting,' has its meaning limited to a given point of time in Jude 6. Aionios means 'enduring through or pertaining to a period of time.' Both the noun and the adjective are applied to limited periods. Thus, the phrase eis ton aiona, habitually rendered 'forever,' is often used of duration which is limited in the very nature of the case. See, for a few out of many instances, the Septuagint, Ex 21:6; 29:9; 32:13; Josh 14:9; 1 Sam 8:13; Lev 25:46; Deut 15:17; 1 Chron 28:4. See also Matt 21:19; John 13:8; 1Cor 8:13. The same is true of aionios. Out of 150 instances in the Septuagint, four-fifths imply limited duration. For a few instances see Gen 48:4; Num 10:8; 15:15; Prov 22:28; Jonah 2:6; Hab 3:6; Isa 61:17.' **Words which are 'habitually' applied to things temporal or material cannot carry in themselves the sense of endlessness**. *Even when applied to God, we are not forced to render aionios 'everlasting.' Of course the life of God is endless; but the question is whether, in describing God as aionios it was intended to describe the duration of his being, or whether some different and larger idea was not contemplated."* [60]

G. Campbell Morgan, also a renowned scholar said:

"Let me say to Bible students that we must be very careful how we use the word "eternity." We have fallen into great error in our constant use of that word. There is no word in the whole Book of God corresponding with our 'eternal,' which, as commonly used among us, means absolutely without end. The strongest Scripture word used with reference to the existence of God is— 'unto the ages of the ages,' which does not literally mean eternally." [61]

Hasting's Dictionary of the New Testament says:

"There is no word either in the O.T. Hebrew or in the N.T. Greek to express the abstract idea of eternity. (vol. III, p. 369): Nonetheless 'eternal' is misleading, inasmuch as it has come in the English to connote the idea of 'endlessly existing,' and thus to be practically a synonym for 'everlasting.' But this is not an adequate rendering of aionios which varies in meaning with the

---

[60] Marvin Vincent D.D. *Vincent's Word Studies in the New Testament*

[61] G. Campbell Morgan, *God's Methods with Man*

variations of the noun aion from which it comes. (p. 370): The chronois aioniois (times of the ages) moreover, are not to be thought of as stretching backward everlastingly, as it is proved by the pro chronon aionion (before the times of the ages) of 2Tim. 1:9; Tit. 1:2." (parenthesis added) [62]

The Interpreter's Dictionary of the Bible, vol. 4, p. 643, says:

"The O.T. and the N.T. are not acquainted with the conception of eternity as timelessness... The O.T. has not developed a special term for eternity... The use of the word aión in the N.T. is determined very much by the O.T. and the LXX. Aión means long, distant, uninterrupted time. The intensifying plural occurs frequently in the N.T....but it adds no new meaning." [63]

Ellicott's Commentary on the Whole Bible, commenting on Matthew 25:46 says:

"Everlasting punishment - life eternal. The two adjectives represent the same Greek word, aionios. It must be admitted (1) that the Greek word which is rendered 'eternal' does not, in itself, involve endlessness, but rather, duration, whether through an age or succession of ages, and that it is therefore applied in the N.T. to periods of time that have had both a beginning and ending (Rom. 16:25), where the Greek is 'from aeonian times;' our version giving 'since the world began.' (Comp. 2Tim. 1:9; Tit. 1:3) - strictly speaking, therefore, the word, as such, apart from its association with any qualifying substantive, implies a vast undefined duration, rather than one in the full sense of the word 'infinite." [64]

These scholars are recognized authorities on definitions of New Testament words based upon actual usage. In spite of the fact that most of them, due to their Augustinian theology, do not embrace Universalism, they nevertheless acknowledge that *aión* and *aionios*

---

[62] Hasting's Dictionary of the New Testament (vol. I, p. 542, art. *Christ and the Gospels*): Eternity.

[63] The Interpreter's Dictionary of the Bible, vol. 4, p. 643

[64] Ellicott's Commentary on the Whole Bible (Matt. 25:46)

refer to time and not eternity. Let us consider some examples of literal translations of Matthew 25:46, which consistently define aionios temporally:

- Concordant Literal Translation: "chastening eonian."
- Young's Literal Translation: "punishment age during."
- Weymouth New Testament: "punishment of the ages."

A final quote is from Christ Triumphant by Thomas Allin:

"Let me state the dilemma clearly. Aion either means endless duration as its necessary, or at least its ordinary significance or it does not. If it does, the following difficulties at once arise; (1) - How, if it means an endless period, can aion have a plural? (2) - How came such phrases to be used as those repeatedly occurring in Scripture, where aion is added to aion, if aion is of itself infinite? (3) - How come such phrases as "for the aion" or "aions and BEYOND"? - ton aiona kai ep aiona kai eti: eis tous aionas kai eti. - See (Sept.) Ex. xv. 18; Dan. xii. 3; Micah iv. 5. (4) - How is it that we repeatedly read of the end of the aion? - S. Matt. xiii 39-40-49; xxiv. 3; xxviii. 20; 1Cor. x. 11; Heb. ix. 26. (5) - Finally, if aion be infinite, why is it applied over and over to what is strictly finite? e.g., S. Mark iv. 19; Acts iii. 21; Rom. xii. 2 ; 1Cor. i. 20, ii. 6, iii. 18, x. 11, &c., &c. But if an aion be not infinite, what right have we to render the adjective aionios (which depends for its meaning on aion) by the terms 'eternal' (when used as the equivalent of 'endless' and 'everlasting?" [65]

Even when *aión* and *aionios* are attributed to God, they do not have reference to His eternity, but rather emphasize that He is the God of the ages. We already know that He is eternal and exists independently from the ages but not because of *aión* and *aionios*. We already saw that God made the ages and is therefore the God of the ages:

*"has in these last days spoken to us by His Son, whom He has appointed heir of all things, through whom also He **made the worlds** (aionas pl. ages)." (Heb 1:2)*

---

[65] Thomas Allin, *Christ Triumphant*

*"...through whom also He did make **the ages**." (Heb 1:2 Young's Literal Translation)*

We also see that the course of the ages was planned out in the wisdom of God, for our glory, before the ages existed:

*"However, we speak wisdom among those who are mature, yet not the wisdom of this age, nor of the rulers of this age, who are coming to nothing. 7 But we speak the wisdom of God in a mystery, the hidden wisdom which God ordained **before the ages** (aiónon pl.) for our glory." (1Cor 2:6-7)*

When it says that He is the *"God of the Ages"* (erroneously translated "everlasting God") what it is saying is that the ages belong to Him – that He is the all wise Designer and Creator of them and that He is ever present in them all:

*"Now to the **King** ~~eternal~~ (aiónon gen. pl. "**of the ages**"), immortal, invisible, to God who alone is wise, be honor and glory forever and ever. Amen." (1 Tim 1:17)*

*"Now to Him who is able to establish you according to my gospel and the preaching of Jesus Christ, according to the revelation of the mystery kept secret since the ~~world began~~ (cronois aionois "**times of the ages**") 26 **but now made manifest**, and by the prophetic Scriptures made known to all nations, according to the commandment of the ~~everlasting~~ **God** (eonian God), for obedience to the faith." (Rom 16:25-26)*

Here in Romans 16:25,26 we see that before the *"times of the ages,"* (to say "times eternal" is an incoherence), the God of the ages had a mystery that He had kept secret, but not eternally, because it has now been revealed to His Church. Also, we see that He exists in eternity before the times of the ages and is the *eonian God*, or *the God of the ages*. He is not referring to His eternity when he says, *"aionios God."*

Aión and Aionios in Greek Literature

The following are illustrations of ancient Greek literature which demonstrate that *aionios* was not understood in the ancient Greek language to mean "eternal" or "everlasting" as it has often been translated in English.

Gregory of Nyssa (AD 335- AD 395), speaks of an "eonian interval" *(aionios diastema)*. It would be absurd to speak of an eternal interval. Chrysostom, (AD 347 to AD 407), says that the reign of Satan is eonian *(aionios)*. He certainly did not mean by that that his reign was co-eternal with God but rather that it was epoch during.

In 1 Enoch 10:10,11 it says of the fallen ones (Nephilim) born of the watchers, that *"they hoped to live an eternal life (zoe eonios)* **and** *(kai) that each one of them would live for five hundred years."* In this text they are presented as hoping to live an "eonian life" which would last for 500 years. In the New Testament we see that in Christ we already have life eonian and in the resurrection we will be made alive unto immortality when death is swallowed up in victory *(1Cor 15:22)*.

AIDÍOS

A Greek Word that came to express the concept of eternity was *aidíos*. It was often utilized by Philo, the Pharisees and Josephus to express eternity in distinction from *aión* and *aionios*. Some linguists believe that *aidíos* was derived from the Greek word *ádes,* translated "Hades" in English. Hades *(ádes)* means "invisible" or "unseen," and is normally used to refer to the realm of departed souls who are awaiting resurrection and judgment. If the root of *aidíos* is *ádes* then it carries the idea of "the invisible or unseen" whether it refers to eternity or other invisible things. *Aidíos* only appears two times in the New Testament. The first occurrence is in Romans 1:20:

> *"For since the creation of the world His invisible attributes are clearly seen, being understood by the things that are made, even* **His eternal (aidíos) power** *and Godhead, so that they are without excuse." (Rom 1:20)*

Here the translation that best agrees with the context would be *"invisible power"* and not *"eternal power"* since the emphasis here is not so much on the eternality of His power as it is with the invisibility of His power - that in spite of it being invisible it can be seen by the things which He created. His invisible attributes can be seen by the things that are made. The Concordant Literal Version translates it in this manner:

> *"For His invisible attributes are descried from the creation of the world, being apprehended by His achievements, besides His*

imperceptible *power and divinity, for them to be defenseless." (Rom 1:20 Concordant Literal Version)*

The only other place where *aidíos* appears is in Jude 6:

"And the angels who did not keep their proper domain, but left their own abode, He has reserved in **everlasting** *(aidían)* **chains** *under darkness for the judgment of the great day." (Jude 6)*

This is an obvious reference to 1Enoch where the Lord tells the angel Rafael to imprison Azazel, one of the angels who left his first estate to cohabit with the daughters of men, engendering giants or Nephilim. In 1Enoch 10:4-6 the Lord commands the angel saying: *"And again the Lord said to Raphael: 'Bind Azazel hand and foot and cast him into the darkness: and make an opening in the desert, which is in Dudael, and cast him therein. And place upon him rough and jagged rocks, and cover him with darkness, and* **let him abide there forever, and cover his face that he may not see light. And on the day of the great judgment he shall be cast into the fire.***"*

Later in the same chapter of 1Enoch we see that "forever" *(aión)* in this instance lasts for seventy generations: *"And the Lord said unto Michael: 'Go, bind Semjaza and his associates who have united themselves with women so as to have defiled themselves with them in all their uncleanness. And when their sons have slain one another, and they have seen the destruction of their beloved ones, bind them fast* **for seventy generations** *in the valleys of the earth,* **till the day of their judgment***..." (1Enoch 10:11,12)*

This is not the only time that Jude cites the book of 1Enoch. In Jude 14,15 he says:

"Now Enoch, the seventh from Adam, prophesied about these men also, saying, "Behold, the Lord comes with ten thousands of His saints, 15 to execute judgment on all, to convict all who are ungodly among them of all their ungodly deeds which they have committed in an ungodly way, and of all the harsh things which ungodly sinners have spoken against Him." (Jude 14-15, cf. 1Enoch 1:9)

That the rendering *"everlasting"* is not a good translation here in Jude 6 is evident because the chains are not eternal, but rather last

***until** the judgment of the great day*. Once again, the translation "invisible" or "hidden" would best fit the description of these chains:

> *"Besides, messengers who keep not their own sovereignty, but leave their own habitation, He has kept in **imperceptible bonds** under gloom for the judging of the great day." (Jude 6 Concordant Literal Version)*

So, we see that neither *olam* of the Old Testament, nor *aión* with its adjective *aionios,* of the New Testament, communicate the idea of eternity. We know by the Names of God and from the construction *olam a-ad (Gr. aión eti)* that He is eternal, and we also know that the just live forever by the same combination of *olam a-ad "to the age and beyond"* which is also applied to them in Daniel 12:2,3. Also we know that the just live eternally because the words "incorruptible" and "immortal" are applied to them. But in the Scriptures the words *olam, aión* and *aionios* express time and not eternity. Even if it could be demonstrated that they *could* mean eternity in some instances, it is only necessary to establish that they don't always mean eternal in order to have an argument against eternal punishment and explain how there could be a universal restoration. Nevertheless, what we have seen is that these words never express in and of themselves eternity in the Scriptures, with the possible exception of *aidíos,* and *aidíos* is never used to describe the duration of the punishment of the unjust.

Chapter six
The Bible and Hell

The Lack of Emphasis on Post-mortem Punishment in the Scriptures.

Many are not aware that the first teaching on "hell" in the Bible was not presented until Jesus taught concerning Gehenna in the gospels. Apart from the reference to shame and self-contempt of the unjust that will last for *olam (a period of undefined duration)* in Daniel, there is no prior mention of punishment after death in the entire Old Testament, and even this punishment of undefined duration is not said to be physical but emotional pain caused by seeing their shameful condition before Him. Therefore, if what Jesus taught was really eternal torment in literal fire without end, then nearly all those who died before His ministry received a horrific surprise upon dying, since they did not receive any prior warning from God.

God simply said to Adam: *"but of the tree of the knowledge of good and evil you shall not eat, for in the day that you eat of it you shall surely die (or "dying you will die") (Gen 2:17)*. It is impossible that Adam and Eve would have understood from the warning *"you shall surely die"* that they would be tormented in a burning hell forever. In fact, we know that that wasn't their destiny. They began dying and died just as warned. However, the majority would say that Adam and Eve are now in the presence of the Lord and are not in torments. So, this warning to them is that they were going to return to dust. Nothing is said of postmortem torments. God, in His mercy expelled them from Eden so that they wouldn't eat of the tree of life and live forever in their fallen physical state in separation from Him, which would have left them much like the legendary vampires.

The place of the departed souls of the dead in the Old Testament was referred to by the Hebrew word *seol* and its equivalent in Greek - *Hades,* which literally means "invisible." It was the invisible realm where the souls of all went upon dying; both the just *(Gen 37:35; Ps 16:10)* and the unjust *(Job 24:19)*.

There was no mention of suffering in *Seol* or in the equivalent *Hades* until Christ gave the parable of the rich man in Hades in Luke

16:23. In this parable both the rich man and Lazarus are in Hades – which is the invisible world of the dead. Lazarus was taken to a realm symbolically described as *"Abraham's bosom."* The rich man on the other hand was taken to a realm also symbolically referred to as *"in this flame."* Of the four times that Jesus mentioned Hades, Luke 16 is the only occasion in which He indicates that it contains a place of punishment.

Jesus used the word *Gehenna* which is translated "hell" eleven times, but only on three different occasions. Only three times during His entire ministry seems to be very little emphasis if it is in reality a literal fire where the majority of His hearers would pass all of eternity in torments that defy description as the traditionalists tell us. But instead of us seeing Jesus focusing upon an eternal hell awaiting the multitudes, we see Him focused upon the good news of the kingdom of heaven. When it says of Him that He had compassion on the multitudes, we would expect that it would have moved Him to preach, warning of the eternal hell, which awaited them if the traditional model were true, but that is not what we find:

*"And when Jesus went out He saw a great multitude; and **He was moved with compassion** for them, and **healed their sick**." (Matt 14:14)*

*"**I have compassion on the multitude**, because they have now continued with Me three days and **have nothing to eat**. 3 And if I send them away hungry to their own houses, **they will faint on the way**; for some of them have come from afar." (Mark 8:2-3)*

Jesus had compassion on the multitudes because they were sick; because they were like sheep without a shepherd, or because they had nothing to eat. But nowhere do we find the loving Savior saying that He had compassion on them because He knew the majority would be eternally tormented in hell. Which would have been more urgent, healing, multiplying food, or warning them that they were headed for an eternal hell?

That is not to take lightly the warnings that Jesus gave to the multitudes (and the disciples) concerning Gehenna. But if Gehenna really was eternal and with literal flames, without any hope of restoration, having been invented for the sole purpose of eternally torturing its occupants, don't you think He would have dedicated more of His time to warning them than doing good deeds and healing all those who were oppressed of the devil?

Paul doesn't even make mention of the words *hell*, *Hades* or *Gehenna*, during his entire ministry as recorded in Acts. Neither does he mention them in all of his epistles with the exception of 1Corinthians 15:55, where he mentions Hades, only to declare the victory Christ obtained over it on our behalf. The rest of the authors of the New Testament do not mention Gehenna either, with the exception of James, who, writing to the Jews who would have been familiar with the garbage dump "Gehenna" burning outside of Jerusalem, used Gehenna to describe the tongue, saying that *"The tongue also is a fire...and is itself set on fire by hell (Gehenna)." (James 3:6).*

Peter mentioned Hades on one occasion, and it was also to proclaim Christ's victory over it in His resurrection *(Acts 2:27,31)*. In Revelation the word Hades is only mentioned three times: In Revelation 1:18 Jesus declares that He has the keys of Hades and Death. In 6:8 it says that the fourth horseman was death and Hades followed after him. The last mention of Hades is in Revelation 20:14, where Death and Hades are cast into the lake of fire.

That is not to say that Jesus and the Apostles did not warn of hell using other terms such as *eonian destruction, eonian correction, eonian fire, and condemnation, etc.* However, they seem to have avoided using the terms *Gehenna, Hades and Tartarus,* since these projected false images. They were terms which were adopted by the Jews in the intertestamental period through the pagan influences of the Persians and Greeks, who dominated the region during that period.

The use of the word *Gehenna*, to refer to a place of fiery purification, originated in the intertestamental period, under Persian influence during the time of Ester. Many of the Jews lived in Persia after the Babylonian captivity and adopted some of the beliefs of the Zoroastrians of that region, adapting them to Judaism. [66] From that

---

[66] The Zoroastrians were monotheists who did not believe in the eternal existence of evil and taught that the purifying fires would eliminate evil bringing about a universal restoration. They are similar to Judaism in many ways. It is believed that the wise men who saw the star and came to worship Jesus were Zoroastrians.
http://en.wikipedia.org/wiki/Zoroastrianism

time forward, the Jewish Gehenna was used by the early Rabbis to refer to a place of fiery purification, which aligned with the Zoroastrian belief in a fiery region in the afterlife that was for purification, and therefore, only lasted as long as was necessary in order to purify sinners. [67] They viewed Gehenna as a place of temporary fiery purification, lasting no longer than 12 months. [68] Most Orthodox Jews to this day hold to this belief. The sect of the Pharisees, however, being more influenced by the Greek concept of eternal punishment, maintained that Gehenna was a place of unending torments.

By the time of Christ, there was much Jewish folklore circulating among the Jews concerning Gehenna and Hades. Therefore, what the Jews understood by these terms was often barbaric and mythical, and required clarification by Jesus and the Apostles in order to avoid misunderstanding. While Jesus used these terms which they were familiar with in order to better communicate with them, at the same time He used other descriptive terms to help them redefine their familiar, yet distorted concepts.

Therefore I believe that, due to the fact that there was so much bizarre folklore associated with *Gehenna,* and also because the terms *Hades* and *Tartarus* were so steeped in Greek mythology with its capricious and vindictive gods, both Jesus and the Apostles normally avoided the use of these terms, instead using other

---

[67] *"GEHENNA: As the concept of the after-life developed in the intertestamental period, the Valley of Hinnom came to represent the eschatological place of judgment (1 En. 27:1f.; 54:1-6 ; 90:25-27 ; etc.) or hell itself (2 Esd 7:36; 2 Bar. 85:13). It is not necessary to see Iranian influence in this development, since* <u>*the purpose of the Zoroastrian molten fire was purgatorial rather than penal*</u> *(Yasna 51:9; but cf. one early rabbinic tradition that Gehenna was a purgatory for those whose merits and sins balanced each other [Tosefta Sanhedrin xiii.3])." International Standard Bible Encyclopedia, revised edition*

[68] *"The overwhelming majority of rabbinic thought maintains that people are not in* Gehenna *forever; the longest that one can be there is said to be 12 months, however there has been the occasional noted exception. Some consider it a spiritual forge where the soul is purified for its eventual ascent to Olam Habah lit."The world to come", often viewed as analogous to Heaven."* http://en.wikipedia.org/wiki/Hell

descriptive words in order to better describe to them God's postmortem correctional punishment.

If Jesus and the Apostles had believed that Gehenna, Hades and Tartarus were places of unending and unusually cruel punishment, as described by the Greeks and as later presented by the doctrine of the traditional Church, then they certainly would have warned of those places of torment, calling them by their real names at every opportunity. Every presentation of the gospel in Acts would have been preceded by the warning of an eternal hell. In reality, most Christians today who believe in an eternal hell; although they often mix hell in with the "good news," must confess that they do not mention the word *hell* nearly enough in order to be consistent with their own beliefs.

So, we see that there is no mention of postmortem punishment in the Old Testament and Jesus said very little concerning it. Rather than focusing on that subject, He dedicated Himself to healing the sick, casting out demons and proclaiming the good news of the kingdom of God, which would not make sense if indeed postmortem punishment is eternal and not restorative - especially if their only opportunity to be saved was during their brief lifespan. In the entire book of Acts, which records numerous evangelistic messages, there is not even one warning of hell. Paul, in all of his epistles, only mentions by name Hades in order to declare Christ's victory over it, and the New Testament ends with the keys of Hades in Christ's hands and Hades being cast into the lake of fire along with death.

If hell is eternal and is the final destiny for the great majority of humanity, why do we find so little emphasis upon it in the Bible? Why is postmortem punishment not even mentioned until the ministry of Christ? We recognize that there is progressive revelation in the Scriptures, but the revelation goes from glory to glory – not from bad to worse. And why didn't Jesus and the apostles warn of hell in every possible occasion, if it is eternal and not restorative? Is it true that Jesus taught that Gehenna is eternal and that all, except for a few elect will suffer there, being consumed with fire that never goes out and eaten by worms with eternal life? Let's examine more closely what Jesus actually taught concerning Gehenna.

Gehenna Fire

On three distinct occasions Jesus warned of Gehenna fire. All three times he was addressing Jews in Israel who were very familiar with Gehenna, which was the Valley of Hinnom on the south side of Jerusalem outside the main wall near the Manure Gate. Gehenna means "Valley of Hinnom." It also went by the name of Topheth which means "drum." In the time of the kings Achaz and Manasseh, they sacrificed children to Molech in that valley *(2Chron 28:3; 33:6; Jer 7:31,32)*. They called it the valley of Topheth because they beat drums in order to drown out the screams of the children being burned in sacrifice. Because of the abominable practices done there, God pronounced judgment and changed its name to the Valley of Slaughter.

> *"They have built the high places of Topheth in the Valley of Ben Hinnom to burn their sons and daughters in the fire —* **something I did not command, nor did it enter my mind***. 32 So beware, the days are coming, declares the Lord, when people will no longer call it Topheth or the Valley of Ben Hinnom, but the* **Valley of Slaughter***, for they will bury the dead in Topheth until there is no more room. 33 Then the carcasses of this people will become food for the birds of the air and the beasts of the earth, and there will be no one to frighten them away. 34 I will bring an end to the sounds of joy and gladness and to the voices of bride and bridegroom in the towns of Judah and the streets of Jerusalem, for the land will become desolate." (Jer 7:31-34)*

According to a twelfth century Jewish Rabbi David Kimhi, in the times of Christ, Gehenna, the Valley of Hinnom was Jerusalem's refuse dumb where they threw "unclean corpses." [69] There they threw all the garbage, manure, remains of animals and cadavers of the poor and criminals. Due to the decomposition there was always an abundance of worms and unquenchable fire caused by spontaneous combustion. [70]

---

[69] Ed Rowell, "Hinnom," Mercer Dictionary of the Bible, 381.

[70] Some, in an attempt to discredit the historicity of Gehenna as a garbage dump, argue that no archeological evidence indicates that it was used in this way. However, it is not to be anticipated that remains would be found since everything would have been reduced to ashes. For that same

As a child I loved exploring the town dumps. At that time there were no environmental controls and the dumps always had smoldering fires and worms in abundance. Both fire and worms were inevitable as long as there were things in a state of decomposition. When Jesus taught concerning Gehenna in Judea, He may well have been indicating with His hand in the direction of Gehenna, Jerusalem's garbage dump. William Barclay said the following of Gehenna in the times of Christ:

> *"Gehenna...means the Valley of Hinnom, a valley to the southwest of Jerusalem. It was notorious as the place where Ahaz had introduced the fire worship of the heathen God Molech, to whom little children were burned... (2Chronicles 28:2-4). Josiah had stamped out that worship and ordered that the valley should be forever after an accursed place...it became the place where the refuse of Jerusalem was cast out and destroyed. It was a kind of public incinerator. Always the fire smoldered in it, and a pall of thick smoke lay over it, and bred a loathsome kind of worm which was hard to kill (Mark 9:44-48). So Gehenna, the Valley of Hinnom, became identified in people's minds with all that was accursed and filthy, the place where useless and evil things were destroyed together with the corpses of criminals."* [71]

Lightfoot also describes Gehenna in the following manner:

> *"It was the common sink of the whole city; whither all filth, and all kind of nastiness, met. It was, probably, the common burying-place of the city (if so be, they did now bury within so small a distance from the city). "They shall bury in Tophet, until there be no more any place," Jeremiah 7:32. And there was there also a continual fire, whereby bones, and other filthy things, were consumed, lest they might offend or infect the city."* [72]

Nevertheless, when Jesus spoke of being cast into Gehenna fire, He was utilizing Gehenna as a metaphor. He was warning of a realm

---

reason they have also not found any remains of the 600,000 cadavers of Jews, which, according to Josephus, were thrown there in AD 70.

[71] Barclay, William. *"The Gospel of Matthew." Daily Study Bible Series.* Philadelphia: Westminster, 1978. 141.

[72] John Lightfoot, "The Valley of Hinnom," ch. 39.

in Hades where the unjust go at death, and not the literal garbage dump outside of Jerusalem:

> *"Then he will say to those on his left, 'Depart from me, you who are cursed, into the **eternal fire** (pur aionios "eonian fire") prepared for the devil and his angels." (Matt 25:41)*

This eonian fire prepared for the devil and his angels is, in all probability, equivalent to the postmortem region "Gehenna" Jesus describes on other occasions. Here we can see that it is a place of punishment prepared specifically for the devil and his angels. It is not the literal garbage dump outside Jerusalem with its smoldering flames and worms consuming garbage and decaying flesh. But is it eternal? As we have already seen, *aionios* refers to that which pertains to the age or ages and does not refer to eternity.

When Jesus spoke of the worms and fire of Gehenna in Mark 9, the King James Version gives the impression that the fire was eternal because it says that the fire "will ***never*** be quenched":

> *"And if thy hand offend thee, cut it off: it is better for thee to enter into life maimed, than having two hands to go into hell, into **the fire that <u>never</u> shall be quenched**: 44 Where their worm dieth not, and the fire is not quenched. 45 And if thy foot offend thee, cut it off: it is better for thee to enter halt into life, than having two feet to be cast into hell, into **the fire that <u>never</u> shall be quenched**: 46 Where their worm dieth not, and the fire is not quenched. 47 And if thine eye offend thee, pluck it out: it is better for thee to enter into the kingdom of God with one eye, than having two eyes to be cast into hell fire: 48 Where their worm dieth not, and the fire is not quenched." (Mark 9:43-48 KJV)*

The King James translators, due to the influence of their traditional belief in eternal punishment, add the word "never" in both instances. "Never" does not appear in the original, but since they assumed the fire is eternal anyway, they just took the liberty to add the word "never" for emphasis in verses 43 and 45. Also Jesus is using the present tense which would read: *"into Gehenna fire where their worm is not dying and the fire is not being quenched."* Some recent translations have corrected this error, simply reading: *"is not quenched"* or *"unquenchable."* The literal versions, such as the Concordant Literal Version also correct the tense saying: *"where their worm is not deceasing and the fire is not going out."*

Translating the passage in this manner, it becomes obvious that He was illustrating from what was literally happening at that moment to the cadavers in the refuse dump of Gehenna. Jesus no doubt indicating with His hand outstretched towards Gehenna said: *"their worms are not dying and the fire is not being quenched."* Being eaten by worms is what happens to dead corpses and not to departed souls in Hades. To apply literally the metaphors and parables of Jesus is an error that many have committed over and over again throughout the centuries. When Jesus said: *"destroy this temple and in three days I will raise it up"* they took him literally and didn't understand what He was saying *(Jn 2:19,20)*. When Jesus said that one must be born again, Nicodemus took it literally and missed Jesus' point *(Jn 3:3-10)*. When He said: *"he that eats my flesh and drinks my blood, has eternal life,"* the majority of His disciples took Him literally and no longer walked with Him *(Jn 6:51-60)*.

Although few today would take literally the words of Jesus when He said we must eat his flesh and drink His blood, many take His allegories like Gehenna as literal and understand Jesus to have said that all who die and go to Gehenna are literally being eaten by worms with eternal life and burning in eternal flames, even though they are disembodied souls. Jesus here is using the same language as used by Isaiah when he prophesied concerning that which would happen to the nations that come against His people Israel and Jerusalem when Christ comes to deliver them from their enemies:

> *"And they shall go forth and look upon **the corpses** of the men who have transgressed against Me. **For their worm does not die, and their fire is not quenched**. They shall be an abhorrence to all flesh." (Isa 66:24)*

The definition of a corpse is a dead body in the state of decomposition. He is saying that the corpses of the enemies of Israel will be piled up outside the walls of Jerusalem and those who pass by will see their corpses smoldering and being consumed by worms and it will be repugnant to all who pass by. By the phrase *"their worm does not die and their fire is not quenched,"* He is saying that as long as there is flesh in decomposition it will smolder in the fire and be eaten by worms until it is entirely consumed. The fact that Jesus makes reference to this passage in Isaiah describing literal corpses outside Jerusalem in decomposition should not be taken to mean that the disembodied souls of the unjust are likewise burned in literal fire and eaten by literal worms. We should rather seek to understand the spiritual meaning behind the metaphor of Gehenna.

Both fire and worms are purifying agents. The Greek word for "fire" is *pur* from which we get such words as *pure, purify, purification, purgatory, etc*. Once sin and resulting death entered the creation, the fire and worms became necessary in order to purify from that which is dead. Without flies and maggots, the corpses in decomposition would contaminate the whole environment, infecting the living. The maggots only consume that which is contaminated and dead. From antiquity maggots have been used to cure patients with severe infections because they only eat that which is dead and infected. Even modern medicine has begun to use them with great results for persistent infections. Fire is also used to destroy harmful bacteria emitted from decomposing corpses.

When Jerusalem was destroyed in AD 70, according to the Jewish historian Josephus, one million two hundred thousand Jews died. Six hundred thousand of them were thrown into Gehenna. There the fire and worms consumed their decomposing flesh, and in that manner the land became free of contaminants. In our time the worms have all died and the fire has long been extinguished, having consumed all rotting flesh. Present day Gehenna is a park where one can go for a stroll without repulsion.

If an *eternal* literal fire is the destiny of all those who have not believed, do you think Jesus and His disciples would have spoken of anything else? They would have been warning people at every opportunity of what awaited all of them if they didn't repent and believe. But perhaps one of the strongest warnings Jesus gave concerning Gehenna was given, not to the multitudes or the Pharisees but to His own disciples:

> *"At that time **the disciples** came to Jesus... If your hand or foot causes you to sin, cut it off and cast it from you. It is better for you to enter into life lame or maimed, rather than having two hands or two feet, to be cast into the everlasting fire. 9 And if your eye causes you to sin, pluck it out and cast it from you. It is better for you to enter into life with one eye, rather than having two eyes, to be cast into hell fire (pur of Gehenna)." (Matt 18:1, 8-9)*

Most would readily agree that Jesus didn't mean that the disciples should literally dismember themselves. If one of them were to have taken Him literally and proceeded to cut off his hand, I am sure Jesus would have intervened to restrain him. Why? Because He was using hyperbolic speech for greater impact, which was not intended to be taken literally. Understanding this, why is it that traditionalists cannot see that Gehenna with its continuous fires and worms was also a hyperbolic illustration for greater impact?

The Unquenchable Fire

> *"If your hand causes you to sin, cut it off. It is better for you to enter into life maimed, rather than having two hands, to go to hell, into the* **fire that shall ~~never~~ (not) be quenched**.*" (Mark 9:43 NKJV)*

> *"And if your hand causes you to sin, cut it off; it is better for you to enter life maimed than with two hands to go to hell, to the* **unquenchable fire**.*" (Mark 9:43 RSV)*

As we saw earlier, in the phrase "the fire that shall *never* be quenched, the word *never* was added by traditional translators to reinforce their belief in eternal fire. Most translations today, however, have corrected this error, translating it as *"unquenchable fire"* as we see in the Revised Standard Version. There is a great difference between *fire that shall never be quenched* and *unquenchable fire.* When I was young, I worked in a sawmill. It had a big silo where sawdust was stored and used to fuel the boilers. One day it started to smoke. A fire had started from within due to the ammonia and heat generated by decomposition. The firemen, after working all night in an attempt to control the fire finally said it was unquenchable. What did they mean when they said it was unquenchable? That it would keep burning forever? No. They left it to burn and after a few days it finally burned itself out. Unquenchable simply means that the fire cannot be put out but keeps burning until all consumables are consumed. Then it goes out by itself even as did the refuse dump in the valley of Gehenna outside of Jerusalem nearly two thousand years ago.

Unquenchable fire is a figure used in the Old Testament to refer to God's judgments. In the examples given, we can see that the unquenchable fire is not referring to *eternal fire* but rather are expressions of severe but temporary judgments:

> *"Son of man, set your face toward the south; preach against the south and prophesy against **the forest land**, the South, 47 and **say to the forest** of the South, 'Hear the word of the Lord! Thus says the Lord God: 'Behold, I will kindle a fire in you, and it shall devour every green tree and every dry tree in you; **the blazing flame shall not be quenched**, and all faces from the south to the north shall be scorched by it. 48 All flesh shall see that I, the Lord, have kindled it; **it shall not be quenched**." (Ezek 20:46-48)*

No one would say that the Negev is in flames today and that the faces of all who pass by even today are scorched from its heat. We understand by unquenchable that it is a fire that cannot be put out by human effort. It continues burning until all that is consumable has been consumed and then it goes out by itself.

We see the same symbolism used by the prophet Jeremiah against Judah and the City of Jerusalem, and it doesn't refer only to people being burned but also animals, trees and crops. The strong terms used in this prophecy are of *temporal* judgment against Judah and Jerusalem. However, the same expressions, when found in the Gospels and in Revelation are said, by the traditionalists, to refer to the *eternal* and not *temporal* wrath against the unjust.

> *"Therefore thus says the Lord God: "Behold, **My anger and My fury will be poured out** on this place — on man and on beast, on the trees of the field and on the fruit of the ground. And **it will burn and not be quenched**." (Jer 7:20)*

If these expressions were directed against the nations and not the people of God, the traditionalists would say that it is here referring to eternal wrath, as they try to do with the same words in Mark 9:43-48. Here, however, we know that it cannot refer to eternal wrath because later in Jeremiah 31 we see God promising the future restoration of Jerusalem, with the promise that it will never be destroyed again:

> *"Behold, the days are coming, says the Lord, that **the city shall be built** for the Lord from the Tower of Hananel to the Corner Gate. 39 The surveyor's line shall again extend straight forward over the hill Gareb; then it shall turn toward Goath. 40 And the whole valley of the dead bodies and of the ashes, and all the fields as far as the Brook Kidron, to the corner of the Horse Gate toward the east, shall be holy to the Lord. **It shall not be plucked up or thrown down anymore forever**." (Jer 31:38-40)*

Here we see in Jeremiah an example of judgment with the same apocalyptic expressions used by Jesus and John in Revelation with *"anger, fury"* and *"fire that shall not be quenched."* But here in Jeremiah it is obvious that it is temporal and corrective, and its end is a permanent restoration, including even Gehenna, referred to as *"the valley of dead bodies and ashes."* So here we see confirmation of what Evangelical Universalists say: Consuming fire is temporal and followed by restoration.

How can we spiritually apply what Jesus said of Gehenna and the worms that do not die and the fire that cannot be extinguished? What is it that Jesus wanted to communicate with the illustration of the Valley of Gehenna?

In the first place, the fire will continue until all the dead works have been consumed - until nothing remains in the individual that could infect or contaminate heaven's environment. As worms and fire are purifiers which consume all that is dead and malignant, so the fire of God will be a Gehenna for those contaminated by the works of the flesh.

> *"He will sit **as a refiner and a purifier** of silver; **He will purify** the sons of Levi, and **purge them as gold and silver**, that they may offer to the Lord an offering in righteousness." (Mal 3:3)*

Fire for Christians?

Our God is a Consuming Fire and wherever there is anything consumable, it will be consumed by Him *(Heb 12:9)*. If we continue in Mark 9 until verse 49, we see that none are exempt from the fire of God – not even His own disciples:

> *"For He **taught His disciples** and said to them… 47 And if your eye causes you to sin, pluck it out. It is better for you to enter the kingdom of God with one eye, rather than having two eyes, to be cast into hell fire - 48 where their worm does not die and the fire is not quenched. 49 For **EVERYONE will be seasoned with fire**, and every sacrifice will be seasoned with salt." (Mark 9:31,47-49)*

What is the fire that all - including His disciples, will be subjected to? If the fire of verse 48 is literal fire, then it follows that the fire of verse 49 is also literal, and that all – including believers, will be burning in a literal fire. Also we know that it is not literal fire since the *eonian fire* was prepared for the devil and his angels *(Matt 25:41)*. A literal physical fire would obviously have no effect upon angelic spirits.

Verse 49 has been very ambiguous to most. Even the ancient scribes that copied the Greek texts seemed to have had difficulty understanding it since the later Byzantine Texts incorporated what seems to have been an explanatory note which later became part of the text itself, making it say: *"For everyone will be salted with fire,* **and every sacrifice will be salted with salt**.*"* However, most modern scholars today consider the earlier shorter reading to be the correct one. There are some 15 different interpretations given for this text and half of the commentaries I consulted refrained from making comments on this verse altogether.

While I believed that the verse referred to the purification process which all without exception must go through, either now or later, in order to become pure of heart and see the Lord, I didn't understand why Jesus made a connection between fire and salt until I began to invesigate concerning the use of fire and sulfur for the refining of gold. I made an amazing discovery which immediately brought clarity of meaning to Jesus' words.

When they refine gold they first melt it and then add sulfur, causing the other metals and impurities to form a dross of sulfides which float to the top. Sulfer is effective in removing other base metals and impurities from gold but is not as effective in separating the silver from the gold. Far before the time of Christ the ancients discovered that salt was more effective in separating the silver from the gold than sulfur. This is called "parting." The Encyclopædia Britannica states: *"By 2000 BC the process of purifying gold-silver alloys with salt to remove the silver was developed."* [73] When the gold containing silver is heated with salt the silver reacts with the salt forming silver chloride which can be easily removed producing pure gold. [74]

---

[73] Encyclopædia Britannica Ultimate Reference Suite, version: 2012.00.00.000000000: *Gold Processing, History*

[74] https://en.wikipedia.org/wiki/Gold_parting

This imagery illustrates God's determination to continue purifying us until we come forth as pure gold. Silver is considered a semiprecious metal, but God will not be conformed to leaving us as a mixture of precious with semiprecious. It is not enough to remove the dross of sinful flesh from our hearts. Even our "good" but independent, dead self-works must be purged from our lives as the silver from gold, until all our works are wrought in God - passing from our life of independence into a perfect oneness with Him.

The Greek noun *"fire"* is in the dative case and could either be translated as instrumental – **"with** fire,*"* or as locative indicating location – *"in fire."* I was never able to understand how we could be salted **with** fire. However, now, understanding that the context is referring to parting gold with salt, it becomes obvious that the correct reading is *"for all will be salted in fire,"* rather than *"with fire."*

Πας	γαρ	πυρι	αλισθησεται
all	for	in fire	will be salted

"for all will be salted in fire."

Many have thought that Mark 9 is referring only to the unjust. However, in the context we see that *all* must pass through a refining process. Even the disciples were not exempt from it. After warning them of the reality of postmortem fire in Gehenna, Jesus explains that everyone will have to pass through the processing of fire in salt which separates the gold even from the semiprecious silver. If we do not submit to the Refiner's fire in this life, becoming purified from all contaminations of flesh and spirit now, perfecting holiness in the fear of God *(2Cor 7:1)*, then we will be hurt by the second death, receiving our part in Gehenna fire which is the purifying lake of fire and sulfur *(Rev 2:11; 21:8)*.

God will not annihilate His enemies in an incinerator, nor did He create an eternal torture chamber when He created the heavens and earth and all that in them is in those first six days. No! His fire is like a refiner's fire and He has declared that His plan for the ages will culminate in the restoration of all when He shall be all in all in eternity:

*"For as in Adam all die, even so in Christ **ALL shall be made alive**.... 28 Now when **all ~~things~~ are made subject to Him**, then*

*the Son Himself will also be subject to Him who put all things under Him, **that God may be all in all**." (1 Cor 15:22,28)* [75]

*"For of Him and through Him and **TO** (eís) Him are **ALL** ~~things~~, to whom be glory forever. Amen." (Rom 11:36)*

*"Say to God, 'how awesome are Your works! Through the greatness of Your power **YOUR ENEMIES SHALL SUBMIT THEMSELVES to You**. 4 **ALL** THE EARTH shall worship You and sing praises to You**; they shall sing praises to Your name." (Ps 66:3,4)*

***"Look to Me, and be saved, ALL you ends of the earth! For I am God, and there is no other. 23 I have sworn by Myself; The word has gone out of My mouth in righteousness, and shall not return, that to Me EVERY KNEE SHALL BOW, EVERY TONGUE SHALL TAKE AN OATH**. 24 He shall say, 'Surely in the Lord I have righteousness and strength.' **TO HIM MEN SHALL COME**, and all shall be ashamed who are incensed against Him." (Isa 45:22-24)*

It is therefore evident that the fire with which all will be purified is a spiritual fire and not literal flames any more than the wood, hay and stubble which will be consumed are literally wood, hay and stubble *(1Cor 3:12)*. Our God is a consuming fire who removes all that which can be moved; all that is of the flesh and all that which is spiritually dead, in order that only the immovable and eternal remains:

*"...Yet once more **I shake not the earth only, but also heaven**. 27 And this word, yet once more, signifieth the removing of those things that are shaken, as of things that are made, **that those things which cannot be shaken may remain**. 28 Wherefore we receiving a kingdom which cannot be moved, let us have grace, whereby we may serve God acceptably with reverence and godly fear: 29 **For our God is a consuming fire**." (Heb 12:26-29 KJV)*

---

[75] Our English word *"things"* does not have an equivalent in Greek. Neither does the neuter form in Greek always indicate objects as in English. When the translators insert "things" in contexts that are obviously referring primarily to persons and not inanimate objects I take the liberty to cross it out in order to keep the focus where it belongs.

The fire of God cannot be extinguished. It continues until it has completely consumed all that is consumable, shakable, earthly and carnal. All that remains is His eternal spiritual kingdom, that which cannot be shaken. The fire is necessary for purification – for the holiness, without which no one will see the Lord *(Heb 12:14)*. If we submit now to the testing by fire in this life, we will be purified, coming forth as gold and will find ourselves in the presence of the Lord in His coming, or upon leaving this body. If, on the other hand, we do not submit ourselves to His consuming fire now, then we will have to experience His fire later.

*"But if that servant says in his heart, 'My master is delaying his coming,' and begins to beat the male and female servants, and to eat and drink and be drunk, 46 the master of that servant will come on a day when he is not looking for him, and at an hour when he is not aware, and will cut him in two and appoint him **his portion with the unbelievers**." (Luke 12:45,46)*

A Christian, even though he is a believer, is not exempt from the purifying fire. Sooner or later all will have to submit themselves to it. If we do not submit now, then we will receive our portion together with the unbelievers. Many think of the gospel as if it were a "fire insurance policy." They rejoice in their salvation, knowing that they are exempt from the eternal fires. Sadly, our consciences can become so calloused that we can have great joy in our own personal salvation and at the same time feel indifference or even satisfaction at the thought of the majority spending all eternity in a flaming hell. However, Jesus said that *all* must be purified with fire because without holiness no one shall see the Lord.

We all desire to be baptized in the Holy Spirit, but how many are willing to receive the baptism in fire? Many think both are one and the same Holy Spirit and in a sense they could be correct, but let's look at what John the Baptist said in context:

*"John answered, saying to all, 'I indeed baptize you with water; but One mightier than I is coming, whose sandal strap I am not worthy to loose. He will baptize you **with the Holy Spirit and fire**. 17 His winnowing fan is in His hand, and He will thoroughly clean out His threshing floor, and gather the wheat into His barn; but **the chaff He will burn with unquenchable fire**." (Luke 3:16-17)*

We see in the context that the fire with which Jesus will baptize is fire that consumes the chaff. If a Christian has chaff in his life when he appears before the Judgment seat of Christ it will be burned, even though he himself will be saved:

*"For **we must all appear before the judgment seat of Christ**, that each one may receive the things done in the body, according to what he has done, whether good or bad." (2Cor 5:10)*

*"Now if anyone builds on this foundation (Christ) with gold, silver, precious stones, wood, hay, straw, 13 each one's work will become clear; for the Day will declare it, because **it will be revealed by fire; and the fire will test each one's work**, of what sort it is. 14 If anyone's work which he has built on it endures, he will receive a reward. 15 If anyone's work is burned, he will suffer loss; but **he himself will be saved**, yet so as **through fire**." (1Cor 3:12-15)*

A very important observation in this passage is that the straw burned is not the individual himself, but rather his dead works which will be exposed to God's consuming fire. If our works have been wood, hay or stubble, they will be consumed in the fire, yet we ourselves will be saved. There will be destruction, but not of our being, as the annihilationists would say, but rather of that which is perishable – the wood, hay and stubble. In Luke 3:17, we also see that it is the *chaff* which is destroyed by fire. The wheat and the chaff are not two classes of people but rather the chaff is the outer shell that is still clinging to the grain of wheat after being harvested. After harvesting, the grain with its chaff is threshed on the threshing floor and the chaff is separated by throwing them into the wind with a winnowing fork. The wheat is saved, whereas the chaff is gathered and burned. It must be separated and destroyed by fire but the grain of wheat, which is the individual self, will be saved. The chaff represents the dead works which will be consumed in the fire, and the wheat, which represents us as individuals, will be saved. The fire is unquenchable. In other words, as much as we would like to spare the chaff in our lives, we cannot stop the fire; it will run its course until all that can be consumed will have been consumed. There's no stopping it.

In this life it is possible for even a believer to evade the fiery trials, but it is better to submit ourselves under the mighty hand of God now, than to receive our part with the unbelievers. Nothing unclean will enter the gates of the New Jerusalem until it has been purified by fire. If we do not prepare ourselves in this life as the Bride of the Lamb, we will be left out in the outer darkness where there will be weeping and gnashing of teeth. There will be weeping and gnashing of teeth, even among some professing believers because they will not be received as part of His Bride in the wedding which will be celebrated at Christ's Second Coming *(Matt 25:1-13; Rev 19:7,8; 21:2; 22:17,27).*

The unbelievers, and also some professing believers, who receive their portion with them, will miss out on the first resurrection and will be hurt by the second death:

"He who has an ear, let him hear what **the Spirit says to the churches**. *He who overcomes shall not be* **hurt by the second death**.*" (Rev 2:11)*

But someone might still ask: Why would anyone be motivated to die to the desires of the flesh and serve God in this life if all are ultimately going to be saved in the end anyway. No one who understands what a glorious future awaits the Bride of Christ would ask that question. Only those who have been made ready will have the privilege of co-reigning with Him in the coming ages as His Bride. The rest will be hurt by the second death which they refused to undergo in this life and will have their part (or portion) in the purifying lake of fire, possibly missing out on the first resurrection and losing the opportunity to celebrate the wedding feast as the Bride of Christ. Paul tells us what his goal was in Philippians 3:10,11:

"that I may know Him and the power of His resurrection, and the fellowship of His sufferings, being conformed to His death, 11 ***if, by any means, I may attain to the resurrection from the dead***.*" (Phil 3:10-11)*

The consuming goal of Paul was to know Christ intimately, suffering with Him and dying to his flesh in this life. Why? To be part of the first resurrection and be in perfect union with Christ, in order to be united with Him as His Bride and co-reining with Him for the ages of the ages. Paul said that Christ is *the Savior of all men, especially of those who believe (1Tim 4:10).* Before Christ delivers the kingdom back to God the Father, all will have been saved and subjected to Him. But what anguish – what weeping and gnashing of teeth would result from seeing what one could have had in glory with

Christ Jesus for the ages but being unable to enter in for having not allowed the fiery trials to prepare them in this life!

> *"For if we died with Him, we shall also live with Him. 12 **If we endure, we shall also reign with Him**. If we deny Him, He also will deny us." (2Tim 2:11-12)*

> *"...heirs of God and **joint heirs with Christ, if indeed we suffer with Him**, that we may also be glorified together." (Rom 8:17)*

Gehenna and the Destruction of Soul and Body

> *"And do not fear those who kill the body but cannot kill the soul. But rather fear Him who is able to destroy (apollumi) both soul (psuque) and body in hell (Gehenna)." (Matt 10:28)*

This passage, taken as commonly translated and out of context, would seem to confirm what the Annihilationists say - that the resurrected bodies of the unjust, together with their souls, will be destroyed or exterminated in Gehenna fire. However, in the same chapter in verse 39, we can see that destroying the soul is not speaking of the cessation of its existence, but rather the subjugation of the life of the soul to the life in the spirit:

> *"He who finds his life ("soul"- psuque) will lose it, and he who loses (apollumi) his life ("soul"- psuque) for My sake will find it." (Matt 10:39)*

Here Jesus uses the same words as in verse 28. What Jesus was actually saying was hidden by the translators who, instead of translating *apollumi* and *psuque* in the same way in both verses, translated it *"destroy the soul"* in 28 and *"lose his life"* in 39. It is obvious that Jesus meant to express the same thing in both instances, but the translators leave us with the impression that He was speaking of two distinct and unrelated things. What is it that Jesus meant to say in the expression *"lose or destroy the soul"*?

The Bible makes it clear that man is a being made up of body, soul and spirit:

> *"Now may the God of peace Himself sanctify you **completely**; and may your whole **spirit**, **soul**, and **body** be preserved blameless at the coming of our Lord Jesus Christ." (1Thess 5:23)*

The complete man, according to Paul is 1) spirit, 2) soul and 3) body. The immaterial part of man is made up of soul and spirit. Even though the natural man cannot distinguish between spirit and soul, in Hebrews we are told that the word of God distinguishes between that which is of the soul from that which is of the spirit:

*"For the word of God is living and powerful, and sharper than any two-edged sword, piercing even to the **division of soul and spirit**, and of joints and marrow, and is a discerner of the thoughts and intents of the heart." (Heb 4:12)*

Man, apart from the revelation of the Word of God, is incapable of distinguishing between that which is of the spirit and that which is of the soul, but the word of God is as a two-edged sword and is able to reveal when we are *soulish*, acting in the soul and when we are *spiritual*, or acting in the spirit.

Our spirit is that which connects us with God who is Spirit. By our spirit we are able to hear God's voice and have communion with Him. God created man to live with his spirit in communion with Himself, with the soul and body submitted to one's spirit.

When man fell, He lost communion with God. Since the spirit no longer heard the voice of God, the soul of man no longer lived aligned with and subjected under the spirit, but rather began to live according to the will of the body or flesh with its five senses. In this fallen condition the soul no longer lived according to the spirit, led by God, but rather according to the desires of his flesh. Man no longer had spiritual perception, he only perceived with his five carnal senses. The spiritual man became "flesh." *(Gen 6:3)*. Those who live in this way, according to the soul and not according to the spirit, are called "carnal" or "soulish." The Greek word for "soulish" is *psuquikos*, which is the adjective of *psuque* or "soul."

*"But the **natural** (psuquikos "soulish") **man** does not receive the things of the Spirit of God, for they are foolishness to him; nor can he know them, because they are spiritually discerned. 15 But he who is **spiritual** (pneumáticos) judges all things, yet he himself is rightly judged by no one... And I, brethren, could not speak to you as to spiritual (pneumáticos) people **but as to carnal**, as to babes in Christ." (1Cor 2:14,15; 3:1)*

> *"These are **sensual** (psuquikos 'soulish') persons, who cause divisions, **not having the Spirit**." (Jude 19)*

> *"This wisdom does not descend from above, but is earthly, **sensual** (psuquikos 'soulish'), demonic." (James 3:15-16)*

The soulish man is carnal, since he does not hear God's voice and therefore lives a sensual life in his soul, according to the five senses of the flesh. He fulfills the desires of the flesh and not those of the Spirit.

When one is born again, it is the spirit which is born from above. Once born of the Spirit we now have the capacity to perceive the things of God and do His will, living according to the Spirit and not according to the flesh. We are now capable of being spiritual and not "soulish;" living the "soul life." *(Jn 3:3,6)*.

Nevertheless, the life of the soul must be destroyed and replaced with the life of the spirit. In Adam our soul was no longer subject to the Spirit. Now with our spirit reborn, it is necessary to put our soul in subjection to our spirit. When Jesus said that it was necessary to lose or destroy (*apollumi*) our soul, I believe He was saying that it is necessary to die to the dominion of the soul, subjecting it to our reborn spirit. The word *apollumi* in the New Testament sometimes means "to destroy or render null or inoperative" and sometimes "to lose." I believe that the idea expressed here is to render inoperative the dominion of the soul in our lives. We should no longer live according to our own emotions and reason, but according to the *rhema* word of God. We should no longer live according to our will but according to the will of God. The soul must be subjected once again to the spirit, in communion with God and no longer following after the flesh in order to fulfill its desires.

> *"Most assuredly, I say to you, unless a grain of wheat falls into the ground and dies, it remains alone; but if it dies, it produces much grain. 25 **He who loves his (soul) life will lose it, and he who hates his (soul) life in this world will keep it for eternal life** (zoe aionios)." (John 12:24-25)*

If we as believers take up our cross, following in the steps of Jesus, laying down our (soul) life for others, we will be spiritual, serving the Lord in spirit. But if we are soulish *psuquikos*, then God must intervene so we are not condemned with the world.

> *"For if we would judge ourselves, we would not be judged. 32 But when we are judged, we are chastened by the Lord, that we may not be condemned with the world." (1Cor 11:31-32)*

Here we see that the disciplinary judgments of the Lord have a correctional purpose - in order that we should not receive our *portion* with the unbelievers, being condemned with the world. The purpose of this discipline can be seen in 1Corinthians 5:5 where Paul says:

> *"deliver such a one to Satan **for the destruction of the flesh**, that his spirit may be saved in the day of the Lord Jesus." (1Cor 5:5)*

The destruction of the flesh is not speaking of the physical body but rather the soul life following after the desires of the flesh and not the desires of the Spirit. In discipline God permits us to receive the consequences of acting in the flesh now, in order that the spirit might be saved in the day of the Lord, and in this way saving us from the Great White Throne Judgment and the second death.

If we submit to God, subjecting our soul to our spirit in this life, God will not have to destroy the dominance of the soul later. If we do not do it in this life, we face the possibility of suffering the destruction of the soul in a physically resurrected body, experiencing the second death in the purifying lake of fire, because without holiness no one shall see the Lord.

Death, Destruction and Annihilation

Those who believe that the destiny of the unjust is to be annihilated, understand death and destruction as the cessation of all existence. On the other hand, the traditionalists who teach eternal punishment in hell insist that neither the first death nor the second death, are the end of existence. The Biblical Universalists, just as the traditionalist, believe that the soul of man does not cease to exist. They differ from the traditionalists in that they believe that the second death is a restorative and correctional process that will culminate in God being all in all. For them, neither death nor destruction mean the annihilation of our being, but rather a transformation and purification. Those who put their faith in Christ in this life and die to the soul life now will not be hurt by the second death afterwards. But those who do not believe or do not submit to the destruction of their soul life in this lifetime risk having to be purified later in the lake of fire, having their portion in the second death or the *eonian* destruction which follows judgment.

In the Bible neither death nor destruction express the concept of annihilation. Nothing in all God's creation will ever cease to exist; it will simply undergo a change of state. The same word *apollumi* appears in 2Peter 3:6 where it says, *"the world that then existed* ***perished****, being flooded with water."* It is evident that the world did not cease to exist since we still inhabit it today. We still breathe the same air, drink its water and till its soil. What is expressed by the word *apollumi* is that it underwent a change in state. In the majority of instances in which it appears in the New Testament, *apollumi* simply means that something *was lost*, only to be found later:

> *"What man of you, having a hundred sheep, if he* ***loses*** *(apollumi) one of them, does not leave the ninety-nine in the wilderness, and* ***go after the one which is lost*** *(apollumi)* ***until he finds it****?" (Luke 15:4)*

> *"Or what woman, having ten silver coins, if she* ***loses*** *(apollumi) one coin, does not light a lamp, sweep the house, and* ***search carefully until she finds it****? 9 And when she has found it, she calls her friends and neighbors together, saying, 'Rejoice with me, for* ***I have found the piece which I lost*** *(apollumi)! Likewise, I say to you, there is joy in the presence of the angels of God over one sinner who repents." (Luke 15:8-10)*

> *"...let us eat and be merry; 24 for this* ***my son was dead and is alive again; he was lost*** *(apollumi)* ***and is found****.' And they began to be merry." (Luke 15:23-24)*

Often, we see *apollumi* used in reference to death, but death in the Bible does not mean "ceasing to exist" as some believe, but rather "a change in existence." This is evident in several texts:

> *"I think it is right to refresh your memory as long as* ***I*** *live* ***in the tent*** *of this body, 14 because I know that* ***I*** *will soon* ***put it aside****, as our Lord Jesus Christ has made clear to me. 15 And I will make every effort to see that* ***after my departure*** *you will always be able to remember these things." (2Peter 1:13-15 NAS)*

> *"For to me, to live is Christ, and* ***to die is gain****. 22 But* ***if I live on in the flesh****, this will mean fruit from my labor; yet what I shall*

*choose I cannot tell. 23 For I am hard-pressed between the two, having a desire to **depart and be with Christ**, which is far better. 24 Nevertheless, **to remain in the flesh** is more needful for you." (Phil 1:21-24)*

*"I know a man in Christ who fourteen years ago — **whether in the body I do not know, or whether out of the body I do not know**, God knows — such a one was caught up to the third heaven." (2Cor 12:2)*

The fact that Paul wasn't sure whether he was in the body or out of the body makes it clear that the soul has a conscious existence separate from the body. Also, he speaks of dying or living as departing from or remaining in the fleshly body – expressions which would not make sense if there is no conscious existence apart from the body or flesh. Peter speaks of himself as living in the tent which is his body and then putting it aside. One can only speak of living in something, departing from something or putting it aside, when ones essential being exists independently of it.

So, we see that the destruction of the body and soul does not have reference to annihilation but rather to the change of state *(apollumi)* of the soul and body, making us subject to Christ through fire, whether it should be fiery trials now or Gehenna fire later. The future destruction of soul and body is said by Jesus to be worse than physical death, but it is not annihilation, nor is it without end, as understood by those who hold to the doctrine of eternal torment.

The Furnace of Fire

*"Therefore as the tares are gathered and burned in the fire, so it will be at the end of this age. 41 The Son of Man will send out His angels, and they will gather out of His kingdom all things that offend, and those who practice lawlessness, 42 and **will cast them into the furnace of fire. There will be wailing and gnashing of teeth.**" (Matt 13:40-42)*

"Again, the kingdom of heaven is like a dragnet that was cast into the sea and gathered some of every kind, 48 which, when it was full, they drew to shore; and they sat down and gathered the good into vessels, but threw the bad away. 49 So it will be at the end of the age. The angels will come forth, separate the wicked from

*among the just, 50 **and cast them into the furnace of fire. There will be wailing and gnashing of teeth**.” (Matt 13:47-50)*

In these passages Jesus speaks of a separation of the just from the unjust. The just enter directly into the Kingdom of God. The unjust will be cast into the furnace of fire. This is in perfect agreement with what Evangelical Universalists believe. They would also insist, along with the traditionalists, that without holiness no one will see the Lord. But the difference between them and those who believe in eternal torment is that the Universalist sees this furnace as the Refiner's fire for purification and not like some eternal medieval torture chamber, or an incinerator, as the annihilationists maintain.

The *furnace of fire* is often used to express the judgment of God but what we see is that the fire is for the purpose of purification, not torture or incineration:

*"The word of the Lord came to me, saying, 18 "Son of man, **the house of Israel has become dross to Me; they are all bronze, tin, iron, and lead, in the midst of a furnace**; they have become dross from silver. 19 Therefore thus says the Lord God: 'Because you have all become dross, therefore behold, I will gather you into the midst of Jerusalem. 20 **As men gather silver, bronze, iron, lead, and tin into the midst of a furnace, to blow fire on it, to melt it; so I will gather you in My anger and in My fury, and I will leave you there and melt you**. 21 Yes, I will gather you and blow on you with the fire of **My wrath**, and you shall be melted in its midst. 22 **As silver is melted <u>in the midst of a furnace</u>, so shall you be melted in its midst; then you shall know that I, the Lord, have <u>poured out My fury on you</u>**." (Ezek 22:17-22)*

Here we see that Israel had become dross or scum, and for that reason God, in His wrath, put them into the furnace of fire and melted them. There are two very important observations that I would like to point out here. In the first place, the furnace of fire was not literal, but rather fiery trials and severe corrective judgments in order to purify His disobedient people who had become scum and needed to be purified in the fires of affliction until they came forth as pure metal. This is the same language as used in the warnings given by Christ and in Revelation, and the furnace here in Ezekiel clearly was neither for annihilation nor eternal torture. In the second place, we see that it ends in restoration. It wasn't in order to burn them up or torture them forever but rather to remove the scum from their lives, making them pure. From chapter 34 onward, God speaks of a purified and restored Israel:

> *"Therefore **say to the house of Israel**.... Then I will sprinkle clean water on you, and **you shall be clean**; **I will cleanse you** from all your filthiness and from all your idols. 26 **I will give you a new heart and put a new spirit within you**; I will take the heart of stone out of your flesh and give you a heart of flesh. 27 I will put My Spirit within you and **cause you to walk in My statutes**, and you will keep My judgments and do them." (Ezek 36:22ª, 25-27)*

Here we see Israel restored and purified after having passed through to the other side of the furnace. They were not exterminated in an incinerator but rather purified in the furnace of affliction. Here we also see the symbolism of pure water used to make them clean rather than the fire. The fiery furnace represents judgment and water represents the Holy Spirit who cleanses us from within. We understand that neither water nor fire are literal in Ezekiel. We also understand that the *"testing by fire" (1Peter 1:6,7)* isn't literal either, but rather affliction that purifies us like gold or silver. Why is it that so many cannot see that the fire mentioned by Jesus and John the revelator isn't literal fire either, but rather fire of affliction to purify the unjust by removing the scum from their lives so that they too will someday come forth as pure gold in the same way that God's wrath purified Israel? Does God show partiality? To burn people - as the false gods demanded - has never entered into the heart of our God *(Jer 7:31)*. That may be the teaching of Baal, Molech and other false gods and it may even be the teaching of the traditional institutionalized church today, but such a thing has never entered into the heart of the God of Love revealed in the Scriptures. The practice of *literalizing* texts which are obviously symbolic can at times be an even more damaging error than spiritualizing literal passages.

The Rich Man and Lazarus

> *"There was a certain rich man who was clothed in purple and fine linen and fared sumptuously every day. 20 But there was a certain beggar named Lazarus, full of sores, who was laid at his gate, 21 desiring to be fed with the crumbs which fell from the rich man's table. Moreover the dogs came and licked his sores. 22 So it was that the beggar died, and was carried by the angels to **Abraham's bosom**. The rich man also died and was buried. 23 And **being in torments in Hades**, he lifted up his eyes and saw*

*Abraham afar off, and Lazarus in his bosom. 24 Then he cried and said, 'Father Abraham, have mercy on me, and send Lazarus that he may dip the tip of his finger in water and cool my tongue; for I am tormented in this flame.' 25 But Abraham said, 'Son, remember that in your lifetime you received your good things, and likewise Lazarus evil things; but now he is comforted and you are tormented. 26 And besides all this, **between us and you there is a great gulf fixed, so that those who want to pass from here to you cannot, nor can those from there pass to us**.' 27 Then he said, 'I beg you therefore, father, that you would send him to my father's house, 28 for I have five brothers, that he may testify to them, lest they also come to this place of torment.' 29 Abraham said to him, 'They have Moses and the prophets; let them hear them.' 30 And he said, 'No, father Abraham; but if one goes to them from the dead, they will repent.' 31 But he said to him, 'If they do not hear Moses and the prophets, neither will they be persuaded though one rise from the dead." (Luke 16:19-31)*

This parable of Jesus is consistent with biblical Universalism which affirms that the unjust will pass through purifying fires upon dying. What Jesus doesn't say here is what traditionalists affirm - that the fire is eternal. Some cite verse 26 where Abraham says that there was a great gulf separating them which did not permit passage from where he was to where they were, and they couldn't pass over to him. But the parable does not say that he would *never* be able to pass over. While one is serving a prison sentence it is very similar to what the rich man was experiencing. A prisoner can receive visits and converse with those on the outside, but as long as he is a prisoner, there is a great wall between them so that they cannot pass to where he is, and he cannot pass to where they are. They can only communicate through a bullet-proof window using a telephone. But once the prisoner has served his sentence, he is free to pass to where they are. It is like when Jesus said: *"Assuredly, I say to you, you will by no means get out of there **till** you have paid the last penny." (Matt 5:26; Luke 12:59).* There is a lot of difference between saying, *"you will by no means ever get out of there"* and *"you will by no means get out of there **until**..."* It is needful to combine all the teachings of Jesus concerning punishments in order to have a more complete understanding of the subject. We must see this parable in light of other occasions in which Jesus spoke of duration: *"you will by no means get out of there **until**"*; *"they will have **their part**"*; and *"beaten with **many stripes**,"* as opposed to *"**few stripes**" (Luke 12:47).*

Also, it is probable that the descriptions of the flame, the tip of Lazarus' finger, and the rich man's tongue, are all figurative and not literal. Lazarus wasn't literally in Abraham's bosom. They are figurative descriptions of two distinct spiritual realms in Hades (the invisible world of the dead). The Pharisees used the expression "Abraham's bosom" in reference to paradise. Also, the parable presents those in paradise as if they were seeing and talking with those tormented in Hades, which probably wouldn't be the case in a literal sense - otherwise paradise would not really be paradise.

This parable is the fifth in a series of five parables, the prior ones being: The Lost Sheep *(Luke 15:3-7),* The Lost Coin *(15:8-10),* The Prodigal Son *(15:11-31),* and The Unfaithful Steward *(16:1-14).* Some would argue that The Rich Man and Lazarus is not a parable because it begins like a real story; *"There was a certain rich man."* However, the parable of the Unjust Steward begins exactly the same way; *"There was a certain rich man."* Also, the parable of The Lost Son begins as though it were a real story saying: *"A certain man had two sons."* The Parable of the Sower also begins as though it were a real story: *"a sower went out to sow,"* but we know it was a parable because Jesus said it was *(Matt 13:3).* If we were to take The Rich Man and Lazarus as a real story and not as a parable, what kind of paradise would it be? Could we be comforted in "Abraham's bosom" while at the same time watching those we love burning in Gehenna and hearing their endless cries for mercy? To me such a paradise would be unthinkable. It would be a torment for those in paradise as much as for those in the flames unless God were to remove all sense of love and compassion from their hearts.

This series of parables was a response to the criticism of the scribes and Pharisees against Jesus for receiving sinners:

"Then all the tax collectors and the sinners drew near to Him to hear Him. 2 And the Pharisees and scribes complained, saying, 'This Man receives sinners and eats with them." (Luke 15:1-2)

All five of these parables are directed - not at the publicans and sinners who drew near to hear Him, but rather against the scribes and Pharisees who criticized Him for receiving them, since they considered themselves to be holy and despised the rest. In the parable of the rich man and Lazarus, Jesus was telling them in so many words what He said to them on a different occasion: *"Assuredly, I say to you that tax collectors and harlots enter the* *kingdom of God **before you**." (Matt 21:31)*. He does not say in the parable that they will never enter, only that the people they despised, like the beggar Lazarus, the tax collectors and the harlots, will enter *before* them into the kingdom.

Jesus, in this parable, took a certain tale of Greek origin well known by them, and changed the personages of the story. In the original story, a rich tax collector named Bar Ma´jan and a poor scribe died. The poor scribe went to paradise but Bar Ma´jan was in torment beside a river desiring to drink of its waters but unable to reach them. [76] There were at least seven other similar folkloric stories circulated among the Jews of Jesus' time. [77]

The scribes and Pharisees must have especially liked this story because it presented them in a good light while presenting the tax collectors, whom they despised, as being the ones in torment. But Jesus changed the story, presenting them in their typical purple dress with fine linen as being the evil ones in this parable, and sinners and beggars as those being received into paradise. This parable was directed specifically at the scribes and Pharisees. Jesus did not intend for us to draw from this parable the conclusion that all beggars go to heaven and all rich people are tormented in flames. Neither did He intend for it to be taken as a description of paradise or hell. Its sole purpose was to expose the hypocrisy of the scribes and Pharisees by utilizing one of their own tales.

---

[76] George W. Sarris *article The Rich Man and Lazarus.*
http://www.georgewsarris.com

[77] Edward William Fudge *The Fire that Consumes,* i Universe.com inc. 2001 p. 203

Chapter seven
The Two-Edged Sword

One who dedicates himself to study the Scriptures and meditates upon them until he discovers the riches contained in them - not conforming himself to simply adopt and defend a creed dictated to him by the institutionalized church, will soon discover that the Scriptures contain many declarations which, for the casual reader, seem paradoxical. Many have thrown the Bible aside saying that it is full of contradictions. But those who have come to know the God of the Bible, and therefore have a passion to know Him more; in their hunger and thirst to better know Him and His ways, discover the secrets hidden in the parables, symbolisms, hyperbolic expressions and even paradoxes contained therein.

Jesus made it clear that He taught in parables in order to keep the truth hidden from those who do not seek Him wholeheartedly.

*"All these things Jesus spoke to the multitude in parables; and without a parable He did not speak to them, 35 that it might be fulfilled which was spoken by the prophet, saying: 'I will open My mouth in parables; I will utter **things kept secret from the foundation of the world**" (Matt 13:34-35 cf. Ps 25:14)*

*"And He said, **To you it has been given to know the mysteries of the kingdom of God, but to the rest it is given in parables**, that 'Seeing they may not see, and **hearing they may not understand**." (Luke 8:10)*

*"At that time Jesus answered and said, 'I thank You, Father, Lord of heaven and earth, that **You have hidden these things from the wise and prudent and have revealed them to babes**." (Matt 11:25)*

Jesus revealed the mysteries – the things hidden from the foundation of the world, only to those who followed Him closely and intentionally hid them from those who lacked hunger for truth. God keeps His secrets for those who fear Him – for those who desire to do His will – for those who call upon Him and hides them from the rest. Not even Satan and the angels with all their knowledge, understand the plan of God for the ages as do His sons and daughters who walk closely with Him:

> "**The secret** of the Lord is **with those who fear Him**, and **He will show them** His covenant." (Ps 25:14)

> "**Call to me and I will answer** you, and will tell you **great and hidden things** that you have not known." (Jer 33:3 NIV)

> "And he said, 'Go your way, Daniel, for **the words are closed up and sealed** till the time of the end. 10 Many shall be purified, made white, and refined, but the wicked shall do wickedly; and **none of the wicked shall understand, but the wise shall understand**." (Dan 12:9-10)

> "**If anyone wills to do His will, he shall know** concerning the doctrine, whether it is from God or whether I speak on My own authority." (John 7:17)

The word of God is compared to a two-edged sword *(Heb 4:12)*. A two-edged sword has two cutting edges – the one opposite from the other. In the same way the word of God often has two sides which seem contrary one to the other. One side seems to be the antithesis to the other, but every stroke of the Word of God fulfills a specific purpose.

For one who considers himself to be righteous in and of himself, the stroke of the law comes to convict him of sin. For the one who already feels the weight of his own sin and guilt, God gives words of acceptance, mercy and grace. This can be illustrated in Romans 11:32:

> "For God has shut up all in **disobedience** so that He may show **mercy** to all." (Rom 11:32 NASU)

In order for man to recognize his need for God's mercy he needs to feel the stroke of the law that commits us all to disobedience. The law was our tutor to bring us to the point of seeing our need for Christ: *"Therefore the law was our tutor to bring us to Christ, that we might be justified by faith. 25 But after faith has come, we are no longer under a tutor." (Gal 3:24-25)*. The law's ministry was death *(2Cor 3:7)*. Were it not for the law we would never see ourselves as sinners in need of Christ. But after the stroke of the law, comes the word of faith, and we commence a relationship with Christ under the grace and mercy of God. Being under grace we are no longer under the old regimen of the law. The Old Covenant is the word of God and it serves its purpose. But if we do not understand that we are now under the New Covenant and try to live under the law being a new creature in Christ, we will live frustrated and confused lives. Both sides, law and grace, are equally the word of God, but if we do not understand that it is a two-edged sword, the word is going to seem contradictory and confusing. The law was our tutor. A child needs a tutor with rules and prohibitions. But now we are "sons" *(huios "mature sons")* and not "children" *(nepios) (Gal 3:24-4:7)*. An adult does not have the same kind of relationship with his father as when he was still a child. Our relationship with God in Christ now is not as a child but as an adult son. The law still exists to convince of sin but not as a regimen of life for one who is in Christ *(1Tim 1:9; Rom 7:6)*.

We see the same two-edged truth of fear and love.

*"The **fear** of the Lord is the beginning of wisdom." (Ps 111:10*
*"...perfect **love** casts out fear." (1John 4:18)*

When one is immature (a child), the fear of the Lord is what predominates in one's relationship with God. But as one is perfected in love, love becomes that which predominates. An adult son no longer needs the fear of correction and discipline in order to do what is right, but rather the discipline of the Lord, having done its work in our character, produces in us the peaceable fruit of righteousness *(Heb 12:11)*. Yes, fear is the beginning of wisdom, but love is its end. One who is immature needs the fear of the Lord in order to learn righteousness, but once he is mature the fear and warnings are replaced with the character of a mature adult son who has been perfected in love.

When we are children, our parents love us the same as when we become adults but that parental love often takes the form of corrective discipline. When we mature, our relationship with our parents changes and we no longer need the corrective words of discipline as before, because we have matured. The same is true in our fear / love relationship with our Heavenly Father.

*"We have come to know and have believed the love which God has for us. **God is love**, and the one who abides in love abides in God, and God abides in him. 17 By this, love is perfected with us,*

so that we may have confidence in the Day of Judgment; because as He is, so also are we in this world. 18 **There is no fear in love; but perfect (mature) love casts out fear, because fear involves punishment,** *and* **the one who fears is not perfected (matured) in love**.*" (1John 4:16-18 NAS)*

It is not that the fear of the Lord is something evil or incompatible with His love. The judgments and discipline of the Lord are just as much an expression of His love as are His favors. But as we mature in character, the fear of correction and punishment is no longer predominant. Diapers are a good thing for a little child, but a time comes when he has been trained and they are then no longer necessary. It is the same way with the warnings of God. *"Therefore consider the goodness and severity of God…" (Rom 11:22).* We find reference both to the goodness of God and His severity in the Scriptures, but for one who has matured in the Love of God, what he predominantly sees is no longer severity but goodness.

Sometimes God acts in a manner that seems contradictory for one who doesn't know His ways, nor understand His purposes. We must understand that His word is a two-edged sword:

"The Lord kills and makes alive; He brings down to the grave and brings up. 7 The Lord makes poor and makes rich; He brings low and lifts up." (1 Sam 2:6-7)

If one doesn't look at the Word of God seeing it as a two-edged sword – one to wound and the other to heal – one to kill and the other to give life – one for destruction and the other for restoration – one to punish and the other to console – one for judgment and the other for mercy, then the Bible will seem like a book full of paradoxes, disjointed truths and contradictions. In order to be able to understand the purpose of God for our lives and for the ages, it is necessary to recognize the reality of contrasts with the full conviction that God is Love. He manifests wrath against all evil but He is Love. He corrects but with Love. He even rejects but not forever because God is Love *(Lam 3:31).* How often we must say together with Paul when contemplating the multifaceted and infinite wisdom of God: *"For who has known the mind of the Lord?"*

Although it would be impossible to sound the depths of the riches of His wisdom, we can always be confident that He is our Father God and that he loves us. The sadistic tortures described in depictions of hell are, at best, inventions of men deprived of any real knowledge of the heart of Father God. These descriptions are found in religious writings but not in the Word of God. Religious men throughout history have submitted others to unimaginable tortures in the name of God but such a thing has never even entered into the heart of our God.

Chapter eight
Texts Used to Prove Eternal Punishment

Taking into account all we have seen so far concerning the real meaning of the words translated "eternal," we can now better understand what the New Testament has to say concerning the duration of punishment.

"They will go away into Everlasting Punishment"

> *"And these will go away into everlasting punishment, but the righteous into eternal life." (Matt 25:46)*

> *"And these shall be coming away into chastening eonian, yet the just into life eonian." (Concordant Literal Version)*

The argument presented by traditionalists is that, if the punishment is not eternal, then neither can the life of the just be eternal, since the same word "eternal" is used of both in the same verse. But as we have seen, *aionios* does not in itself express "eternity" in the New Testament, even when referring to eternal life. This fact is recognized even by many who hold to the doctrine of eternal punishment. Ellicott's Commentary on the Whole Bible says the following on Matthew 25:46:

> *"Everlasting punishment - life eternal. The two adjectives represent the same Greek word, aionios. It must be admitted (1) that the Greek word which is rendered "eternal" does not, in itself, involve endlessness, but rather, duration, whether through an age or succession of ages, and that it is therefore applied in the N.T. to periods of time that have had both a beginning and ending."* [78]

Marvin Vincent, in *Vincent's New Testament Word Studies,* says the following concerning the eonian life and eonian punishment in this verse:

---

[78] *Ellicott's Commentary on the Whole Bible (Matt. 25:46)*

> *"**Zooee aionios** 'eternal life,' which occurs 42 times in the New Testament, but not in the Septuagint, is not endless life, but life pertaining to a certain age or aeon, or continuing during that aeon. I repeat, life may be endless. The life in union with Christ is endless, but the fact is not expressed by aionios.*
> ***Kolasis aioonios**, rendered 'everlasting punishment' (Matt 25:46), is the punishment peculiar to an aeon other than that in which Christ is speaking."* [79]

Also, the duration expressed by the adjective *aionios* in each instance depends upon the noun that accompanies it and not upon its proximity with another occurrence of the same adjective. For example, if we were to say, "the *eonian* hills belong to the *eonian* God" we would not mean by that that the hills have the same duration as God, even as we wouldn't understand the phrase, "my *long* legs are going to get uncomfortable on such a *long* trip," as meaning that my legs are the same length as the trip.

Apart from Matthew 25:42, we have another instance in Scriptures where *aionios* is also used two times in the same verse, and yet the duration in each case is different:

> *"in hope of **eternal** (aionios) life which God, who cannot lie, promised **before time began** (pro kronon aionion "before the times eonian")." (Titus 1:2)*

In this case the King James Version translators hid the second occurrence of *aionios* by translating "before times *aionion*" as *"before time began."* However, in both instances it is the same word *aionios;* the first in singular and the second in plural, (agreeing with its noun "times"). The Concordant Literal Version translates it correctly:

> *"in expectation of **life eonian**, which God, Who does not lie, promises before **times eonian**." (Titus 1:2 CLV)*

In the first place, we know that *"the times"* are measurements of time created by God and have no relationship with eternity. Eternity doesn't have "times," but rather time was created in eternity. In eternity before creation there were no days. Before the moon

---

[79] Vincent's Word Studies in the New Testament - Additional note on *aion* and *aionios* in 2Thessalonians 1:9

existed, there were no months. Before the sun, there were no years. Eternity doesn't have times and ages. The ages were created by God:

> "has in these last days spoken to us by His Son, whom He has appointed heir of all things, through whom also **He made the ~~worlds~~** *(aionios, "the ages")." (Heb 1:2)*

In the second place, returning to Titus 1:2, it doesn't make sense to say that God promised eternal life before eternity since eternity doesn't have a beginning or end. But it does make sense to say that He promised before the times of the ages. So, the first occurrence of *aionios* in Titus 1:2 is "eonian life" or "life of the ages" referring to future ages, while the second occurrence, *"before eonian times"* or *"before the times of the ages,"* refers to all past ages since the beginning of time. *Aionios* doesn't speak of the same duration (or even the same time period) in both occurrences. Therefore, the argument that *"aionios correction"* must have the same duration as *"aionios life"* because it appears in the same verse is not a valid argument.

Although we know that the just will receive immortality in the resurrection, *zoe aionios* (translated "life eternal") only means "eonian life" or "the life of the ages." Everlasting life is expressed by other words such as "immortality," "incorruptible" or "for the age and beyond," as we saw in Daniel 12:2,3:

> *"And many of those who sleep in the dust of the earth shall awake, some to* **everlasting (olam) life**, *some to* **shame and everlasting (olam) contempt**. *3 Those who are wise shall shine like the brightness of the firmament, and those who turn many to righteousness like the stars* **forever and ever** *(olam a-ad "olam and beyond")." (Dan 12:2-3)*

A literal translation better expresses the distinction between "age during" or "eonian," and "eonian and beyond":

> *"And the multitude of those sleeping in the dust of the ground do awake, some* **to life age-during**, *and some* **to reproaches--to abhorrence age-during**. *3 And those teaching do shine as the brightness of the expanse, and those justifying the multitude as stars* **to the age and forever** *(lit. "and beyond")." (Dan 12:2,3 Young's Literal Translation)*

In these two verses we see that the eonian life of the just continues beyond the shame and self-contempt of the unjust. The same can be said of Matthew 25:46.

Also, we see that the punishment cannot be eternal because of the meaning of the Word translated "punishment." The Greek word *(kolasis)* means "corrective punishment" in contrast with *timoreo* which often expresses "vindictive punishment or torture." William Barclay, a Greek scholar, in his commentary, <u>The Daily Study Bible and New Testament Words</u> says the following of *kolasis:*

"The Greek word for punishment here [Mt. 25:46] is kolasis, which was not originally an ethical word at all. It originally meant the pruning of trees to make them grow better. I think it is true to say that in all Greek secular literature kolasis is never used of anything but remedial punishment." [80]

Thomas Talbott, professor of Philosophy in the University of Willamette in Oregon and author of *"The Inescapable Love of God"* explains:

"According to the Aristotle, there is a difference between revenge and punishment; the latter (kolasis) is inflicted in the interest of the sufferer, the former (timoria) in the interest of him who inflicts it, that he may obtain satisfaction. Plato also appealed to the established meaning of kolasis as support for his theory that virtue could be taught: 'For if you will consider punishment (kolasis)...and what control it has over wrong-doers, the facts will inform you that men agree in regarding virtue as procured.' Even where a punishment may seem harsh and unforgiving, more like retribution than parental chastisement, this in no way excludes a corrective purpose. Check out the punishment that Paul prescribes in I Corinthians 5:5. One might never have guessed that, in prescribing such a punishment—that is, delivering a man to Satan for the destruction of the flesh—Paul had in mind a corrective purpose, had Paul not explicitly stated the corrective purpose himself ("that his spirit may be saved in the day of the Lord Jesus"). So as this text illustrates, even harsh punishment of

---

[80] William Barclay, *The Daily Study Bible and New Testament Words*

a seemingly retributive kind can in fact serve a redemptive purpose." [81]

The majority of the Pharisees believed in eternal punishment as does the traditional Church today, but they did not use the phrase *"kolasis aionios" (eonian correction)* that Jesus used. In order to express everlasting vindictive punishment, they used the phrases *"aidíos timoria"* (eternal torture), *"eirgmos aidíos"* (eternal prisons), and *"timorion adialeipton"* (unending torment). The Jewish historian Josephus (AD 37-100), said of the Pharisees: *"They believe that the evil spirits are kept in eternal prisons (eirgmon aidíon). The Pharisees say that all souls are incorruptible, but while the souls of good men are taken to other bodies, the souls of wicked men are subjected to eternal punishment (aidíos temoría)."* In another place he says of the Essenes, *"...they consign the souls of the evil to a dark and tempestuous place, full of endless torture (timoría adialeipton), where they suffer an "immortal torment" (athanaton timorion)."* Josephus always used *aidíon (eternal) and athonaton (immortal)* and *timoría* in reference to eternal punishment. In the Bible, however, the word *aidíos* "eternal" and *athonaton* "immortal" are not used in reference to the punishment of the unjust. When Jesus spoke of the punishment of the unjust, He said, *"correction eonian" (kolasis aionios)* which are terms used by Josephus and the Pharisees to refer to temporal and corrective punishments, and He avoided terms then in use to describe eternal punishment. He always spoke of a correctional punishment with a positive end in view. [82]

The great Greek scholar Archbishop trench in *Trench's New Testament Synonyms*, also explains the difference between the vindictive punishment *timoria* and the corrective punishment *kolasis:*

"Punishment: timoria, kolasis
Timoria*... The classical use of timoria emphasizes the vindictive character of punishment. It was punishment that satisfied the inflictor's sense of outraged justice and that defended his own*

---

[81] from Gerry Beauchemin, *Hope Beyond Hell*

[82] Hanson, J.W. (2014-09-16). Universalism: The Prevailing Doctrine of the Christian Church During Its First 500 Years (Kindle Location 585). . Kindle Edition.

honor or that of the violated law. The meaning of timoria, then, agrees with its etymology.
Kolasis *refers to punishment that is designed to correct and better the offender. Thus Plato uses kolaseis and noutheteseis together. Several times in one passage in the Protagoras, Plato's use illustrates the distinction we have drawn."* [83]

This explains why the early Church fathers who were Greek speaking had no problem understanding that *kolasis* referred to correctional punishment with limited duration. Clement of Alexandria AD 150 to AD 215 says of God's punishment of the wicked:

"But God does not punish, for punishment is retaliation for evil. He chastises, however, for good to those who are chastised, collectively and individually." [84]

"Punishment is, in its operation, like medicine; it dissolves the hard heart, purges away the filth of uncleanness, and reduces the swellings of pride and haughtiness; thus restoring its subject to a sound and healthful state." [85]

"God's punishments are saving and disciplinary leading to conversion...and especially since souls, although darkened by passions, when released from their bodies, are able to perceive more clearly because of their being no longer obstructed by the paltry flesh." [86]

Even when *kolasis* is used in a context which appears to be purely vindictive and penal, one must keep in mind that the root meaning of the word *kolasis* is *correction*. In the judgments of any just society penalties are not purely vindictive but also correctional in nature. While those condemned to serve a sentence in penitentiaries, correctional institutions, or reformatories are being punished for their

---

[83] *Trench's New Testament Synonyms: Punishment*

[84] *Ante-Nicene Fathers, Volume 2, Chapter 16*

[85] Clement of Alexandria, *Paedagogus* 1.8 as cited in Thayors Léxicon.

[86] Clement of Alexandria, *Hanson, John Wesley, Universalism: The Prevailing Doctrine of the Christian Church During Its First Five Hundred Years.* p. 117

crimes, the primary objective is to reform - to produce penitence and correction in order to ultimately restore the offender to society.

Although dictatorships have existed which administer vindictive punishment without reformative motives, they are rightly considered to be primitive, barbaric and unjust by any civilized society. How much more can we say of God's own judgments that they are good! *(Ps 119:39)*. Even the best correctional institutions often fail to reform some of the most obstinate individuals, but contrary to the traditional doctrine of eternal reprobation for the majority, God's judgments will ultimately restore even the most obstinately rebellious:

> *"Say to God, 'How awesome are Your works! Through the greatness of Your power* **Your enemies shall submit themselves to You. 4 All the earth shall worship You** *and sing praises to You; They shall sing praises to Your name." (Psalm 66:3-4)*

Contrary to what traditionalists would have us believe, every biblical example of God's judgments are for correction and end in restoration. Fiery wrath and perpetual desolations are declared upon Israel and Judah only to be followed up by their final restoration *(Jer 25:9, cf. Jer 29:10; Ezek 22:17-23,31 cf. Ezek 36:24-26; Jer 30)*. This is not only true of God's elect but also of the nations. From Jeremiah 45 thru 51 we see apparently irremediable destruction declared against nations such as Egypt, Moab, Ammon and Elam followed up by promises of restoration *(cf. Isa 19:22)*. The very nations in Revelation which come up against Christ in His coming will walk in the light of the New Jerusalem in the post White Throne Judgment new earth *(Rev 21:24-26)*. If even Sodom and those who were disobedient in the days of Noah are restored, how can we still insist that the judgment of the nations and the White Throne Judgment will not finally result in restoration? *(Ezek 16:53,54; 1Peter 3:19,20)*.

> **All nations** whom You have made
> Shall come and worship before You, O Lord,
> And shall glorify Your name. *(Ps 86:9)*

If God's punishment were purely vindictive and for His own benefit and pleasure, then one might argue that His punishment *could* last forever, although eternal vengeance would still be unjust, excessive and contrary to God's loving nature. However, seeing that the word Jesus used is "correction" *(kolasis),* it is evident that it *could not* last forever. A punishment for the purpose of correction only lasts until the desired result has been achieved – the correction of the offender. Once corrected, the *eonian* correction ceases. It may last a very long time or a rather short time, depending upon the time necessary to accomplish its purpose. In Jonah's case it lasted for an eon of just three days. Justice always suspends punishment when the correction has been achieved. According to the meaning of the word *kolasis*, we see that the punishment in Scriptures is always a measured punishment according to the works of each one. Even in the apocalyptic lake of fire each one receives only that which is *his part:*

> *"But the cowardly, unbelieving, abominable, murderers, sexually immoral, sorcerers, idolaters, and all liars shall have **their part** (meros) in the lake which burns with fire and brimstone, which is the second death." (Rev 21:8)*

The expression *"their part" (meros)* does not correspond with an infinite punishment. That which is "a part" is a measured punishment. The prodigal son said to his father: *"Father, give me the portion (meros) of goods that falls to me." (Luke 15:12)*. The same Greek word *meros* is used in each instance. We get our English word "merit," which refers to *that which one deserves; a portion or part pertaining to someone*. Their *part* is limited to what corresponds to each one – no more, no less. If the punishment were infinite, then it couldn't be said to be a *part* or *portion*. Jesus said of the evil servant: *"and will cut him in two and appoint him his portion with the hypocrites. There shall be weeping and gnashing of teeth." (Matt 24:45)*. Again we see that it is a portion and not infinite. Here the phrase *"will cut him in two"* simply means "cut or lacerate." It was common practice to scourge disobedient servants, leaving them lacerated, but they didn't normally dismember them. If a master were to cut his servant in two for disobeying, what benefit would it be to him? He would just have one less servant. Kenneth Wuest's translation gives the more logical meaning: *"and he shall scourge him severely and shall appoint his part with the actors on the stage of life who play the role of that which they are not."* [87]

---

[87] *The New Testament: An Expanded Translation* by Kenneth S. Wuest Copyright © 1961 by Wm. B. Eerdmans Publishing Co.

There is another phrase utilized in the Scriptures for punishment which also limits the duration of punishment. *"Assuredly, I say to you, you will by no means get out of there **till** you have paid the last penny." (Matt 5:26 cf. Luke 12:59).* In the context of this parable Jesus is speaking of *"hell (Gehenna) fire" (v. 22),* and He said that one will not get out ***till***. A punishment cannot be forever and at the same time last **until**, but it can be an eonian or age during punishment, lasting **until**. Forever does not have an end but an age or ages last **until** the purpose for the age or ages has been fulfilled – whether it should be three days or millenniums. Another example we find is in Matthew 18:34,35:

*"And his master was angry, and delivered him to the torturers **until** he should pay all that was due to him. 35 **So My heavenly Father also will do to you** if each of you, from his heart, does not forgive his brother his trespasses." (Matt 18:34-35)*

If we do not forgive others their debts against us, then our Father will deliver us to torments, however, not eternally, but rather **until**. Nor is it without significance that Jesus refers to God in this instance as Father, emphasizing His paternal correction. Also, in the Lord's Prayer we see that the forgiveness is paternal and not penal or judicial *(Matt 6:14,15)*. What father among mankind would continue punishing beyond that which is necessary for the correction of his child? Didn't Jesus say that we are evil fathers in comparison to Him? The traditional Church has degenerated to the point of presenting our Father God as infinitely crueler than the worst earthly father. Jesus, in contrast, said that every sin will be forgiven men *(Matt 12:31)*. Also, we see in Scriptures that the wrath of God is not eternal as tradition teaches, but rather *"**until**"*:

"The anger (wrath) of the Lord will not turn back Until He has executed *and performed the thoughts of His heart. In the latter days you will understand it perfectly." (Jer 23:20)*

On still another occasion Jesus made it clear that correction only lasts as long as necessary. It is found in Matthew 21:31:

*"...tax collectors and harlots enter the kingdom of God **before you**." (Matt 21:31)*

Here Jesus presents two groups of individuals: 1) Those who already knew they were sinners, (tax collectors and harlots) and 2) sinners who thought they were holy, (self-righteous, religious scribes and Pharisees). Many would say that neither category would ever enter the kingdom of Christ, but Jesus said that both groups will enter, but those in the first group enter **before** those of the second group for the obvious reason that those of the second group are slower to recognize their need for the Savior. Without holiness no one will see the Lord *(Heb 12:14),* but the correction only lasts *until* one comes to repentance, faith and holiness.

Another important consideration is the morphology of the noun *"punishment," (kolasis).* According to the Greek scholar A.T. Robertson, when Greek substantives end in *–ria, -ma,* or *–sis* as in *kolasis,* they are nouns which lay emphasis upon the *result* of an action rather than the action itself. [88] These Greek result nouns are translated into English with the endings *–ment* and *–ion.* Words like "punish*ment*," "judg*ment*," "atone*ment*," "salvat*ion*," "redempt*ion*," "destruct*ion*," etc., all lay emphasis upon the result of an action. Although it includes any action necessary to its accomplishment, the emphasis is always upon the end result. Christ's redemptive work was completed within hours, but the abiding result is *eternal redemption.* A father's punishment of his child results in his child's having been corrected. Therefore, the morphology of the noun *kolasis* implies a punishment with a final result or end. This is not compatible with "eternal punishing" or "eternal destroying," as traditionalists understand it. *Eonian correction* does not mean eonian action but eonian results. How can we speak of the results of an action which continues for eternity without ever coming to completion? There are no results unless the action completes its purpose.

Returning to our consideration of Matthew 25:46, it is important to understand that Jesus isn't referring to the Great White Throne Judgment mentioned in Revelation 20, which will take place at the end of the 1,000 year millennial reign of Christ, but rather he is referring to a separation of those of the nations who will be alive on the earth at the time of the Second Coming of Christ, when He begins His reign on the earth:

"When the Son of Man comes in His glory, *and all the holy angels with Him,* **then** *He will sit on the throne of His glory. 32* **All**

---

[88] Robertson, *A Grammar of the Greek New Testament*, p.152.

the nations *will be gathered before Him, and He will separate them one from another, as a shepherd divides his sheep from the goats. 33 And He will set the sheep on His right hand, but the goats on the left. 34 Then the King will say to those on His right hand, 'Come, you blessed of My Father, inherit* **the kingdom** *prepared for you from the foundation of the world." (Matt 25:31-34)*

Here we see that those who treated the brothers of Jesus kindly are the sheep that will be permitted to enter into the kingdom of Christ *(35-40)*, while those who did not treat his brethren kindly are the goats who will not be permitted to enter alive into the kingdom but will go into eonian correction. He is not talking about eternal salvation but rather about the separation of the nations which will take place right after His Second Coming. The entrance isn't based upon having put one's faith in Christ but upon their treatment of His brethren. And who are the brothers of Jesus? Many think they are the persecuted Jews living during the great tribulation. Without discounting the probability that it includes them, [89] we see that those who are actually called the brethren of Jesus are those who make up His Church; those born in His likeness:

"For whom He foreknew, He also predestined to be conformed to the image of His Son, **that He might be the firstborn among many brethren."** *(Rom 8:29, cf. Heb 2:11)*

The "brethren" of Jesus, therefore, are those of the new creation – Christ Jesus being the first-born among them. We become His brethren and enter the kingdom of heaven through the new birth - not for our treatment of the brethren. This passage only has reference to those of the nations who will be alive in the time of the Second Coming; they are not Christians (the brethren) who have already been born again and possess eternal life. The brethren will have already been caught up to meet Christ in the air in His Second Coming. Those being separated here are living individuals of the nations who either will be permitted to enter into the life of the age/s, or sent into eonian correction, depending upon their treatment of believers. Matthew 24 and 25 is a response of Jesus to the question made by the disciples concerning the end of the age *(Matt 24:3)*. Jesus is speaking specifically of a separation of those who are alive

---

[89] see my book *"Focusing in on End Times Events".*

after the great tribulation when Christ returns *(Matt 24:29, cf. 25:31)*. Nor does He say that they will be transformed in that moment, receiving glorified bodies. It simply says that the sheep will be granted entrance into the kingdom of Christ – "the eonian life" or the "life of the *age/s*." John 3:36 says that those who have believed in Jesus already, in this present age, have the eonian life for having believed in Him. In 1John 5:11,12 it says:

> *"And this is the testimony: that God* **has given us eternal life**, *and this life is in His Son. 12 He who has the Son* **has life**; *he who does not have the Son of God does not have life." (1John 5:11,12)*

We who have believed don't have to wait until Christ comes to know whether or not we will enter into eonian life because in Christ we already possess it. We are no longer of the nations but rather the Church of the firstborn ones, the brothers of Jesus.

Temporal vs. "Eternal" in 2Corinthians 4:1

Some have argued that in 2Corinthians 4:18 *aionios* must mean "eternal" rather than "eonian" since it is contrasted with that which is *temporal*. The text, as often translated, *could* seem to warrant that conclusion. The New King James Version reads:

> *"while we do not look at the things which are seen, but at the things which are not seen. For* **the things which are seen are temporary** *(proskairos), but* **the things which are not seen are eternal** *(aionios)."*

It is argued that this verse is making a contrast between time and eternity and that *aionios* in this instance must mean "eternal" rather than "eonian." However, it is more than significant that the word translated *"temporary"* is not from the Greek word *kronos,* used by Plato to distinguish *chronological* time from eternity. Instead Paul uses the word *proskairos,* which is from the word *kairos,* and refers to *that which is momentary* in contrast with that which is *enduring*. Strong's defines *proskairos* as: *"for the occasion only, i.e. temporary."* Therefore, the antonym of *proskairos,* as with *kairos,* would be *enduring* – not *eternal*. Plato's antonym for *eternal* was *kronos* – not *kairos*.

What is being contrasted in 2Corinthians 4:18 is that which is *temporary or momentary* with that which is *enduring* - not time with eternity. The other two uses of the word *proskairos* in the New Testament are not used to express time as opposed to eternity but the momentariness of something as opposed to that which is enduring *(cf. Matt 13:21; Heb 11:25)*. Therefore, all that Paul meant to convey in this comparison is that, that which is seen and tangible is momentary and fleeting as opposed to that which is not seen and age-during.

That the invisible might also be eternal would be beside the point and beyond the meaning conveyed in the word *aionios* itself. Paul is not contrasting *aionios* with *kronos* but with *kairos* – not time vs. eternity but *momentary* vs. *enduring*.

That *aionios* refers to chronological time and not eternity in the Scriptures becomes evident when we look at passages like Romans 16:25,26 which, although carefully hidden by traditional translators, literally says: *"...according to the revelation of the mystery kept secret* ~~since the world began~~, *(kronois aioniois – lit.* **"in times eonian"**) *but now made manifest…"* In the first place we must bear in mind that eternity does not have times *(kronois)*. Also, an "*eternal* secret" could not be said to have *now been made manifest,* since an eternal secret would never be revealed.

Also, in 2Timothy 1:9 and Titus 1:2 the phrase, *pro kronon aionion*, literally means *"before the times of the ages."* To render it as "before times eternal" would be an anomaly since eternity has neither a beginning nor times. That is apparently why the King James translators concealed *pro kronon aionion,* by mistranslating it to read: *"since the world began."* These examples, among others we have already seen, demonstrate that *aionios* cannot mean eternal as Augustinian theologians would have us believe.

Eternal Destruction

> *"…when the Lord Jesus is revealed from heaven with His mighty angels, 8 in flaming fire taking vengeance on those who do not know God, and on those who do not obey the gospel of our Lord Jesus Christ. 9* **These shall be punished with everlasting destruction (olethros aionios) from the presence** *of the Lord and from the glory of His power" (2Thess 1:7-9)*

Keeping in mind that *aionios* means "eonian" or "that which pertains to the age/s," it becomes clear that the eonian destruction *(olethros aionios)* is not eternal but rather that it lasts for a long but indefinite time.

The word *olethros* appears four times in the New Testament and means: "destruction, ruin or corruption." It does not mean annihilation, as the annihilationists affirm, since it is used to describe the condition or state of persons still physically alive, or things that still are in existence. 1Timothy 6:9 is an example: *"But those who desire to be rich fall into temptation and a snare, and into many foolish and harmful lusts which drown men in destruction (olethros) and perdition (apoleia)."* Many who have sunken into the world of sin and vices, reach the point where their lives are in ruins. It is not that they have ceased to exist, but they have made shipwreck of their lives. Jesus said that the prodigal son lived wildly. He didn't come to himself until his life was destroyed and in ruins.

I spent several months learning Spanish in the beautiful city of Antigua Guatemala where there are many ruins. The buildings were "destroyed" by earthquakes but nevertheless they didn't cease to exist. Some are still in ruins while others have been restored. Destruction is not synonymous with annihilation.

In what sense could one suffer temporal destruction resulting in his own benefit? We don't have to look far in the New Testament to find the answer. Paul gave orders to the Corinthians, saying they were to deliver over to Satan the man who was in fornication with his father's wife unto a destruction which had a positive result in view:

*"In the name of our Lord Jesus Christ, when you are gathered together, along with my spirit, with the power of our Lord Jesus Christ, 5 deliver such a one to Satan **for the destruction (olethros) of the flesh, that his spirit may be saved** in the day of the Lord Jesus." (1Cor 5:4-5)*

Here we see a restorative purpose in excluding this man from the community of the saints. He was delivered to Satan for destruction. However, not the destruction of himself as an individual, but rather that of his fleshly self – his sinful flesh. If one persists in sin, the destruction eonian is for his own good, and not just for the good of the community. In the same way, those who die physically without having died to the flesh, will undergo correctional punishment *(kolasis)* for as long as is necessary for the destruction of his flesh or soul life. It will be an eonian destruction but not eternal. It may last two or three days, or it may last for ages. What we do know is that it will continue until the fleshly appetites are destroyed, because without holiness no one will see the Lord *(Heb 12:14)*.

The destruction eonian, according to the King James Version in 2Thessalonians 1:9, is *"**from** (apo) the presence of the Lord."* *"Destruction **From** the presence"* can either mean *"destruction **excluded from** the presence"* or *"destruction **proceeding from** the presence of the Lord."* The New International Version says *"shut out from"* which conveys the former idea. The English Standard Version also says, *"destruction **away from** the presence"* but gives the alternate reading *"or destruction **that comes from** the presence."* Several Spanish versions render it *"destruction **by** the presence"* or *"destruction **proceeding from** the presence" (por la presencia Reina Valera 1909, Spanish Sagradas Escrituras, Peshitta Español "procedente de la presencia")*.

Grammatically, the Greek preposition *apo* could be translated either way, and practically speaking I believe the eonian destruction will be both "destruction *proceeding from* the presence of the Lord" and also "destruction *away from* the presence of the Lord." In Revelation 14:10 it says that *"he shall be **tormented** with fire and brimstone **in the presence** of the holy angels and in the presence of the Lamb."* We will see this in more detail farther along. Suffice it to say for the moment that one's torment will be occasioned by the gaze of Him whose eyes are penetrating as a flame of fire, exposing all for what it is. They will suffer eonian shame from (or by) the presence of the Lord; which presence is inescapable. But at the same time, they will be away from the presence of the Lord as long as they remain in their condition, because without holiness no one will see the Lord.

Their torment will be both being seen by Him and seeing from afar the kingdom in its glory and not being able to draw near because of their uncleanness which cannot be hidden in the light of His presence. As the apostle John exhorted us as believers: *"And now, little children, abide in Him, that when He appears, we may have confidence and not be **ashamed before (apo) Him** at His coming." (1John 2:28).* Here again the Greek preposition *apo* appears which could express both the idea of shrinking **from His presence** or being ashamed **by His presence**. I believe that both meanings apply. If we don't abide in Him, our shame will make us want to run and hide before the presence of the Lord, just as Adam did in his shame.

I believe that the second death is this eonian destruction both *by* the presence and *from* the presence of the Lord. We must all die two deaths. One is physical death and the other is death to the independent ego and the flesh. Jesus says to us: *"For whoever desires to save his life will lose it, but whoever loses (apollumi "lose, destroy") his life for My sake will find it." (Matt 16:25).* Both deaths are inevitable. It is preferable to die now in this life than to *be hurt by* the second death after physical death and judgment *(Rev 2:11; 21:8).* "And whoever falls on this stone will be broken; but on whomever it falls, it will grind him to powder." *(Matt 21:44).* Those who believe in this life and submit to God's discipline in order to be sanctified will *be broken* in this life. It is the painful process of death to the soul life and the flesh. But it is much to be preferred over that which awaits those who do not submit themselves under the mighty hand of God in this life. That's why Paul said that He is *"the Savior of all men, **especially** of those who believe." (1Tim 4:10-11).* One day every tongue will confess that Jesus is Lord *(Phil 2:11),* but more blessed are those who choose Him now in this life.

But who would be the beneficiary of a punishment consisting of "eternal" destruction without an end? Our God and Father, Creator of all? Is it conceivable that the God of Love; infinite in wisdom, would predestine a cosmic garbage dump in which the majority of His rational creatures will pass eternity in a miserable state of conscious torment and ruin without any plan for restoration? Is it possible that it would give God satisfaction to contemplate the suffering of so many billions of his creatures for all of eternity? How can we reconcile such a concept of God with such passages as the following?

> *"The Lord is merciful and gracious; slow to anger, and abounding in mercy. 9 He will not always strive with us, **nor will He keep His anger forever**." (Ps 103:8-9)*

> *"For the Lord **will not cast off forever**. 32 Though He causes grief, yet He will show compassion according to the multitude of His mercies. 33 For **He does not afflict willingly**, nor grieve the children of men." (Lam 3:31-33)*

> *"For **His anger is but for a moment**, His favor is for life; Weeping may endure for a night, but joy comes in the morning." (Ps 30:5)*
> *"For I am merciful,' says the Lord; **I will not remain angry forever**. Only acknowledge your iniquity…" (Jer 3:12-13)*

*"**He does not retain His anger forever**, because He delights in mercy." (Mic 7:18)*

Have you heard someone speak of God's "eternal wrath"? Did you know that that expression does not appear in the Scriptures? On the contrary, what we do see is that His wrath is only for a moment in comparison with His favor which is forever. It says that He will not keep His anger forever. It is His love that never ceases – not His wrath! *(1Cor 13:8)*. How is it possible for God, who doesn't reject *forever*, to give the *"eternal"* sentence of destruction, excluded from His presence *forever*? On the other hand, if we can see that the destruction has reference to the soul life and the flesh, and if we can see that it is eonian instead of eternal; then we can begin to comprehend how the God of Love could permit it, understanding that it is only *eonian,* or until all should be perfected. When the second death has fulfilled its purpose, then the last enemy - death, will have finally been destroyed. The purpose of God for the ages is *that in the dispensation of the fullness of the times He might gather together in one all things in Christ, both which are in heaven and which are on earth — in Him,* and it shall be done just as He has purpose. *(Eph 1:10).* Halleluiah! *"For **of** Him and **through** Him and **to** Him are **all things**, to whom be glory forever. Amen." (Rom 11:36).*

There are occasions in which, according to the traditional translations, the wrath of God seems to be eternal. But in each case the context reveals that it is not "eternal" but for a time *(olam).* Reading in the King James Version what Jeremiah prophesied against Judah, leaves us with the impression that His punishment of them is eternal:

*"And you, even yourself, shall let go of your heritage which I gave you; and I will cause you to serve your enemies in the land which you do not know; For you have kindled a fire in **My anger which shall burn forever**." (Jer 17:4)*

If we were to understand this prophecy against Judah as translated here, we would arrive at the conclusion that He is indeed referring to eternal wrath. Also, chapter 25 verse 9, understood as translated, gives us the impression of eternal destruction or annihilation:

"behold, I will send and take all the families of the north, 'says the Lord,' and Nebuchadnezzar the king of Babylon, My servant, and

*will bring them against this land, against its inhabitants, and against these nations all around, and will **utterly destroy them**, and make them an astonishment, a hissing, and **perpetual (olam) desolations**." (Jer 25:9)*

Nevertheless, *"eternal wrath"* and *"perpetual destruction"* in this instance are clearly only for a time *(olam)*. In the case of Judah, He specifies that *olam,* which was translated *"eternal"* and *"perpetual,"* only lasts seventy years, as we see in the following verses:

*"And this whole land shall be a desolation and an astonishment, and these nations shall serve the king of Babylon **seventy years**. 12 'Then it will come to pass, **when seventy years are completed**, that I will punish the king of Babylon and that nation, the land of the Chaldeans, for their iniquity, says the Lord; and I will make it a perpetual desolation." (Jer 25:11-12)*

*"For thus says the Lord: **After seventy years are completed at Babylon, I will visit you and perform My good word toward you**, and cause you to return to this place. 11 **For I know the thoughts that I think toward you, says the Lord, thoughts of peace and not of evil, to give you a future and a hope**. 12 Then you will call upon Me and go and pray to Me, and I will listen to you. 13 And you will seek Me and find Me, when you search for Me with all your heart. 14 I will be found by you, says the Lord, and I will bring you back from your captivity; I will gather you from all the nations and from all the places where I have driven you, says the Lord, and I will bring you to the place from which I cause you to be carried away captive." (Jer 29:10-14)*

In the case of Judah, as confirmed by history, the eonian wrath and destruction lasted for 70 years. Take note that, even in His wrath, His thoughts towards them were still *thoughts of peace and not of evil, to give them a future and a hope. (v.11)* His wrath and destruction were corrective and ended when the 70-year sentence was fulfilled. It was not an eternal destruction but a long-lasting destruction *(olam)*. How can we say that the wrath of the Lord that burns *"forever"* and the *"perpetual"* desolation in Judah's case was only for a limited time, and then insist that the *"eternal"* destruction of 1Thessalonians 1:9 never comes to an end? Doesn't Romans 2:11 say that *there is no partiality with God?* God does not keep His anger "forever" nor reject "forever" because God is Love. Love only shows anger for the purpose of correction. It only rejects *until* we seek Him - not forever.

"Shall not see Life"

> *"He who believes in the Son has everlasting life; and* **he who does not believe the Son shall not see life, but the wrath of God abides on him."** *(John 3:36)*

Clearly, John chapter 3 speaks of a *krisis* [90] judgment which can only be averted by believing in Christ. However, the tendency we have, due to our traditional mindset of an eternal unending wrath, is to subconsciously *"eternalize"* judgment texts (ie. read *"eternity"* into texts even though that is not what is stated). We unconsciously tend to read it this way: *"He who is not believing shall* **never** *see life, but the* **eternal** *wrath of God abides on him* **forever-and-ever."**

If indeed Jesus meant to say that those who were not believing would *never* see life, then all of us would also be eternally excluded since there was a time when we were not believers.

We need to be renewed in the spirit of our minds because tradition has programmed us into unconsciously altering almost every text we read related to God's judgments and His wrath. If we read it like it is actually stated, we could even apply John 3:36 to our corrections in our own paternal relationships with our children: *"Go to your room until you change your mind. Until you do, I will continue to be angry with you and you will not see the light of day."*

In the Scriptures we see God's wrath as *age during*, when warranted, but not eternal. His anger lasts *"until"* - not forever. The obstinate may not see life for a year, 70 years or ages but it is still *"until"* and not *"never."* All who died in Adam will be made alive in

---

[90] *krisis* simply means "judgment," sometimes with a positive outcome and other times negative. Translators often go beyond the meaning of *krisis* rendering it "condemnation." Condemnation is *katakrisis,* which is the negative outcome of a *krisis* judgment. *Krisis* judgment may lead to a condemnatory sentence but *krisis* does not preclude condemnation. Traditional translators often render *krisis* judgment as "damnation" which assumes more than what is expressed in the word *krisis.*

Christ. We see in Scripture that His wrath does not continue on forever:

> *"For I will not contend forever, **nor will I always be angry**; **For the spirit would fail** before Me, and **the souls which I have made**." (Isa 57:16)*

> *"For the Lord **will not cast off forever**. 32 Though He causes grief, yet **He will show compassion** according to the multitude of His mercies. 33 For **He does not afflict willingly**, nor grieve the children of men." (Lam 3:31-33)*

From these verses and others, we can see that it is His love and compassion which never come to an end – not His wrath. Repentance and faith in Christ will always be the only way to salvation, but in the coming ages as now, salvation will be a gift of God and not of works, since by the works of the law no flesh will ever be justified before God, whether in this life or beyond. The everlasting (eonian) gospel never changes into another gospel *(Rev 14:6)*.

Are there few who are saved?

> *"And He went through the cities and villages, teaching, and journeying toward Jerusalem. 23 Then one said to Him, '**Lord, are there few who are saved**?' And He said to them, 24 'Strive to enter through **the narrow gate**, for many, I say to you, will seek to enter and will not be able. 25 When once the Master of the house has risen up and shut the door, and you begin to stand outside and knock at the door, saying, 'Lord, Lord, open for us,' and He will answer and say to you, 'I do not know you, where you are from,' 26 then you will begin to say, 'We ate and drank in Your presence, and You taught in our streets.' 27 But He will say, 'I tell you I do not know you, where you are from. Depart from Me, all you workers of iniquity.' 28 There will be weeping and gnashing of teeth, when you see Abraham and Isaac and Jacob and all the prophets in the kingdom of God, and yourselves thrust out. 29 They will come from the east and the west, from the north and the south, and sit down in the kingdom of God. 30 And indeed **there are last who will be first, and there are first who will be last**." (Luke 13:22-30)*

> *"Enter by the **narrow gate**; for wide is the gate and broad is the way that leads to destruction, and there are many who go in by it.*

14 Because narrow is the gate and difficult is the way which leads to life, and there are few who find it." (Matt 7:13-14)

The passages we are examining here are the response of Jesus to the question: *"Are there few who are saved?"* Something very important to keep in mind in the teachings of Jesus is that, even though He was the mediator of the New Covenant, He still ministered under the Old Covenant. And if the law was the ministry of death *(2Cor 3:7)*, some of the sayings of Jesus were like the nails that closed the coffin once and for all to those who hoped in salvation by works. To those who said that they had never killed anyone, Jesus said that they were in danger of Gehenna for just saying damaging words to others. To those who boasted that they had never committed adultery He said that just looking at a woman with sexual desire constituted adultery. He took the law, which is humanly impossible to keep and made it infinitely more impossible for man to fulfill.

To some, who already recognized their need for salvation, Jesus revealed that salvation was by grace through faith. To Nicodemus, He compared salvation to the healing of the rebellious Israelites when they were saved from dying of snakebites by just one look of faith in the direction of the serpent of bronze *(Jn 3:14-16)*. To others, who still considered themselves to be righteous, He pointed out something in their life where they were lacking in order to remove all hope of being saved by their own works.

When the rich young ruler in Mark 10 asked Jesus: *"Good Teacher, what shall I do that I may inherit eternal life?"* Jesus responded by mentioning one by one the 10 commandments. The law promised life for those who observed it perfectly, which obviously no one has ever been able to do except for God Himself in the person of Christ. Nevertheless, the rich young ruler, thinking that he was righteous according to the law, responded saying: *"Teacher, all these things I have kept from my youth."* Then Jesus, in order to destroy any illusion that he could save himself by his own works said: *"One thing you lack: Go your way, sell whatever you have and give to the poor, and you will have treasure in heaven; and come, take up the cross, and follow Me.*

What was Jesus' intention in making such a demand upon this man? Was He reinforcing his belief that salvation depended upon his own works? No. He had followers like Lazarus and others who were rich and yet He did not place this requirement upon them. The motive of Jesus is obvious. He wanted to remove from him all hope of saving himself, causing him to seek the grace and mercy of God as his only hope of salvation. When the rich young ruler asked: *"Good teacher, what must I do to be saved?"* Jesus began His response by emphasizing that there is no one good except God alone. His motive was to commit *all to disobedience, that He might have mercy on all (Rom 11:32).*

Why did Jesus say that *"those who are well had no need of a physician, but those who are sick, and that He didn't come to call the righteous, but sinners, to repentance?" (Mark 2:17).* Because those who consider themselves to be righteous don't sense any need of mercy. A person only begins to seek God when he becomes aware of his condition as a sinner. All are sinners, but for an individual to seek salvation he must first come to see his need. He must realize that his only hope of righteousness is the righteousness of God in Christ, received as a free gift of grace, apart from works *(Rom 3:19-25).*

We see that Jesus put no demand upon the criminal being crucified beside Him. The criminal simply said to Jesus: *"Lord, remember me when You come into Your kingdom,"* and Jesus replied: *"Assuredly, I say to you, today you will be with Me in Paradise." (Luke 23:42,43).* And He extends the same invitation to all: *"If **anyone** thirsts, let him come to Me and drink." (John 7:37).*

He offered salvation freely to the Samaritan woman who had had five husbands and was presently living with a man out of wedlock, saying: *"If you knew the gift of God, and who it is who says to you, 'Give Me a drink,' you would have asked Him, and He would have given you living water." (John 4:10).* In contrast, when speaking to the self-righteous, He made salvation by self-works even more hopelessly impossible. Why? To exclude them? No, but rather to commit them all to disobedience in order to ultimately have mercy on them all.

After His conversation with the rich young ruler, Jesus said to his disciples in so many words, that it was impossible for a rich man to be saved. In Matthew 19:25 we see their reaction to the demand Jesus made to the rich young ruler: *"When His disciples heard it,* **they were greatly astonished***, saying, '****Who then can be saved****?"* In Jesus' reply we discover what it is that He wants all of mankind to understand concerning their salvation: *"But Jesus looked at them and said to them, 'With men this is impossible, but with God all things are possible." (v. 26).*

Jesus didn't just say this in reference to the rich, but to all. What Jesus wanted to make clear, before going to the cross and initiating the New Covenant in His blood, was that self-salvation isn't just difficult – it's impossible. But for God nothing is impossible, and He desires that all be saved, and so shall it be. Nevertheless, the prostitutes and the tax collectors will enter the kingdom *before* the self-righteous religious people. Why? Because the self-righteous religious people are the last to recognize their need for God's mercy and salvation *(Matt 21:31,32).*

"For God has committed ~~them~~ [91] all to disobedience, that He might have mercy on all." (Rom 11:32)

Returning to the passage in Luke 13 where Jesus answers the question: *"Lord, are there few who are saved?"* there are some very important observations which we should make. In the first place it is clear that those who are lost are not eternally lost, as is traditionally taught. What Jesus says is that some will not be permitted entrance into the kingdom of heaven initially, but He makes no reference to eternal exclusion. On the contrary, what we see in verse 30 is that those esteemed as being the first candidates to enter, such as the Pharisees and religiously self-righteous, will actually be the last to enter, while those least expected to enter, such as the harlots and tax collectors, will enter first. The word "first" in Greek is *protos* and in this context refers to those who are first in *time* or *sequence.* Also, the word "last" is *eschatos,* which here refers to those who are last in sequence to enter. "First" and "last" are not necessarily referring to importance in the kingdom but rather to sequence. Jesus elsewhere refers to first and last in importance but uses different terms: *"least" elachistos* and *"greatest" megos (Matt 5:19; 11:11).* If the exclusion of the lost was eternal, then Jesus would not have spoken of some who would be the first to enter and others who would be eschatologically the last to enter.

Neither do we see eternal perdition presented in the parallel passage in Matthew 7:13,14. Due to the traditional dogma of an

---

[91] *"them"* is not in the original Greek text, but was added by the translators.

eternal hell, we unconsciously assume that the word *"destruction" (apoleia)* means *eternal* destruction. But how can destruction be eternal if Jesus said: *"for the Son of Man has come to seek and to save that which was lost [apollumi "destroy or lose"?] (Luke 19:10).* Will He somehow not be able to do what He came to do? Jesus used the same word in both cases; "destruction" being the noun form and "was lost" being the verb form. He is the Good Shepherd who leaves the 99 sheep in the fold to seek the only lost one **until He finds it** *(Luke 15:4).* Is it possible that, in spite of this, some will be eternally lost? No! A thousand times No! He is the One who said: *"And I, if I am lifted up from the earth, will draw (drag)* **all ~~peoples~~ to Myself.***"* *(John 12:32).* [92] Is it possible for Him to have said it and not be able to do it? Percentage wise, the traditional view often presents Christ as ultimately eternally losing 99% of those He died to rescue, with only the 1% safe in the fold. Did not the Good Shepherd lay down His life for the whole world?

In the second place, when we compare the passages concerning the narrow gate with the last chapters of Revelation, beginning with the Second Coming of Christ for His Bride, we see that the initial exclusion of the majority from the kingdom of heaven is not an eternal exclusion. Those who are not already His at His coming will not take part in the wedding feast and therefore will not be of the Bride of Christ, the Lamb's wife, and they will not dwell in the New Jerusalem *(Rev 21:9,10).* However, that is not the end of the story.

After the Great White Throne Judgment of Revelation 20, which takes place a thousand years after the Second Coming, those who did not enter by the narrow gate and are not found in the book of life, will be cast into the lake of fire. Tradition would tell us that from this point on all will have gone to their final destiny where they will be forever, without any possibility of restoration for those who are in the lake of fire. All the saints will be in heaven and all the rest will be in hell forever. However, in Revelation we see a different scenario.

In Revelation 21 we see the New Jerusalem, the wife of the Lamb, descending out of heaven upon the new earth. At that point another distinct group of people is introduced – the nations who will walk in

---

[92] The word *"peoples"* is not in the Greek text but was added by the translators, allowing Calvinists to say it only refers to *"all peoples"* or *"people groups"* rather than everyone.

the light of the New Jerusalem, the habitation of the Bride, the wife of the Lamb *(21:24)*.

Now we no longer have just two groups – the Church in the New Jerusalem and the condemned in the lake of fire – but also the third group - the saved of the nations *(21:25)*. Who are they? Obviously, at first they will only consist of those found written in the book of life at the Great White Throne Judgment. They will be made alive and glorified at that time, but since the wedding already took place a thousand years prior to this judgment, they will not make up part of the wife of the Lamb who inhabits the New Jerusalem, but rather *they will walk in the light of the New Jerusalem (21:24)*.

However, we also see others of the nations in the outer darkness who cannot enter the New Jerusalem while they remain unclean and do not yet have their names written in the book of life *(21:27)*. The book of Revelation ends with the Spirit and the Bride of the Lamb extending the invitation to all those who are outside and are thirsty and want to partake of the water of life to enter and drink freely. Her gates shall not be shut. However, they will remain outside in outer darkness *until* they repent and wash their robes in order to be able to enter. Nevertheless, the invitation continues to be extended to all those who are thirsty and wish to enter, just as it is now.

> *"Blessed are those who wash their robes, that they may have the right to the tree of life and may go through the gates into the city. 15 Outside are the dogs, those who practice magic arts, the sexually immoral, the murderers, the idolaters and everyone who loves and practices falsehood." (Rev 22:14-15 NIV)*

Some who are in outer darkness will enter sooner, while others will be the last to enter, but when all is said and done, God will be all in all *(1Cor 15:28)*, when in the dispensation of the fullness of time, both those in heaven and those on earth will have been reunited in Christ *(Eph 1:10)*. After the Great White Throne Judgment, those being made alive and glorified will be made alive on an individual basis - *"each one in his own order." (1Cor 15:23)*. But in the end, all will have submitted to Him, bowing the knee and confessing Him as Lord to the glory of God. Then the time will have finally come when all will have entered in by the narrow gate which leads to life.

In the third place, in the context of the passage concerning the narrow gate, Jesus wasn't speaking to individuals who already recognized that they were sinners and in need of salvation as many think, but rather He was confronting the Pharisees and self-righteous religious people who trusted in themselves. They were the ones unwilling to humble themselves low enough to enter by the narrow gate. They are the ones who will be standing outside and knocking when it is too late to enter into the marriage feast. In Luke 18:13,14 we see that it was the tax collector, and not the Pharisee, who was received by the Lord. Jesus explained the reason saying: *"...for everyone who exalts himself will be humbled, and he who humbles himself will be exalted." (Luke 18:14)*. Only the poor in spirit will inherit the kingdom of God, because only they are willing to humble themselves and enter by the gate which is too uncomfortably narrow for the self-righteous.

Therefore, there is nothing in Christ's teaching about the narrow gate which implies eternal perdition. To the contrary, what He taught is in harmony with the final restoration of all, beginning with those who early recognize their need of God's mercy.

Forever and Ever

> *"...He shall be tormented with fire and brimstone in the presence of the holy angels and in the presence of the Lamb. 11* **And the smoke of their torment ascends <u>forever and ever</u>*;* and they have no rest day or night***, *who worship the beast and his image, and whoever receives the mark of his name." (Rev 14:10-11)*

Due to the influence of tradition, the translators have rendered *"into the ages of the ages" (eis tous aiónas ton aiónon)* as "forever and ever" in English. This rendering does not even make common sense, because it isn't possible to add "ever" to forever. When we speak of eternity, we are not speaking of units of time which can be compounded one upon the other. Adding ages to ages does not equal eternity but rather a very long period of time. In Spanish they translate it more realistically, rendering it *"for the centuries of the centuries" (por los siglos de los siglos)*. Although an age is usually longer than a century, this is at least a logical translation. Nevertheless, because of the influence of tradition, even Spanish speaking readers, when they read *"por los siglos de los siglos,"* understand it as meaning eternity. But the phrase, "into the ages of the ages" refers to time; a very, very, long time perhaps, but time nonetheless. It is a common misconception to think of eternity as an infinite succession of ages. If that were so the Scriptures would not speak of the *"end of the ages" (Heb 9:26 lit. sunteleia ton aionon)*. Every age has its end, and when the last age, or "the Age of ages" ends, time will then be no more, and eternity is all that remains.

It should also be pointed out that not everyone who enters into the eonian punishment will remain in the lake of fire for the full amount of time indicated by *"the ages of the ages."* The prepositional phrase *"eis tous aiónas ton aiónon"* (*"**into** the ages of the ages"* mistranslated *"forever and ever"*) literally has reference to a non-specific amount of time within the ages of the ages and not necessarily the entirety of all future ages. The phrase, when introduced by *eis, only* indicates open-ended **entrance into** the ages of the ages without specifying duration. The preposition *eis* is defined in Strong's as: *"to or into (indicating the point reached or entered), of place, time, or (figuratively) purpose (result, etc.)."* I meticulously examined all 1,767 occurrences of the preposition *eis* in the New Testament and in each case, although variously translated, it is always used to express the idea of *"to"* or *"into,"* just as Strong's defines it. When used of time, it always has reference to time of indefinite duration. Although it is often translated as *"for,"* the only idea expressed is entrance *"into"* an indefinite timespan without specifying one's duration within that time span.

To illustrate the concept expressed by *eis "into,"* if I were to say that I continued working *into* my lunch hour I am not necessarily saying that I worked all the way through my lunch hour. If I worked the entire duration of the lunch hour, I would have said instead that I worked *through my lunch hour (Gr. dià)*. If the revelator had said that the torment continued *"through"* or *"throughout" (dià)* the ages of the ages, then we would understand it to refer to the whole timespan, but that is not the idea expressed by the Greek preposition *eis*.

The use of *"for"* by the translators instead of *"to"* or *"into"* could read more meaning into the word *eis* than intended by the text, giving the impression that everyone who enters into the punishment of the ages will be punished equally throughout the entirety of the ages of the ages. However, we know from other passages that not everyone who enters into the eonian punishment will be punished for the same amount of time. Each will be judged according to their works and will receive their *"part"* or *"portion"* in the lake of fire. They will not all be punished the same amount of time. Some will receive *"many lashes"* while others will receive *"few lashes" (Lu 12:47,48)*. Some will enter the kingdom *before* others *(Matt 21:31)*. Some will be *first* to enter the kingdom of heaven and others will be *last (Lc 13:30)*, but each and every one will be made alive *"in his own order" (1Cor 15:23)*.

We see this illustrated in the Lord's declaration of punishment upon Judah and Jerusalem in Jeremiah:

"behold, I will send and take all the families of the north,' says the Lord, 'and Nebuchadnezzar the king of Babylon, My servant, and will bring them against this land, against its inhabitants, and against these nations all around, and will utterly destroy them, and make them an astonishment, a hissing, and **perpetual desolations (eis** *oneidismon aionion "***into** *eonian desolations").*" *(Jer 25:9)*

When Nebuchadnezzar invaded Judah they entered "**into** *(eis)* eonian desolations" *(LXX)*. Did they remain desolate? No. The desolation of Jerusalem only lasted 70 years, as stated a few verses later:

"For thus says the Lord: **After seventy years are completed at Babylon**, *I will visit you and perform My good word toward you, and* **cause you to return to this place**.*" (Jer 29:10)*

In this instance, the Lord told them that they would go "into eonian desolations," but that after 70 years Jerusalem would be inhabited again. As with eonian punishment, eonian desolation was only entered into for the time necessary to complete the correctional punishment. They went into *(eis)* eonian punishment but came *out of* it *(ek)* after 70 years of desolations

Whenever reference is being made to a specific amount of time, it is never introduced by the preposition *eis*. For example, we see that the overcomers will reign with Christ for a thousand years in Revelation 20:4: *"And they lived and reigned with Christ for a thousand years."* Here the word *"for"* is not from the Greek preposition *eis*. The word "for" was added by the translators. The text simply says: *"they lived and reigned with Christ a thousand years."* The same is true in every other instance where a specific timespan is in view (*"for seventy years"* Jer 25:11; *"for three days,"* Acts 28:7; *"we stayed there seven days,"* Acts 20:6; 21:4; *"oppress them four hundred years,"* Acts 7:6, etc.).

Every instance where a time of *punishment* is in view in the New Testament it is always preceded by the preposition *eis "into."* Therefore, whenever we see reference to the duration of punishment it only states that one enters "into" it without indicating the duration involved. The time factor remains in the Lord's hands. Only He can judge each individual with just judgment. However, since we know that His judgments are just and correctional, we know they will not last longer than that which is just and necessary for the restoration of each individual.

Since *"into the ages"* sounds awkward in English we could better understand it as *"in the ages of the ages"* without significantly changing the meaning. *"In the ages of the ages"* expresses something which will take place within the ages of the ages without specifying how much of that timespan it will occupy. When we say something like: *"in the 21st Century man will be on Mars,"* we are simply stating that something will take place within that century without specifying the time necessary to accomplish that objective

It also says that *"they have no rest day or night."* As we see in Genesis one, the day and the night were created by God. The same applies to centuries and ages which are simply larger measures of time *(cf. Heb 1:2, "made the ages")*. Eternity, on the other hand, is not created – it always is. All the terms used here designate time, and therefore cannot be referring to eternity. "Forever and ever" is an incorrect rendering of ages which contain days and nights. It should have been translated "into the ages of the ages" just as it appears in the original Greek. The punishment of each individual will continue for the time necessary to achieve the objective of God in administering it – no more and no less.

Should we understand literally the terms used here to describe the punishment of the unjust? Will they be in a literal lake of molten lava and burning sulfur? Will heaven be literally filled with their smoke into the ages of the ages, or even worse, in eternity? Will they literally be burning without ever being burned up? Will the nostrils of the saints and the Lamb literally be filled with the stench of smoking flesh and burning sulfur, even after the ends of the ages in eternity? As incredible as it seems, many of us have insisted that such is literally the case, and that it is not merely an invention of fallen man's imagination, but rather something designed by God Himself before time began. But the Bible is full of graphic symbolic expressions and hyperboles – especially the book of Revelation, and if we don't recognize them for what they are, and we take them literally, we can convert God into a monster infinitely more frightful than anything Hollywood could possibly conjure up.

A rule of Bible interpretation is, *"when the plain sense makes common sense, seek no other sense."* On the other hand, if the obvious sense does not make common sense, we should seek understanding of the truth communicated in the allegory or symbolism used in the passage. Otherwise we will end up with some very strange and contradictory beliefs.

In Revelation 12, when it describes the pregnant woman clothed with the sun and the moon under her feet with a crown of twelve stars, do we take it literally or do we seek to understand the symbolism described by the revelator? In chapter thirteen, when John says he was standing by the sea and a beast arose from the sea having seven heads and ten horns, do we take it literally or symbolically? When we see the harlot in Revelation seventeen, sitting on many waters and drunk with the blood of the saints, do we take it literally or symbolically? I could continue giving example after example showing that Revelation is a book with truths hidden in symbolisms. Hardly anything in the whole book of Revelation is to be taken literally. They are symbols and allegories given in visions which require wisdom and understanding to interpret *(Rev 13:8, cf. Dan 12:8,9),* Is the lake of fire the only exception, or should we also seek understanding as to the symbolic meaning behind that expression as well?

The apostle John here used the same metaphorical and symbolic expressions as did Isaiah to describe the destruction of Edom in Isaiah 34:8-10:

> *"For it is the day of the Lord's vengeance, the year of recompense for the cause of Zion. 9 Its streams shall be turned into pitch, and its dust into brimstone; its land shall become burning pitch. 10* **It shall not be quenched night or day; its smoke shall ascend forever** *(olam). From* **generation to generation** *it shall lie waste; No one shall pass through it forever and ever (netash netash 'continually', i.e. 'continually from generation to generation')." (Isa 34:8-10)*

These graphic, symbolic descriptions are hyperbolic and therefore were not literally fulfilled. Their streams did not turn to pitch, and its dust to sulfur, and its smoke did not ascend forever *(olam)*. Today, if one were to visit Edom, the only smoke he is bound to see would be from fires kindled by the women preparing meals. John the revelator was using the same hyperbolic and symbolic expressions used by Isaiah. Even if one were to take it as being an eschatological prophecy of something yet future, it is hardly likely that that geographical region will be a waste-place beyond the new creation, or that its smoke will be literally ascending in eternity.

Tormented with Fire

> *"He shall be **tormented** (basanízo) with fire and brimstone in the presence of the holy angels and in the presence of the Lamb. 11 And the smoke of **their torment** (basanismós) ascends forever and ever; and they have no rest day or night, who worship the beast and his image, and whoever receives the mark of his name." (Rev 14:10-11)*

What is the nature of this *"torment"* that the unjust will suffer in the lake of fire? Will it simply be torture for the satisfaction and entertainment of the saints as some say, or does it have a restorative purpose?

The word translated *"tormented"* here is the Greek word *basanízo*. Thayer's Greek Lexicon defines it: *"a testing by the touchstone or by torture."* [93] Touchstones were made of basalt and were used to test the purity of gold. By rubbing the gold on the touchstone, it would leave a mark by which the trained eye could determine the purity by the color. Also, acid was applied to determine the purity with more exactitude and the impurities would be consumed by the acid, producing smoke.[94] This explains what is meant by the saying: *"the smoke of their basanismós ascends."*

In a refiner's context, the touchstone *(basanízo)* is not speaking of torture at all, but rather the refiner's use of a touchstone in order to determine the gold's purity. Kittel's Theological Dictionary of the

---

[93] *Thayer's Greek Lexicon*

[94] https://www.gia.edu/bench-tip-use-the-touchstone-method-for-testing-purity-karat-gold
 https://en.wikipedia.org/wiki/Touchstone_(assaying_tool)

New Testament gives us a thorough definition of *basanízo* and its related words:

> *"NT:931 básanos, basanízo, basanismós, basanistés*
> *The básanos originally belongs to the calling of the inspector of coins. It is linked with the Heb. root ("to test") and the Egyptian bhn ("basalt")... the testing of gold and silver as media of exchange by the proving stone, was first developed by the Babylonians, then came to the Aramaeans and Hebrews by way of Lydia...*
> *In the spiritual sphere it has the figurative sense, which is closely related to the original concrete meaning, of **a means of testing**. The word then undergoes a change in meaning. The original sense fades into the background. Basanos now comes to denote "torture" or "the rack," espec. used with slaves... In the testing of metal an essential role was played by the thought of **testing and proving genuineness**. The rack is a means of **showing the true state of affairs. In its proper sense it is a means of testing and proving**, though also of punishment."* [95]

As we see, the word *basanízo* eventually was applied to bringing out the truth in man and over time the meaning degenerated, becoming nothing more than torture carried out by perverse men. However, contrary to what Kittel insinuates, I believe that in the context of these passages - full of references to the purifying fire, it is not speaking of torture at all, but rather retains its original significance to the refiner, which was to test in order to determine the level of purity in those subjected to the Refiner's consuming fire.

This explains what it means when it says that they will be *"tested as with a touchstone" (not tormented) in the presence of the holy angels and in the presence of the Lamb."* Christ and the angels will not be merely observing as the spectators did in the Roman arena but will be ever present, overseeing the progress of those being refined as gold. I see them as something similar to the review board in a correctional institution which reviews each inmate periodically to determine whether or not the correction has produced its desired result, so that they can be integrated into society once again. As soon as the *basanízo* reveals that the fire has fulfilled its desired result of purification, the individual will be freed from the lake of fire and his

---

[95] Kittel's Theological Dictionary of the New Testament (10 vol.)

name will be written in the book of life, permitting him to enter the gates of the New Jerusalem and receive healing from the tree of life *(Rev 22:2,14).*

As the touchstone is the Refiner's tool which reveals the level of purity, so also the fire is the Refiner's fire which is kindled – not in order to torment but in order to purify. Even the severe judgments accompanying the Second Coming of Christ are for disciplinary and restorative purposes. They are poured out for the purpose of purifying and cleansing, as we see in Malachi 3:2,3:

> *"But who can endure **the day of His coming**? And who can stand when He appears? For **He is like a refiner's fire and like launderers' soap**. 3 **He will sit as a refiner and a purifier of silver; He will purify the sons of Levi, and purge them as gold and silver**, that they may offer to the Lord an offering in righteousness." (Mal 3:2-3)*

Here we can see that the fire of God isn't inconsistent with His love. He comes like fire to purify and soap to cleanse. Why should we think that the lake of fire and Gehenna fire are distinct from this in their purpose?

The consuming fire purifies our lives in His judgments and afflictions through which we must pass as we walk with Him in life. Israel's slavery in Egypt is referred to as an *"iron furnace." (Deut 4:20; Jer 11:4; 1Kings 8:51).* It is obvious that none of these expressions have reference to literal fire, but rather refer to purifying afflictions. Also, we know that the eonian flames for the just are not eternal. In the same way, we should not understand *"eonian fire"* as though it were literal fire, lasting forever.

Fire in Scriptures is used often in reference to God. *"Our God is a consuming fire." (Heb 12:29).* The fire of God only consumes that which is consumable - the impurities and evil. The word translated fire in the Greek, as we have already seen, is *pur.* Our words, pure, purify, purification, purgatory etc., are derived from this word. Even Christians will be purified with fire, and all that is wood hay and stubble will be consumed. Nevertheless, they themselves will be saved, but *"as through fire." (1Cor 3:13-15).* All that remains of the soul life, the flesh and dead works, will be consumed. Those who have part in the first resurrection will not be hurt by the second death *(Rev 20:5,6).* What is the second death? It is the death of the soul life and of the sinful flesh. I don't believe that we should *literalize* eschatological references to fire any more than we would take literally the fire which will prove the works of every Christian.

I believe that just a glance from the glorified Christ whose eyes are *like a flame of fire (Rev 1:14; 2:18)*, will expose all that remains of the soulish self and the flesh in the spiritual believer, and will burn all the wood, hay and stubble with His penetrating gaze. John exhorts us:

"And now, little children, abide in Him, that when He appears, **we may have confidence and not be ashamed before Him at His coming***." (1John 2:28)*

When the prophet Isaiah saw the Lord in His glory, he became exposed to his own vileness and cried out:

"Woe is me, for I am undone! Because I am a man of unclean lips, and I dwell in the midst of a people of unclean lips; for my eyes have seen the King, the Lord of hosts." (Isa 6:5)

In every revival where God has visited His people, the initial experience is a fiery conviction of sin and guilt, just as Isaiah felt. The contrast between His love and holiness and our selfishness and sin is nearly unbearable.

I have come to the conclusion that the eonian fire is God's consuming fire: the brightness of His countenance, which exposes the ungodly to eonian shame and self-contempt.

"Now Enoch, the seventh from Adam, prophesied about these men also, saying, "Behold, **the Lord comes** *with ten thousands of His saints, 15 to execute judgment on all,* **to convict** *(expose the shame of)* **all who are ungodly** *among them of all their ungodly deeds which they have committed in an ungodly way, and of all the harsh things which ungodly sinners have spoken against Him." (Jude 14-15, cf. Vine's Expository Dictionary of Biblical Words, "elencho").*

The light of His presence exposes us, and none can hide their shame from His presence. The torment is described as *shame and contempt* in Daniel 12:2. Exposed by the fire of His glorious presence, in all His holiness and love, they will cry out to the rocks,

*"Fall on us and **hide us from the face of Him** who sits on the throne and from the wrath of the Lamb!" (Rev 6:16-17).* They will be forced to retreat away from the presence of the Lord into outer darkness where there will be eonian shame, contempt, weeping and gnashing of teeth. Those who repent and move towards the light will be purified by the very fire of His presence, but those who hate the light will remain in darkness *(John 3:19,20).* From afar they will see the glory of the New Jerusalem, whose gates are never shut, but there shall by no means enter into it anything that defiles, because the Lord God and the Lamb will be its light *(Rev 21:23-27).*

I believe that the fire that brings about the second death will be that which is produced by the presence of the Lamb and His glory upon His saints. Their shameful condition, exposed by the brightness of His presence will be unbearable to all those who have not died to the selfish, independent soul life and the flesh during their mortal existence. Either we suffer the second death - the destruction of the soul life here and now, or later in *the lake of fire, which is the second death.* The result of not dying in this life is that they will not be able to endure the consuming fire of His presence. The presence of the Lamb which was slain out of love for all will produce such shame and self-contempt that their reaction will be to withdraw into outer darkness to mitigate their shame and anguish.

An alternate reading of 2Thesalonisenses 1:9 says: *"They will suffer the punishment of eternal (eonian) destruction, **which comes from the presence of the Lord** and from the glory of his might."* [96] As we saw earlier, the eonian destruction of the flesh is that which comes from the presence of the Lord, but at the same time it will cause them to be excluded from His presence because without holiness no one can endure seeing the Lord. Both being before the Lamb and the saints, as well as being excluded from the New Jerusalem in their defiled condition, is what I believe will produce the second death, which they didn't submit themselves to during their lifetime. I believe that their primary torment will be their shame and self-contempt, as mentioned in Daniel 12:2.

---

[96] *English Standard Version footnote for 2Thess 1:9*

Fire and Sulfur

The lake is not only said to be of fire but also of brimstone or sulfur. How are we to understand this? Many, including most Bible translators, being unfamiliar with the refiner's process for purifying gold, have missed entirely the imagery of this expression.

As explained in an enlightening article written by Michael Webber entitled: *"What is the Lake of Fire?"* [97] the expression, *"the lake of fire"* rightly understood and translated accordingly, is not referring to a divine incinerator nor to an eternal torture chamber, but rather to the refiner's crucible or melting pot.

From antiquity sulfur was added to the impure gold upon reaching the molten state. In the fire the impurities and most other baser metals unite with the sulfur, being converted into sulfides which float to the surface as dross and are then removed. To the refiner of gold and precious metals of biblical times, the connection between fire and sulfur would have been very obvious. Even to this day sulfur is commonly used in the same manner, although other more sophisticated methods have been developed. [98]

Also, the word translated *"lake"* in our translations obscures the real meaning of the passage. The word in Greek is *límne.* Although it can sometimes refer to a lake, in other contexts it often means *"a pool"* or *"a pond."* Strong's Concordance defines it as *"a pond (large or small)."* The same word, which is used in the New Testament referring to something as large as Lake Gennesaret in Galilee, can also refer to a pool or a puddle. In certain contexts, according the Liddel, Scott, Jones Greek-English Lexicon, *límne* can actually refer to the *receptacle* containing the pool. [99] In the context of the refiner's

---

[97] http://thetotalvictoryofchrist.com/whatisthelakeoffire.pdf

[98] https://www.911metallurgist.com/blog/sulphur-refining-gold

https://www.911metallurgist.com/blog/gold-refining-methods#goldrefining-by-sulphurisation

https://en.wikipedia.org/wiki/Gold_parting

[99] Liddell, Scott, Jones - A Greek-English Lexicon: *limne.*

fire and sulfur, the *"pool"* would be the pool of precious molten metal and the *"receptacle"* would be the refiner's crucible or melting pot.

The Bible translators, either unfamiliar with the process of gold refining, or else unduly influenced by the traditional doctrine of eternal torments, or both, all rendered it as *"lake"* instead of *"pool,"* with the exception of the Douay-Rheims Bible which reads: *"the pool of fire and brimstone."* Nevertheless, once one understands the refiner's process of purifying gold, the meaning becomes clear.

All throughout Scripture we see that God's consuming fire is as a *"refiner's fire."* He passes us through the fire of affliction until we come forth as pure gold (*Mal 3:2,3; Prov 17:3; Ps 66:10-12; Deut 4:20; Ezek 22:17-22; Isa 48:10; Zech 13:9; 1Peter 1:7; Rev 3:18*). Just as apostate Israel was cast into the furnace of fire to refine them, so it will be in the end of the age. God's fire is intended to purify the heart because only the pure in heart can see God *(Matt 5:8; Heb 12:14)*. It will not be quenched until it has consumed all that is impure – either now in this life or in the future. His purifying fire will continue until He has made all new *(Rev 21:5)*. The apocalyptic *"lake of fire and sulfur"* is the divine crucible which will serve to refine the hearts of even God's most obstinate enemies, bringing about the restoration of all in the coming ages, to the praise of the glory of His grace.

Therefore, recognizing that *"for forever and ever"* is actually *"into the ages of the ages"* and thus a measure of time that doesn't have relation to the eternal state, and also taking into account the fact that the book of Revelation is a book of symbolisms and that God is described as a consuming fire *(pur);* who comes with fire to purify and launderer's soap to cleanse; that fire together with sulfur refer to the purification of gold; that *"torment"* basanizo literally means *to examine, testing to determine purity*, instead of torture without purpose, we can see two things: First, that the punishment is not eternal, and second, that it has a purpose and end result that is corrective and restorative. When the time of the restoration of all comes to completion, the second death will have fulfilled its purpose, and all will have become subjected to Christ. Only then will Christ have destroyed the last enemy – death. Then *"God will wipe away every tear from their eyes;* **"there shall be no more death**, *nor sorrow, nor crying. There shall be no more pain, for the former things have passed away." (Rev 21:4).*

Eternal Fire

> *"Then He will also say to those on the left hand, 'Depart from Me, you cursed, into the **everlasting fire** (pur aionios) prepared for the devil and his angels." (Matt 25:41)*

We have already seen that *aionios* only has reference to time and not to eternity. Therefore, the fire is eonian and not eternal. Some understand the fire to be literal. Some would even say that the fire is much hotter than any fire on earth, because they believe that the lowest part of hell is at the center of the earth, which we now estimate to be 10,000 degrees Fahrenheit. From where do they draw this conclusion? From descriptions of hell taken from other religions and from the vivid imagination of men like Dante in his novel "Divine Comedy," but not from the Bible. We can see in the example of Sodom that the eonian fire is not eternal:

> *"**as Sodom** and Gomorrah, and the cities around them in a similar manner to these, having given themselves over to sexual immorality and gone after strange flesh, are **set forth as an example**, suffering the vengeance of **eternal fire**." (Jude 7)*

Sodom, Gomorrah and the surrounding cities, are not burning today. The eonian fire only lasted until all consumables were consumed and then the fire went out. If one were to say that it is referring to eternal fire in hell, then it could not be said that they are *set forth as an example,* because a *sign* is something observable, whereas Hades is invisible. [100] As we have already seen, fire in the

---

[100] Jude 7 literally says that Sodom and the surrounding cities, *"lie there as an example or specimen of eonian fire (próskeintai deigma)."* Peter, in 2Peter 2:6, tells us that they were reduced to ashes as an example or exhibition (jupódegma) of God's judgment. Josephus relates how the ashen remains were visible in his day. He said the following: *"The country of Sodom borders upon it. It was of old a most happy land, both for the fruits it bore and the riches of its cities, although it be now all burnt up. It is related how, for the impiety of its inhabitants, it was burnt by lightning; in consequence of which there are still the remainders of that Divine fire, and the traces [or shadows] of the five cities are still to be seen.... And thus what is related of this land of Sodom hath these marks of credibility which our very sight affords us."* (Josephus: Wars of the Jews, §54 [4.54]) Although more deteriorated by time the remains are still seen to this day in the extensive ash and sulfur formations near the southern Dead Sea coast.

Scriptures is a purifier. The trials and afflictions are fires which are permitted in our lives to purify us:

*"Beloved, do not think it strange concerning the **fiery (purosis) trial** which is to try you, as though some strange thing happened to you." (1Peter 4:12)*

*"that the proof of your faith, (being) more precious than gold that perisheth though it is proved **by fire** (pur), may be found unto praise and glory and honor at the revelation of Jesus Christ." (1Peter 1:7 ASV)*

Also, we see in Isaiah 33:14-16 that fire is used to refer to God and clearly is not literal since the righteous are the only ones who can abide in it without being hurt by it:

*"Now will I arise,' says the Lord. 'Now will I be exalted'... 14 The sinners in Zion are terrified; trembling grips the godless: 'Who of us can dwell **with the consuming fire**? Who of us can dwell **with everlasting (olam) burning**?'*
*15 He who walks righteously and speaks what is right, who rejects gain from extortion and keeps his hand from accepting bribes, who stops his ears against plots of murder and shuts his eyes against contemplating evil — 16 this is the man who **will dwell on the heights**." (Isaiah 33:10, 14-16 NIV)*

In answer to the question of who can dwell on the heights in the presence of God who is "a consuming fire" and an "everlasting *(olam)* burning" and not be consumed by Him, Isaiah answers that they are those who walk righteously. The expression *"consuming fire"* appears eight times in the Bible and always refers to God. The fire will not harm the righteous, but it will burn up the chaff and straw of the ungodly *(11,12)*. Clearly these expressions "consuming fire" and "eternal flames" are not literal flames, but spiritual flames, which consume all dead works – all consumables like chaff and straw. The flames are just as symbolic as is the chaff.

We decide. Either we pass through the purifying fire now, voluntarily submitting ourselves under the mighty hand of God, or we will have to pass through the fire while the sons of the kingdom are reigning in glory. If we follow Christ now, taking up our cross, then He promises that He will be with us in the fire:

"When you pass through the waters, I will be with you; And through the rivers, they shall not overflow you. When you walk through the fire, you shall not be burned, nor shall the flame scorch you." (Isa 43:2).

The "Unpardonable" Sin

*"Therefore, I say to you, every sin and blasphemy will be forgiven men, but the blasphemy against the Spirit will not be forgiven men. 32 Anyone who speaks a word against the Son of Man, it will be forgiven him; but whoever speaks against the Holy Spirit, it will not be forgiven him, **either in this age or in the age to come**." (Matt 12:31-32)*

*"Assuredly, I say to you, all sins will be forgiven the sons of men, and whatever blasphemies they may utter; 29 but he who blasphemes against the Holy Spirit ~~never~~ has forgiveness, but is subject to **eternal condemnation**." (Mark 3:28-29)*

When the scribes attributed the power that Jesus had to cast out demons to Beelzebub, the prince of demons, Jesus sternly responded with this warning. The blasphemy of the Holy Spirit is to see an evident manifestation of the power of the Holy Spirit, and while knowing it is the Holy Spirit, attribute it to the devil.

The majority in the Church today would say that the blasphemy of the Holy Spirit is a sin that will *never ever* be forgiven by God. And since it is difficult to pin down exactly what constitutes the blasphemy of the Holy Spirit, many live in constant fear that they may have committed the "unpardonable" sin. The traditional understanding of this passage has caused emotional breakdowns and even suicides of sensitive individuals, and many more have gone back into the world without hope of salvation, thinking that in some way they have committed this sin. These passages as traditionally translated and preached from some pulpits have become an instrument in the hands of the accuser, causing the destruction of many throughout history.

It is worthy of note that many of the early Church fathers who spoke the same Greek in which these words were originally written, did not understand this sin as "unpardonable." Saint Athanasius of Alexandria *(AD 295 to AD 373)* wrote: *"If they repent they may obtain pardon, for there is no sin unpardonable with God to them who truly repent."* [101] Saint Chrysostom, AD 386 said: *"We know that this sin was forgiven to some that repented of it."* [102]

How could it be that those who lived closer to the time of the Apostles believed that it was possible to be forgiven for the blasphemy of the Holy Spirit, while today the majority denies the possibility of forgiveness? They were familiar with the Scriptures in the original language and defended Scripture's absolute authority even as we do. I see three main reasons.

In the *first* place, the Greek fathers were not reading a translation influenced by tradition but were reading the New Testament in Greek as originally written. The influence of the traditional doctrine of eternal punishment can be seen in the majority of translations when compared with the original. Let's take a closer look at these verses. Mark 3:29 has been translated in the following manner:

> *"Assuredly, I say to you, all sins will be forgiven the sons of men, and whatever blasphemies they may utter; 29 but he who blasphemes against the Holy Spirit* ~~never~~ **has forgiveness**, *but is subject to* **eternal condemnation.**" *(Mark 3:28-29 NKJV)*

We see that the translators translated *aión* which means "age" with the word "never" giving the impression that there would never be any possibility of ever receiving God's forgiveness. The text simply says, *"he does not have forgiveness into the age (eis ton aiona)."* There is a great difference between *"into the age"* and *"never."* The phrase rendered *"eternal condemnation"* is *aionios krisis "eonian judgment."* That means that one who blasphemes the Holy Spirit is guilty of a sin with age during consequences. We have already seen that *aionios* has reference to a long but indefinite period of time, "that which pertains to an age," and should not be translated "eternal." A literal translation of verse 29 communicates better what Jesus actually said:

> *"but whoever may speak evil in regard to the Holy Spirit hath not forgiveness* **to the age** *but is* **in danger of age-during judgment**. *(Young's Literal Translation)*

---

[101] Thomas Allin, *Christ Triumphant*

[102] Thomas Allin, *Christ Triumphant*

Reading a literal translation, we can now understand how the Greek Church fathers could say that the "unpardonable" sin was pardonable. Now let us examine the words of Jesus according to Matthew:

"Therefore I tell you, people will be forgiven for every sin and blasphemy, but blasphemy against the Spirit will not be forgiven. 32 Whoever speaks a word against the Son of Man will be forgiven, but whoever speaks against the Holy Spirit will not be forgiven, **either in this age or in the age to come***." (Matt 12:31-32)*

First Jesus says in verse 31 that the blasphemy against the Holy Spirit will not be forgiven, without saying for how long. In verse 32, He explains that one will not receive forgiveness *"in this age or in the age to come."* He did not say that one would never be forgiven for all eternity but that one will not be forgiven either in this age or in the coming age. "This age" was the age in which Jesus was ministering. The coming age would be the millennium or, according to some, "the Church age." That is far from saying that one will not be forgiven forever. Even if He would have said "into the ages of the ages" the time of forgiveness would eventually arrive because ages are segments of time and have no relationship to eternity. The *end of the ages* will eventually arrive.

Also, not receiving forgiveness does not automatically mean exclusion from the kingdom of heaven in hell. When Michal despised David for dancing before the Lord, the Lord made her barren for the rest of her life. Though she wasn't forgiven for the rest of her life she continued as the queen with many privileges as David's wife *(2Sam 6:14-23)*. We should not interpret *"will not be forgiven"* as being synonymous with going to hell forever. If I hire a brother to do some work in the church and I discover that he is stealing building materials I probably wouldn't give him employment again anytime soon, but that doesn't mean that I would forever exclude him from the fellowship or that he would cease being my friend.

The *second* reason why the Greek Church fathers had no problems with believing that the blasphemy of the Holy Spirit could be forgiven was because they knew the merciful and forgiving heart of God. From the Scripture they knew that *"the Lord will not cast off forever." Though He causes grief, yet He will show compassion according to the multitude of His mercies" (Lam 3:31-32)* - that He *"will not always strive with us, nor will He keep His anger forever" (Ps 103:9)*, and that *"His mercy endures forever" (Ps 107:1)*. That *"He is gracious and merciful, slow to anger and of great kindness and **He relents from doing harm.**" (Joel 2:13)*. There are many examples in the Scriptures of God, in His infinite mercy and great kindness, relenting of punishment declared against people, and the Church fathers had no reason to think God had changed.

One example is Nineveh. The word of the Lord declared against Nineveh was: *"yet forty days, and Nineveh shall be overthrown." (Jonah 3:4)*. However, when the people of Nineveh repented, the Lord repented of the punishment He had declared against Nineveh. When Jonah realized that God had repented of the evil declared against them, he was very angry and he said to the Lord: *"I know that You are a gracious and merciful God, slow to anger and abundant in loving-kindness, One who relents from doing harm." (Jonah 4:2)*. Both Jonah and the early Church recognized something of the nature of God that the traditional Church today still needs to rediscover - that God is *abundant in loving-kindness: One who relents from doing harm.*

Another example is the case of Coniah (Jeconiah cf. 1Chron 3:17), God swore an oath against him, saying that none of his descendants would rule again in Judah:

*"As I live, 'says the Lord,' **'though Coniah the son of Jehoiakim, king of Judah, were the signet on My right hand, yet I would pluck you off'**; 30 Thus says the Lord: 'Write this man down as childless, a man who shall not prosper in his days; For **none of his descendants shall prosper, sitting on the throne of David, and ruling anymore in Judah."** (Jer 22:24,30)*

God said that even if Coniah were the signet ring on His right hand, he would pluck it off. He even declared him childless. These words didn't leave room for any hope that any of his descendants would ever again reign in Judah. But was the curse pronounced against him and his descendants carried out as declared or did God relent of the punishment He had pronounced? Coniah was carried away captive to Babylon where he died. But when the 70 years of captivity were fulfilled, the king Cyrus permitted the Jews to return to Jerusalem. God relented of the evil declared against the descendants of Coniah, and his grandson Zorobabel was placed as ruler of Judah *(cf. 1Chron 3:17-19)*. The Lord prophesied through Haggai declaring a reversal of the curse declared against Coniah and his descendants:

"And again the word of the Lord came to Haggai on the twenty-fourth day of the month, saying, 21 'Speak to Zerubbabel, governor of Judah, saying: '...I will take you, Zerubbabel My servant, the son of Shealtiel,' says the Lord, **'and will make you like a signet ring; for I have chosen you,'** *says the Lord of hosts." (Hag 2:20-23)*

Here we can see that truly God is a God full of mercy who relents of punishments declared against the sons of men. He clearly declared to Coniah that He would pluck him off the throne like a signet ring off His hand and that none of his descendants would ever rule in Judah. Now, 70 years later, He says to his grandson: *"I will make you like a signet ring; for I have chosen you."* This declaration is a direct repeal of what was declared against Coniah, his grandfather, 70 years earlier.

The Greek fathers, before the influence of Saint Augustine and the institutionalized Church, still saw the Lord as *a gracious and merciful God, slow to anger and abundant in loving-kindness, one who relents from doing harm (Jonah 4:2)*. They still believed that mercy triumphs over judgment. However, the Church, under supervision of the governing authorities, changed the face of God and introduced the Church to the cruel god of the dark ages.

So, we can see that the Greek fathers, reading the warnings of blasphemy against the Holy Spirit in the original text, would not have had any problem accepting the possibility of eventual forgiveness of all sins, including the blasphemy of the Holy Spirit. This, combined with a knowledge of the forgiving heart of God, knowing that He doesn't reject forever and that He is merciful and full of loving kindness and relents of punishment, brought them to the conclusion that God will eventually forgive all sins; even the sin of blasphemy of the Holy Spirit.

Better for Judas Not to have been born

> *"The Son of Man indeed goes just as it is written of Him, but woe to that man by whom the Son of Man is betrayed!* **It would have been good for that man if he had not been born.***" (Matt 26:24)*

Many understand this passage as though it said that it would have been good for Judas not to have ever *existed*, but what it actually says is that it would have been good for Judas not to have *been born*. In other words, it would have been better for him to have been aborted before birth. In Ecclesiastes 6:3 it says: *"If a man begets a hundred children and lives many years, so that the days of his years are many, but his soul is not satisfied with goodness, or indeed he has no burial, I say that* **a stillborn child is better than he.***" (Eccl 6:3)*. A stillborn is a child who was conceived and therefore exists, but since he was aborted, he would go to heaven without having to face judgment. While it is certain that an aborted child loses the great opportunity of an earthly development, if one were to live and not fulfill his purpose in life and die without burial, it would have been good for him not to have even been born. Therefore, when it says that it would have been good for Judas not to have been born, it is saying that it would have been better for him to have died an aborted child than to live and face the consequences of betraying the Son of God. It is not saying that it would have been better for him to have never existed, as many suppose.

Jesus uses the same expression that Salomon uses elsewhere in Ecclesiastes 4:3. In this passage Salomon explains the reason why he considered it better for one not to have been born:

> *"But better off than either are those who have never been born (gínomai), who have never seen the injustice that goes on in this world." (Eccl 4:3 TEV)*

The reason Salomon gives as to why it would be better not to be born, is because of the evil one faces on earth in this life. He says nothing concerning the afterlife in this regard. Surely, Judas' recognition that he had played into Satan's hands, betraying the Savior and shedding innocent blood, made him wish he had never been born. When he realized how Satan had used him, he refused to receive the payment and threw the money at the feet of the chief priests and elders. Then, wishing he had never been born, he went out and hanged himself.

According to the traditional view of eternal punishment for the vast majority, it would have been better for almost all rational beings to have never *existed* and not just Judas, since according to them the majority will be tormented throughout all eternity. Also, tradition says that all who commit suicide will go to hell forever, and since Judas committed suicide, they would say that, for that reason also, it would have been better if he had never existed. However, in the Scriptures there is total silence concerning the destiny of those who commit suicide. Therefore, to my way of reasoning, we should not presume to know that which God has not revealed. If we wish to make a pronouncement concerning suicide, I believe that we are safer to cite the words of Jesus when He said: *"...every sin and blasphemy will be forgiven men..." (Matt 12:31)*

Chapter nine
The Testimonies of Near-Death Experiences

Near-death experiences refer to the visions related by those whose souls have left their bodies while being close to death. Although there are records in existence of these experiences since before the time of Christ by individuals of many different religions of the world, they have been much more frequent in the last few decades. In 1981, a survey in the United States revealed that 15% of Americans reported having had near-death experiences. With improved urgent care and life support systems, those figures have increased even more in recent years. In a survey conducted in hospitals by Kenneth Ring, he discovered that a third of those who were close to death or pronounced clinically dead and came back, reported having had a transcendental experience. [103] Although the majority of these experiences are positive, some had negative experiences where they found themselves in hell or purgatory.

I have read extensively on the subject during the last 20 years. In October of 2013, I was hospitalized for 17 days and for three days I was between life and death. Due to the immune suppressants I take to prevent the rejection of my transplanted liver, an insect bite developed into an abscess and quickly became life threatening. After flying out of the jungle in a small plane I was received by an ambulance in Villavicencio, and after 4 hours on the winding highway I arrived at the hospital in Bogota, where they drained the abscess, removing over a liter of infected material. My blood was poisoned with a bacterium called staphylococcus aurous, which often causes death.

During those three days I left my body three times. Each time I would fall abruptly back into my body and would feel its limitations in my weakened state. While out of body, I floated over beautiful terrains and saw colors I had never seen since my days on LSD and other hallucinogenic drugs during the 1960s, and I saw geometric images that defied the imagination. In one instance I found myself talking to someone dressed in white just before reentering my body. I knew that we had been conversing for some time, but I don't

---

[103] Kenneth Ring, *Life at Death*

remember the conversation, except for the last part when I was about to pass through a veil beyond which I could see the hospital with sleeping patients in different beds. I knew it was time to reenter my body and I remember asking the person in white how I would know if I had entered the right body. He said that I would know when I repeated the number "361."

The next moment I felt myself fall abruptly into a body and startled I lifted my head, looking around the room and at my body in an effort to determine where I was. I couldn't even recognize my own body and was feeling quite agitated. It was 2:00 a.m. and there was a nurse beside me taking my vital signs. She told me to be still. I looked around the room again but couldn't tell where I was. When I saw the monitor, I saw several numbers and looked for "361" but they were all different numbers. I looked around the room and at my body once again, and then looked back at the monitor just as it registered my temperature. It read 36.1 Centigrade. As soon as I repeated "361" out loud I suddenly recognized my own body.

I confess that that was a very strange experience. I don't even remember most of the conversation. I just remember that I was in a place where there was much light and I had a sense of peace and well-being. The person I was with emanated love and wisdom. I would have concluded that I was just hallucinating if it were not for the fact that I was given the sign "361" before returning to my body and seeing it appear later on the monitor.

While I do not discount the authenticity of some of these out of body experiences as encounters with the spiritual realm, I do not believe that we should let these subjective experiences have any influence upon the formation of our doctrines concerning the afterlife when these experiences are not in agreement with the Scriptures, and especially when they go directly against what the Scriptures teach. The fact is that much of what individuals report having seen and heard in near-death experiences directly contradicts the Bible.

Jesus said: *"I am the way, the truth, and the life. No one comes to the Father except through Me." (John 14:6)*. Though there are many testimonies of both Christians and non-Christians that confirm these words of Jesus, the vast majority of those who have had near-death experiences worldwide are of other religions or even atheists who testify of having gone towards the light and having had ecstatic experiences without any mention whatsoever of Jesus Christ.

Because of this, many giving more weight to these subjective experiences than to the words of Jesus Himself, have ceased to believe that it is necessary to come to God through Christ. For them, it is no longer essential to put one's faith in Jesus Christ, since Buddhists, Hindus, Muslims, Indigenous animists and even Atheists, have found themselves in heaven in these experiences without the need for repentance and faith in Christ.

The Scriptures are very clear in emphasizing the need of holiness to be in the presence of the Lord:

"Pursue peace with all people, and holiness, without which no one will see the Lord." (Heb 12:14)

"Now the works of the flesh are evident, which are: adultery, fornication, uncleanness, lewdness, 20 idolatry, sorcery, hatred, contentions, jealousies, outbursts of wrath, selfish ambitions, dissensions, heresies, 21 envy, murders, drunkenness, revelries, and the like; of which I tell you beforehand, just as I also told you in time past, that **those who practice such things will not inherit the kingdom of God***." (Gal 5:19-21)*

"For this you know, that **no fornicator, unclean person, nor covetous man, who is an idolater, has any inheritance in the kingdom of Christ and God***. 6 Let no one deceive you with empty words, for because of these things the wrath of God comes upon the sons of disobedience." (Eph 5:5-6)*

"Its gates shall not be shut at all by day (there shall be no night there)… 27 But **there shall by no means enter it anything that defiles, or causes an abomination or a lie***, but only those who are written in the Lamb's Book of Life." (Rev 21:25,27)*

In spite of these clear declarations of the Scriptures, even some pastors say - based upon the testimonies of persons who have had near-death experiences, that holiness of life is not necessary in order to inherit the kingdom of God at death. I just finished reading a book written by a pastor concerning near-death experiences called: *"Revealing Heaven – The Christian Case for Near-Death Experiences"* by John W. Price. [104] Based upon testimonies of

---

[104] John W. Price, *Revealing Heaven – A Christian Case for Near-Death Experiences*, Kindle format

pleasant near-death experiences related by practicing homosexuals, he relegates the prohibition of these practices, and many others which are censured in the Scriptures, to "cultural taboos" that have been converted into "religious dogmas."

We must decide whether we are going to base our convictions upon subjective near-death experiences or by what the Word of God says. The Bible is very clear concerning these sins:

*"**Do you not know that the unrighteous will not inherit the kingdom of God**? Do not be deceived. Neither fornicators, nor idolaters, nor adulterers, nor homosexuals, nor sodomites, 10 nor thieves, nor covetous, nor drunkards, nor revilers, nor extortioners will inherit the kingdom of God." (1Cor 6:9-11)*

"as Sodom and Gomorrah, and the cities around them in a similar manner to these, having given themselves over to sexual immorality and gone after strange flesh, are set forth as an example, suffering the vengeance of eternal fire." (Jude 7)

"But the cowardly, unbelieving, abominable, murderers, sexually immoral, sorcerers, idolaters, and all liars shall have their part in the lake which burns with fire and brimstone, which is the second death." (Rev 21:8)

The present day increase in the frequency of these near-death experiences and visions is in part due to improved urgent care and life support systems making it possible to revive more individuals from the brink of death. However, another factor that we should take into account is the source of the revelations. They return with revelations from the spirit realm, but are they always true revelations of spiritual realities beyond this life? Paul warns us that *"Satan himself disguises himself as an angel of light"* (2Cor 11:14). I am convinced that, at least in part, the increase of these experiences in these last days; especially the revelations which contradict the word of God, are revelations of deceiving spirits of whom we have been warned in Scriptures:

"for the time will come when they will not endure sound doctrine, but according to their own desires, because they have itching ears, they will heap up for themselves teachers; 4 and they will

turn their ears away from the truth, and be turned aside to fables." (2Tim 4:3,4)

Paul says here that they will not endure sound teaching but rather, according to their own desires, they will seek out teachers for themselves who will tell them myths instead of the truth. And where do these fables originate? From the imagination of the teachers, or is there something more sinister hidden behind their fables? In another passage Paul reveals the true source of many of these teachings:

"Now the Spirit expressly says that in latter times some will depart from the faith, giving heed to deceiving spirits and doctrines of demons." (1Tim 4:1)

Without discounting the reality that many of the near-death experiences are genuine encounters with God and revelations of heaven and hell; as with any revelation, vision, prophecy or miracle, we need discernment so as not to believe every spirit but rather to test the spirits to see if they are of God *(1John 4:1)*. In 1John 4:3 John says that every spirit that doesn't confess Jesus is not of God, but rather is antichrist. The great majority of revelations of near-death experiences are antichrist because they exclude the need of Christ for salvation. They are very similar to the increasingly frequent revelations from communications given by "extra-terrestrials" and supposed messages received from the dead - phenomenon which are also on the rise in these last days.

In the same way that we need to exercise discernment concerning revelations of heaven, we also need more discernment concerning supposed revelations of hell. We must examine them in the light of the Scriptures. Many of these revelations deceive by taking from the Word, but others deceive by adding many details which are not found in Scripture. I have read or heard many testimonies of visions of hell and the most outstanding characteristic to me is their many conflicting details. They often contain details which are not in Scripture, contradict the Word, or defy all logic.

Jesus said of the eonian fire, that it was prepared for the devil and his angels. The obvious idea expressed here is that it is a place of punishment prepared for them, where they will be tormented along with all of the unjust among mankind, who will also be punished there with them. Nevertheless, the typical testimony of hell describes it as if hell belonged to Satan and as if the demons and fallen angels were the tormentors rather than the tormented.

Many give descriptions of worms eating the bodies of the tormented. In the case of the seven Colombian youth who describe what they saw in hell, the worms were giants, although the rest who mention worms describe them as normal in size.[105] These testimonies which describe worms in hell seem to have been influenced by misapplications of texts which simply speak of corpses being consumed by maggots:

> "And they shall go forth and look upon **the <u>corpses</u> of the men** who have transgressed against Me. For **their worm does not die, and their fire is not quenched**. They shall be an abhorrence to all flesh." (Isa 66:24)

This passage is a judgment declared against those who come against Jerusalem. It is not a description of the torments of hell. It simply says that those near Jerusalem will see the corpses of their enemies being eaten by worms in the fire and their stench will be an abhorrence to all who pass by. The worms do not die off and the fire doesn't go out until the corpses are fully consumed.

> "They will all respond, they will say to you, 'You also have become weak, as we are; you have become like us.' 11 All your pomp has been brought down to the grave, along with the noise of your harps; **maggots are spread out beneath you and worms cover you**." (Isa 14:10-11)

Here, as in Isaiah 66, he is speaking of the decomposition of corpses. Here it refers to the corpse of the king of Babylon. It is saying that all who were awed by his splendor will be amazed to see his despicable death. In verse 18 through 20 it gives more detail saying:

> "All the kings of the nations lie in state, each in his own tomb. 19 But you are cast out of your tomb like a rejected branch; **you are covered with the slain, with those pierced by the sword**, those who descend to the stones of the pit. Like a corpse trampled

---

[105] *www.youtube.com/watch?v=C3CwknAC8RI*

*underfoot, 20 **you will not join them in burial.**" (Isa 14:18-20 NIV)*

It should be obvious that what is being described here is not the king's soul being tormented in hell, but rather his dead corpse, in a heap with others slain in battle, being consumed by maggots. It speaks of him as being deprived of his own royal tomb, which was an important legacy for great kings. Such a despicable death for the mighty king of Babylon would have caused great wonder to all who observed his end. If it caused worldwide astonishment to see the end of dictators like Hitler, Saddam Hussein and Gadhafi, one can just imagine how it would be for a world ruler like the king of one of the greatest empires of the ancient world.

Therefore, the testimonies of hell which describe disembodied souls being eaten by worms is not based upon what the Scriptures actually teach. They were most likely influenced by hellfire sermons which misinterpreted the verses which speak of maggots consuming the corpses of the dead. These descriptions can also be produced by deceiving spirits who are known for misapplying Scriptures to their own advantage in order to malign the character of God.

There is a website where one can read of visions of hell from several different world religions. [106] On their page that is dedicated to the Christian hell there are some 30 visions of hell within Christianity from 100 years before Christ up to the fifteenth century. The belief in purgatory was promoted and formally adopted by the Catholic Church in the eleventh century. It is interesting to observe that the visions subsequent to that usually included not only a description of hell, but also of purgatory, although today, at least among Protestants, there is no longer mention of purgatory in their testimonies. During the dark ages, most of the visions and near-death experiences were negative, telling of torments, fire and darkness. Nowadays, in a time when hellfire and condemnation is no longer focused upon in most pulpits, the majority relate pleasant experiences of light, peace and love.

One testimony I listened to was of a young girl who attended a legalistic church who said she was shown a place in hell reserved for women who had short hair and wore pants during their lifetime and

---

[106] http://www.hell-on-line.org

died without repenting. Knowing that many of those with long hair and long dresses were also gossips and slanderers I wondered how it would be decided which compartment in hell would be most appropriate for each one.

Others, who attended churches where tithing was imposed, testified to seeing people swimming in a lake of molten lava with signs on their chests which said: "I didn't tithe." It is very common to hear testimonies in which sin groups are compartmentalized in hell – one place for those who didn't tithe, another place for fornicators, another for liars, etc., etc. This would not be logical since most would fall into several different categories. The fornicator most likely didn't tithe either, and probably lied, slandered and wore pants and makeup as well. Judgment will be according to all our works and not just one predominate category.

This concept of categories does not come from Scripture but from other religions such as the Hindus and Buddhists, and from writers with a morbid imagination like Dante. A woman who sold many copies of her book on her supposed visions of hell, described hell as a lake of fire about the size of a football field. I couldn't help wondering how all would be able to fit in a lake the size of a football field if 90% of humanity, plus Satan and his angels and the demons are in it. One best-seller said that in hell nobody had any memory of God. On the other hand, many others say that that which most torments those in hell is not being able to stop thinking about God, while knowing that there no longer exists the possibility of being reconciled to Him.

Some testimonies giving details of hell have been exposed as intentional fraud to mock Christians for their gullibility. Others were invented by "evangelists" in order to have more converts. Others have gained a fortune selling their books and videos of supposed visions of hell.

I think it is worthy of note that nearly all who have had negative near-death experiences of hell were delivered and allowed to come back into their bodies when they cried out to God for mercy. This would be in agreement with Christian Universalism and the Scriptures we have seen thus far:

*"The Lord is gracious and full of compassion, slow to anger and great in mercy. 9 The Lord is **good to all, and His tender mercies are over all His works.**" (Ps 145:8-9)*

*"For **the Lord will not cast off forever**. 32 Though He causes grief, yet He will show compassion according to the multitude of His mercies. 33 For **He does not afflict willingly**, nor grieve the children of men." (Lam 3:31-33)*

*"Like water spilled on the ground, which cannot be recovered, so we must die. But God does not take away life; instead, **he devises ways so that a banished person may not remain estranged from him**." (2Sam 14:14 NIV)*

In my teens, under the effects of hallucinogenic drugs, I had several hellish experiences. Nevertheless, looking back on those experiences now with a clearer perspective and with a personal knowledge of God, I do not attribute those hellish experiences to God but rather to the enemy. We should not derive our beliefs concerning hell from visions and near-death experiences. Paul said that even if an angel from heaven were to preach another gospel different from the pure good news of Jesus Christ, let him be accursed *(Gal 1:8)*. Neither should our convictions be based upon the imagination of writers like Dante, but solely upon the Word of God. Even then we need to learn to distinguish between that which is literal and that which is metaphorical.

Most of all, we need our eyes opened to *be able to comprehend with all the saints what is the width and length and depth and height - to know the love of Christ which passes knowledge; that we may be filled with all the fullness of God (Eph 3:18-19)*. Many of God's people do not comprehend the immensity of His love. Instead of opening up to receive the fullness of God, they open themselves up to fear motivated religion and end up being instead "filled with all the fullness of fear" - fear of a sadistic and angry god. The enemy is not only our accuser, accusing us before God, but he is also God's accuser, accusing God before us. He does everything within his power to blind our eyes so that we cannot see the good news of the gospel in all its glory. Many of the descriptions of hell discount the salvific work of the cross of Christ and limit the love and mercy of God, which endure forever.

I personally have arrived at the conclusion that the majority of the testimonies of hell do not agree with the testimony of Scripture and do not produce good fruit in the lives of those impacted by them. There are no examples in Scriptures of "evangelizing" lost souls with threats of hell, traumatizing people with graphic details of endless torments in order to motivate them to accept Christ. The threat of hell was used in the dark ages by institutionalized religion in order to keep the masses in line and the coffers full, but that is not what we find in the early Church. Jesus said: *"But I, when I am lifted up from the earth, will draw all ~~men~~ to myself." (John 12:32 NIV).* [107] Think about it; what was it that drew you to Christ – the threat of hell or the love of God in Christ Jesus?

As Christians, what is it that transforms us into the image of Christ? The fear of hell? Many ministers enslave the people of God, using the fear of hell as a whip to drive them to work harder and give more, but does that really make us more like Christ? We can only become like Him through a personal relationship with Him – a relationship based upon love and trust. Fear-based religion often produces dead works, but only a relationship of love can produce the fruits of a life transformed by His presence.

---

[107] The word *"men"* is not in the Greek text but was added by the translators.

Chapter ten
Her Gates are Always Open

Revelation chapter 20 ends with the Great White Throne Judgment, where the dead are judged according to their works, and all whose names are not found written in the book of life are cast into the lake of fire. From the traditional point of view, the eternal destiny of every rational being will then be eternally sealed without any further possibility of salvation for those not found written in the book of life at that time. In chapter 21, after the judgment, we see the New Jerusalem descend from heaven upon the new earth. The rest of the chapter is a description of this heavenly city. Until one comes to the end of the chapter, one might think that, as the door of Noah's ark, so also the door of opportunity is forever closed for those outside who might wish to enter. And that is what tradition teaches us. Nevertheless, from verse 24 onwards, we see that the gates of the New Jerusalem are always open and will never be shut to the nations:

> "And the nations of those who are saved shall walk in its light, and the kings of the earth bring their glory and honor into it. 25 **Its gates shall not be shut at all** by day (there shall be no night there). 26 And they shall bring the glory and the honor of the nations into it. 27 **But there shall by no means enter it anything that defiles, or causes an abomination or a lie, but only those who are written in the Lamb's Book of Life**. 22:1 And he showed me a pure river of water of life, clear as crystal, proceeding from the throne of God and of the Lamb. 2 In the middle of its street, and on either side of the river, was the tree of life, which bore twelve fruits, each tree yielding its fruit every month. **The leaves of the tree were for the healing of the nations**. 3 And there shall be no more curse, but the throne of God and of the Lamb shall be in it, and His servants shall serve Him." (Rev 21:24-22:3)

There are several things in these verses which indicate there will be restoration beyond the Great White Throne Judgment. In the *first* place, we see in verse 8 of chapter 21 that those sentenced in the judgment will receive *"their part"* in the lake of fire. Since they are not found written in the book of life they will be judged and sentenced, each one according to his works. This in itself implies a measured sentence that has an end. In the same way that the words of Jesus: *"you will not get out **until**...* and *"**many stripes**...**few stripes**,"* necessitate a sentence of limited duration; the expression *"**their part**"* also implies a measured punishment of a limited time. "Many stripes" cannot mean "eternal stripes" any more that "many ages" can mean eternity. That which is measured is not infinite.

In regard to those who are not found written in the book of life, there is nothing in all of Scriptures that indicates that one's name cannot be written in it at a later time. Indeed, we see that in Christ, *all* without exception will be made alive, each *in his own due time (1Cor 15:22,23)*. In fact, we do see mention of the book of life after the White Throne Judgment. No one will be able to enter the gates of the New Jerusalem unless their names are found written in the book of life *(21:27)*. If there were no possibility of leaving the lake of fire and having one's name subsequently written in the book of life, why would the book of life be mentioned with reference to entering the gates of the New Jerusalem?

In the last verses of Revelation, after the Great White Throne Judgment in the new earth, the invitation is still open for all those who desire, to enter into the gates of the New Jerusalem and drink of the water of life freely:

> *"Blessed are those who wash their robes, that they may have the right to the tree of life and may go through the gates into the city. 15 Outside are the dogs, those who practice magic arts, the sexually immoral, the murderers, the idolaters and everyone who loves and practices falsehood." (Rev 22:14-15)*

> *"And the Spirit and **the bride** say, 'Come!' And let him who hears say, 'Come!' And let him who thirsts come. Whoever desires, let him take the water of life freely." (Rev 22:17)*

Here we see the Spirit and the Bride giving the invitation to *"whoever desires"* to *"wash their robes"* and have their names written in the book of life so as to be able to enter through the gates and drink freely of the water of life. At that time, in the new earth, the Church is the Bride, the Wife of the Lamb, who dwells with Him in the New Jerusalem. The water of life flows from the throne of God in the New Jerusalem, forming the river of life, with the tree of life on either side, which tree is for the healing of the nations *(22:1,2)*. Psalms 87 also seems to refer to a yet future time when the nations will enter the gates of Zion in which are springs of living water *(v.7)*. They will have their names recorded as having been spiritually reborn there *(v.5,6)*.

None of the details of this invitation by the Bride in Revelation 22 would have had any application to the old pre - White Throne Judgment earth. Prior to the Second Coming, the Church was not yet the Bride - the Wife of the Lamb, but here it is the *Bride* who says *"come."* The New Jerusalem didn't descend upon the new earth until after the White Throne Judgment, and therefore there was no place on the pre-judgment earth where one could enter the gates and partake of the tree of life and drink from the river of life. These are new earth conditions and yet we see that there are still those outside being invited by the Lamb's Wife to enter and drink freely from the river. If the lake of fire is eternal and hidden away in the core of the earth, then where do these unclean sinners come from that need to wash their robes? Traditionalists have great difficulty explaining how people can still be present on the new earth in need of cleansing and healing after all the unjust have already been cast into the Lake of Fire following the Great White Throne Judgment, but it harmonizes perfectly with the final universal restoration of all.

It is my conviction that the lake of fire is not a geographical lake in a literal sense any more than it is a literal sea out of which the beast arises in chapter 13 *(13:1)*. Neither do I believe it is literal fire and brimstone.

> *"...He shall be tormented with fire and brimstone in the presence of the holy angels and in the presence of the Lamb. 11* ***And the smoke of their torment ascends forever and ever****; and they have no rest day or night" (Rev 14:10-11)*

In the description of the judgment declared against Edom by the prophet Isaiah, we see very similar description which few would take in a literal sense:

> *"Its streams shall be turned into pitch, and its dust into brimstone; its land shall become burning pitch. 10 It shall not be quenched night or day;* ***its smoke shall ascend forever*** *(olam).* ***From generation to generation*** *it shall lie waste; No one shall pass through it* ***forever and ever.****" (Isa 34:9-10)*

These expressions are very graphic and obviously hyperbolic. Their streams and land did not literally turn to pitch, or their dust into sulfur, and their smoke isn't still ascending today. It says that no one would be able to pass through Edom continually from generation to generation, but one can pass through Edom without any problem today. Also, we see that Isaiah's prophecy, although it singles out Edom, is directed against all nations in verses 1-3:

*"Come near, you nations, to hear; and heed, you people! Let the earth hear, and all that is in it, the world and all things that come forth from it. 2 For the indignation of the Lord is against **all nations**, and His fury against all their armies; He has utterly destroyed them, He has given them over to the slaughter. 3 Also their slain shall be thrown out; their stench shall rise from their corpses, and the mountains shall be melted with their blood." (Isa 34:1-3)*

This prophecy is full of hyperbolic expressions of judgment which we understand as being symbolic and not literal, such as *"the mountains will be melted with their blood," "the hosts of heaven shall be dissolved," "The sword of the Lord is filled with blood, it is made overflowing with fatness," "its streams shall be turned into pitch and its dust into brimstone" "its smoke shall ascend forever,"* etc. Even taking this prophecy as a preview of an eschatological event, we would still understand these expressions as hyperbole emphasizing severity of judgment and not literal. The mountains will not literally be melted by their blood; the rivers will not literally turn to pitch and their smoke will not literally ascend forever. Much less should we understand that every individual of these nations is burning and putting off smoke or will be doing so forever. The smoke arises from their cities and not the inhabitants, even as the unquenchable fire in Ezekiel 20:46-48 is *"the forest of the South"* and not its inhabitants. These expressions of judgment, even though they are graphic, do not ever speak of judgments that go beyond physical death and the destruction of their cities.

Also, we see later in the same book of Isaiah that the judgment against the nations is not eternal. In Isaiah 60 we see a clear reference to the healing of the nations who will be saved and walk in the light of the New Jerusalem and will enter her gates which will always be open, just as we see in Revelation 21 and 22:

"Arise, shine; for your light has come! And the glory of the Lord is risen upon you. 2 For behold, the darkness shall cover the earth, and deep darkness the people; But the Lord will arise over you, and His glory will be seen upon you. 3 The **Gentiles shall come to your light**, *and kings to the brightness of your rising. 4 Lift up your eyes all around, and see: They all gather together, they come to you; your sons shall come from afar, and your daughters shall be nursed at your side. 5 Then you shall see and become radiant, and your heart shall swell with joy; because the abundance of the sea shall be turned to you, the wealth of the Gentiles shall come to you.* **Therefore your gates shall be open continually; they shall not be shut day or night.**" *(Isa 60:1-5,11)*

It is probable that the lake of fire is a spiritual condition rather than a geographical location, and those who are in it can see the New Jerusalem but will not enter until they have fulfilled their "part" or sentence in the lake of fire. The invitation of the Bride is extended to all, but it will be just as it is now; no one responds to the call until they are granted repentance and are drawn by the Spirit. Although they will see the light of the New Jerusalem and will hear the invitation of the Bride to enter, they will continue in the lake of fire until they repent of their sins and have been purified of their uncleanness by the purification of fire and sulfur. Another description of their spiritual condition in addition to the expression "lake of fire" is "the outer darkness." Outer darkness is an expression which, if taken literally, is incompatible with literal fire, which always produces light, especially in dense darkness:

"And I say to you that many will come from east and west, and sit down with Abraham, Isaac, and Jacob in the kingdom of heaven. 12 But the sons of the kingdom will be cast out into **outer darkness. There will be weeping and gnashing of teeth**." *(Matt 8:11-12, cf. 22:13; 25:30).*

The symbolisms are utilized to express the experience of those who live in rebellion towards God, who is a consuming fire, and to describe how it is to live far from Him who is the Light. The lake of fire and sulfur emphasizes corrective punishment and purification, and the outer darkness emphasizes the separation away from the glory and radiance of His presence *("but outside are dogs…" Rev 22:15)*. I believe that the weeping and gnashing of teeth will be occasioned by observing from afar the joy of the saints in the New Jerusalem and not being able to enter until they have fulfilled their part in the lake of fire in outer darkness, and until the Spirit draws them into the New Jerusalem through the invitation of the Bride.

Another cause of their weeping and gnashing of teeth will be the result of being excluded from the wedding feast. They will never enjoy the privilege of being the Bride, the Wife of the Lamb. The marriage will have already been consummated in the Second Coming of Christ when He comes for his Church. Christ will receive His Bride unto Himself to dwell with Him in the New Jerusalem, which He has prepared for His Wife. From the heavenly New Jerusalem, she will reign with Him for a thousand years upon the earth.

At the end of the thousand-year millennium all the rest will be judged before the Great White Throne; God will make a new heaven and earth and then the New Jerusalem will descend from heaven upon the new earth. The rest *"of the nations of those who are saved"* will inhabit the new earth but not the New Jerusalem, which is the exclusive habitation of the Bride, the Wife of the Lamb: *"And the nations of those who are saved shall walk in its light, and the kings of the earth bring their glory and honor into it."* (Rev 21:24). The saved of the nations who are not the Bride - the Wife of the Lamb, will walk in the light of the New Jerusalem but they will not be of the New Jerusalem.

Those in outer darkness, in the lake of fire, suffering the second death, remain away from the presence of the Lord and His glory in the outer darkness. They can only see from afar, weeping and gnashing their teeth in the awareness of what they lost. Someday they will be granted repentance and their names will also be written in the book of life. Then they will be able to walk in the light of the New Jerusalem like the other saved individuals of the nations and enter through its gates which will never be shut, but they will never be the Bride, the Wife of the Lamb.

Those who respond to the invitation and wash their robes will be able to enter through the gates and drink of the water of life and partake of the tree of life but, as I understand it, they will never enjoy the privilege of being the Bride - the Wife of the Lamb, who exclusively has the privilege of entering into the intimacy of the inner chamber of the Lamb. Until the end, we see the distinction between the Wife inhabiting the New Jerusalem and the nations who walk in her light. That is not to say that at the end of the ages, in eternity, this distinction will still exist, since by that time God will be all in all –

all having become subjected to Christ *(1Cor 15:28)*. However, for the ages of the ages (i.e. as long as time exists), the wife will continue inviting whoever wills to enter in and drink freely of the water of life until the last soul has been restored.

So, we see that the gates of the New Jerusalem in the new earth will never be shut. The invitation will continue to be extended to those who are outside to wash their robes and enter through the open gates to partake of the river of life and the tree of life for their healing. His mercy really does endure forever! Christ will reign until all are subject to the Father that He might be all in all. This would not be possible with a traditional model which doesn't allow for another opportunity after the Great White Throne Judgment, but it harmonizes perfectly with Universalism which anticipates the eventual restoration of all, when in the fullness of time, all will be reunited in Christ, both those who are in heaven and those who are on earth *(Eph 1:10)*.

Chapter eleven
The Age of Ages

> *"to him be glory in the church and in Christ Jesus throughout all generations, for ever and ever ("into the **age** of the ages" tou aionos ton aionon)! Amen." (Eph 3:21)*

As we have seen, the Greek phrase traditionally translated "forever and ever" is in reality *"into the ages of the ages" (eis tous aiónas ton aiónon)*. However, in one instance the Greek construction is very distinct. In Ephesians 3:21 it is not *"the ages of the ages"* but rather *"the Age of the ages."* The verse should be translated as we find in the literal translations:

> *"to Him be the glory in the ecclesia and in Christ Jesus for all the generations **of the eon of the eons**! Amen!" (Concordant Literal Version)*

Although traditional translations make no distinction between *"the ages of the ages"* and *"the age of the ages,"* we know that it was intentional and not just an orthographic error made by Paul, and there is a great difference between *"the ages of the ages"* and *"the Age of the ages."* When we use the singular followed by the same word in plural in this manner, we are expressing the idea that that which is in singular form has preeminence over that which appears in plural. In every instance where we find this construction in the Bible, we understand that the first, which appears in singular form, is singular in importance, significance or eminence, compared to the rest which follow in the plural form. When we say, *"King of kings,"* or *"Lord of lords,"* we understand that it is saying that that particular King is preeminent over all other kings. The expression *"Song of songs"* means the most outstanding Song of all songs. The same is true with the *"Holy of holies"* which is usually translated *"the Most Holy"*:

> *"...The curtain will separate the **Holy Place** from the **Most Holy Place** (tou hagiou ton hagion)." (Ex 26:33)*

> *"...and the veil hath made a separation for you between **the holy** and **the holy of holies**." (Ex 26:33 Young's Literal Translation)*

The tabernacle was divided by the veil separating *"the holy"* from the *"Holy of holies"* which is usually rendered *"most holy."* We all understand this distinction, and it is surprising that the translators, who were consistent in translating *"King of kings," "Lord of lords" "Song of songs"* and *"Holy of holies"* or *"most holy,"* failed to distinguish between *"the ages of the ages"* and *"the Age of the ages."* When we understand that the Age of the ages is the age which is preeminent among all others - the culmination of all ages, then the full import of the passage in which it is employed, is revealed:

*"to Him be the glory in the ecclesia and in Christ Jesus for all the generations **of the eon of the eons**! Amen!" (Concordant Literal Version)*

Or expressing the full sense of the word "generations" *(genos)* one could say:

*"to Him be the glory in the Church **and** in Christ Jesus **to all descendants of all generations**, into the age of the ages, Amen!"*

The conjunction *"and" (kai)* is included in most translations based upon the Nestle-Aland Greek New Testament, which further clarifies that both the Church and Christ Jesus will be revealing the glory of God to coming generations. Also, a more precise translation reveals who will be seeing the Glory of God revealed in Christ and in His Church. It will not just be the angels. The phrase *"throughout all generations"* indicates that it will be revealed in the Church and in Christ Jesus *"to all descendants of all generations up to and including those of the final Age of ages."* The word *"generations"* refers to descendants or generations – not so much as to a period of time as to those born or generated. Angels do not generate and therefore do not have generations. Therefore, it is saying that, in the Age of ages, all will see the glory of God as displayed in Christ and His Bride, the Church. The prophecies of Scripture speak of a time coming when all people of all generations will see the Glory of the Lord and here we see that it will be revealed in Christ and in His Church, the bride:

*"The **glory of the Lord shall be revealed, and all flesh shall see it together**; for the mouth of the Lord has spoken." (Isa 40:5)*

*"For **the earth will be filled with the knowledge of the glory of the Lord, as the waters cover the sea**." (Hab 2:14)*

*"Arise, shine; for your light has come! And the glory of the Lord is risen **upon you**. 2 For behold, the darkness shall cover the earth, and deep darkness the people; But **the Lord will arise over you, and His glory will be seen upon you**. 3 **The Gentiles shall come to your light**, and kings to the brightness of your rising." (Isa 60:1-3)*

Many mistakenly think that the last age before entering eternity is the millennium, which they consider as being the full extent of Christ's reign. Afterwards, according to them, all will be judged and go to their eternal destiny, whether it be heaven or hell. Nevertheless, we see reference to several future ages and not just one:

*"that **in the ages to come** He might show the exceeding riches of His grace in His kindness toward us in Christ Jesus." (Eph 2:7)*

Each time we see *"forever and ever"* in traditional translations it must be kept in mind that it is literally *"into the ages of the ages,"* referring to future ages and not "forever." Eternity is not divided up into time units such as days, years, centuries and ages but is rather a reality which always is and exists independently from time. It is a misconception to think of eternity as an infinite succession of ages. We do not know how many ages there will be before the final Age of ages comes to a close, but the Scriptures would not speak of the *"end of the ages" (Heb 9:26 lit. sunteleia ton aionon)* if everlasting meant a succession of ages without end.

Although we do not know how many future ages are included in God's plan for the ages, we know that there is more than one future age and that in the final age – the Age of ages, His glory will have been seen by all flesh - by all generations through the Church and through Jesus Christ *(Eph 3:21)*, and all will have been made subject to Him, bowing the knee and confessing Him as Lord, before the final Age of the ages comes to an end, because it says:

*"**Then comes the end**, when He delivers the kingdom to God the Father, when He puts an end to all rule and all authority and power.... 28 Now **when all things are made subject to Him**, then the Son Himself will also be subject to Him who put all things under Him, **that God may be all in all**." (1Cor 15:24,28, cf. Phil 2:10,11)*

What is it that Christ will be doing together with His Bride in the coming ages? Tradition tells us that the kingdom of Christ ends after the millennial age. In Ephesians 2:6,7 we see that we are already seated with Him and that we will be reigning with Him, not only in the coming age but in the coming *ages:*

"and raised us up together, and made us sit together in the heavenly places in Christ Jesus, 7 **that in the ages to come** *He might show the exceeding riches of His grace in His kindness toward us in Christ Jesus." (Eph 2:6-7)*

The word *"show"* has the idea of "exhibiting or displaying." To whom are we going to demonstrate or exhibit the abundant grace of God if not to those who are in outer darkness, in need of His grace? The nations will walk in her light *(Rev 21:24; Is 60:1-3)*. The Father will then be glorified *in the Church and in Jesus Christ to all the descendants of all generations (Eph 3:21)*. We are His workmanship, created in Christ Jesus to manifest His abundant grace, producing in others *the praise of the glory of His grace:*

"just as **He chose us in Him before the foundation of the world***, that we should be holy and without blame before Him in love… 6* **to the praise of the glory of His grace***, by which He made us accepted in the Beloved… 9 having made known to us the mystery of His will, according to His good pleasure which He purposed in Himself, 10* **that in the dispensation of the fullness of the times He might gather together in one all things in Christ***, both which are in heaven and which are on earth — in Him." (Eph 1:4,6, 9,10)*

What is the mystery of the ages? That He chose us in Christ from before the foundation of the world that we might manifest the abundant riches of His grace to all generations, and that in the dispensation of the fullness of time – the Age of ages, all shall be gathered together in Christ, both those who are in heaven and those who are on the earth. The mystery of the ages is His plan for the ultimate restoration of all, with all finally being brought together in Him and subjected to Him. Then comes the end when Christ Himself will subject Himself to the Father and God will be all in all *(1Cor 15:28; Phil 2:10,11)*.

The ages of the ages

The expression *"the ages of the ages"* refers to ages which are preeminent over all past ages. Even as the Age of the ages focuses on one particular age, and we show its particularity by capitalizing the singular "Age," *"the ages of the ages"* refers to a plurality of ages which are more significant than any prior ages and for that reason are called *"the ages of the ages."* They are more significant because they commence with the millennial reign of Christ and culminate with the greatest and final Age of the ages when, having subdued all to Himself at the end of time, He delivers up the kingdom to the Father. It is significant that in the Old Testament the expression *"the ages of the ages"* does not appear. It isn't until we enter into the New Covenant that this phrase is used expressing that all future ages will stand out above all prior ages. Christ will not reign forever and ever, as some mistranslations would have us think, but rather "for the ages of the ages," or until His enemies have been made His footstool.

> *"Then the seventh angel sounded: And there were loud voices in heaven, saying, 'The kingdoms of this world have become the kingdoms of our Lord and of His Christ, and* **He shall reign forever and ever** *(into the ages of the ages)!" (Rev 11:15)*

> *"Sit at My right hand,* **_till_** *I make Your enemies Your footstool?" (Heb 1:13)*

> *"For He must reign* **_till_** *He has put all enemies under His feet. 26 The last enemy that will be destroyed is death. 27 For 'He has put all things under His feet.' But when He says 'all things are put under Him,' it is evident that He who put all things under Him is excepted. 28 Now* **when all things are made subject to Him, then the Son Himself will also be subject to Him who put all things under Him**, *that God may be all in all." (1Cor 15:25-28)*

Revelation 11:15 is not a contradiction of Hebrews 1:13 and 1Corinthians 15:25-28. *"Forever and ever,"* as we have seen, is only for *"the ages of the ages"* and ends at the end of the ages when all enter into God in eternity. However, the *"ages of the ages"* are the greatest ages of all ages, *"the times of all times"* because Christ will be reigning with His Bride, the Church, and all the earth will be covered with the knowledge of the glory of God as the waters cover the sea. Then we enter into eternity where God is all in all and there will no longer be need of hierarchies.

The end does not come with some in heaven and the majority in an eternal hell, but with the restoration of all, resulting in God being all in all. What a glorious end of the ages! Until God becomes all in all, the ages will continue. There will not be an eternal dualism with some in God and others eternally in opposition to Him, but rather He shall truly be **all in all**. Glory to His name!

Chapter twelve
Universalism in the History of the Church

One of the obstacles which kept me from seriously considering Universalism was that I didn't know anyone who held this doctrine and I thought it was of recent origin and only taught by some liberals and modernists that gave little importance to the authority of the Scriptures. I was surprised to discover that Christians, many of whom are known for their devotion and knowledge of the Scriptures and the original languages, were Universalists. [108] The following is a partial list of some Universalists known by many:

- William Law
- La Fontaine
- Sir Isaac Newton
- Isaac Watts
- Dr. Edward Young
- Immanuel Kant
- George MacDonald
- James Montgomery
- Washington Irving
- Hans Christian Andersen
- Henry Ward Beecher
- William Barclay
- G. Campbell
- John Murray
- Robert Ingersoll
- John Young L.L.D
- Andrew John Jukes
- Rev. Charles A. Pridgeon
- John A. T. Robinson,
- William Barclay,
- A.E. Knoch
- J. Preston Eby, author
- Hanna Hurnard, author of "Hind's Feet on High Places."
- Hannah Whitall Smith, author of "The Secret of a Happy Life."
- Benjamin Franklin

---

[108] http://www.tentmaker.org/tracts/Universalists.html

- President George Washington
- President Abraham Lincoln

Abraham Lincoln was not only one of the most outstanding of all the presidents of the United States, but he was also a great man of God. What many do not know is that he was also a Universalist. In Abraham Lincoln's Biography, *"Abraham Lincoln the Christian"* it says:

> *"Abraham Lincoln did not nor could not believe in the endless punishment of anyone of the human race. He understood punishment for sin to be a Bible doctrine; that the punishment was parental in its object, aim, and design, and intended for the good of the offender; hence it must cease when justice is satisfied. All that was lost by the transgression of Adam was made good by the atonement."* [109]

Universalism – The Doctrine of the Majority until Saint Augustine and the Dark Ages

Many are also surprised, just as I was, to discover that the majority of the most prominent Church fathers in the early Church taught the *Apocatastasis,* or final restoration of all. Of the primary six theological schools which existed during the first five centuries of the Church only one taught eternal punishment. Another taught annihilation and the other four all taught Universalism. J.W. Hanson, who made an in-depth study of the writings of the early Church fathers says the following:

> *"The school in Northern Africa (Carthage) favored the doctrine of endless punishment; that in Asia Minor annihilation. The two in Alexandria and Caesarea were Universalistic of the school of Origen; those at Antioch and Edessa were Universalistic of the school of Theodore of Mopsuestia and Diodore of Tarsus."* [110]

---

[109] Johnson, William J. *Abraham Lincoln the Christian.* Milford, MI: Mott Media, 1976. p.62

[110] J.W. Hanson D.D., *Universalism The Prevailing Doctrine Of The Christian Church During Its First Five Hundred Years* pp. 174,175

The great Church historian, Philip Schaff, although not a Universalist, confirms what Hanson said:

> "In the first five or six centuries of Christianity there were six known theological schools, of which four (Alexandria… Antioch, Caesarea, and Edessa or Nisibis) were Universalist, one (Ephesus) accepted conditional immortality; one (Carthage or Rome) taught endless punishment of the wicked. Other theological schools are mentioned as founded by Universalists, but their actual doctrine on this subject is unknown." [111]

> "Under the instruction of these great teachers [Clement, Origen, Gregory, and Theodore of Mopsuestia] many other theologians believed in universal salvation; and indeed the whole Eastern Church until after AD 500 was inclined to it." [112]

Gieseler, another well-known Church historian, makes it clear that Universalism was not limited to Origen's followers in the Eastern Church:

> "The belief in the inalienable capacity of improvement in all rational beings, and the limited duration of future punishment, was so general, even in the West, and among the opponents of Origen, that, even if it may not be said to have arisen without the influence of Origen's school, it had become entirely independent of his system." [113]

Even Saint Augustine, known as the father of Roman Catholic theology and the one who popularized the doctrine of eternal punishment, recognized that even in his day (AD 354 to AD 430) there were many who taught Universalism and referred to them in a positive light:

> "There are very many in our day who, though not denying the Holy Scriptures, do not believe in endless torments."

---

[111] Schaff, Phillip, *The New Chaff-Herzog Encyclopedia of Religious Knowledge – Vol 12*, Baker Book House, 1950

[112] Philip Schaff, *The New Schaff-Herzog Encyclopedia of Religious Knowledge*. Vol XII, p.96.

[113] Gieseler, *Ecclesiastical History*, vol. 1. para. 82.

"And now I see I must have a gentle disputation with certain tender hearts of our own religion, who are unwilling to believe that everlasting punishment will be inflicted, either on all those whom the just Judge shall condemn to the pains of hell, or even on some of them, but who think that after certain periods of time, longer or shorter according to the proportion of their crimes, they shall be delivered out of that state."

The fact that the majority of the Greek fathers such as Clement and Origin were Universalists should draw our attention. They had first-hand knowledge of the Greek of the New Testament, since it was their first language. Saint Augustine, on the other hand, spoke Latin and confessed his disdain and lack of knowledge of Greek. He based his interpretations on a Latin translation made by Jerome, which is now recognized as a very poor translation of the original Greek.

In addition to the fact that the fathers of the early Church had first-hand knowledge of the New Testament Greek, they were also the nearest in time to the ministry of the twelve Apostles, increasing the probability that their doctrines reflected the teachings of the original Apostles. When the emperor Constantine (AD 306 to AD 337) "converted" to Christianity, the Church was employed as an institution of the government and this religion was imposed upon all. Before this the Church was a persecuted minority which continued in the doctrine of the apostles and the early fathers; separate from the government and without its intervention. However, from Constantine onward the government had an ever-increasing control over the formation and imposition of Church doctrines, converting it into an instrument of the state, in order to keep the people in subjection. This sank the Church into the dark ages which lasted more than a millennium.

Therefore, it is to be anticipated that the doctrine of the Greek fathers before the institutionalization of the Church by the Roman Empire would have been purer and closer to that taught by the New Testament writers. Many of them died as martyrs for their convictions at the hands of the government and established religion. After Constantine and the theology of Saint Augustine, primarily set forth in his work "The City of God" which presented the state as an arm of the Church, it was the Church itself, together with the government, that persecuted the Christians. To whom should we give more weight, to the persecuted Church or to the persecuting Church?

What do the early Church Fathers say about the Apocatastasis (Universal restoration)? Since what remained of the great library of Alexandria was finally destroyed by Pope Theophilus, the 23rd pope of Alexandria, who sought to wipe out Origenism, destroying most of Origen's works as well as the works of other Universalists, and since the Church of the Dark Ages destroyed all materials deemed to be heretical, very few writings of the early Church fathers remain today.

In addition to that, many of those who believed in universal restoration in that epoch practiced what they called "reserve," only sharing this teaching among those whom they considered mature and therefore less apt to convert the grace of God into a license for immorality. They often justified this practice of reserve by passages such as 1Corintians 2:6,7 which says: *"However, we speak wisdom among those who are mature… we speak the wisdom of God in a mystery, the hidden wisdom which God ordained before the ages for our glory."* Origen said:

> "all that might be said on this theme is not expedient to explain now, or to all. For the masses need no further teaching on account of those who hardly through the fear of eternal punishment restrain their recklessness." [114]
>
> "But we must still remember that the Apostle would have this text accounted as a secret, so that the faithful and perfect may keep their perceptions of it as one of God's secrets in silence among themselves, and not divulge it everywhere to the imperfect and those less capable of receiving it." [115]

Due to the practice of reserve on the part of some, their references to universal restoration are not very abundant in their writings. Some of their public sermons do not make any mention of it or at best only make a few indirect references to that doctrine.

Nevertheless, in spite of the above-mentioned reasons, there are references to universal restoration which are sufficiently clear and abundant so as to establish that they believed in the restoration of

---

[114] Origen, *Quoted in Hanson, John Wesley, Universalism: The Prevailing Doctrine of the Christian Church During Its First Vive Hundred Years*, 1899. p. 56.

[115] Origin, *Commentary In Epist. Ad Rom. lib viii. cap. xi.*

all. Below are some quotes from the most prominent fathers of the early Church. [116]

Clement of Alexandria AD 150 to AD 215.

> "The Lord, he says, is a propitiation, 'not for our sins only,' that is, of the faithful, 'but also for the whole world.' Therefore He indeed saves all universally; but some as converted by punishments, others by voluntary submission, thus obtaining the honor and dignity, that 'to Him every knee shall bow, of things in heaven, and things in earth, and things under the earth,' that is angels, and men, and souls who departed this life before His coming into the world." [117]

> "If in this life there are so many ways for purification and repentance, how much more should there be after death! The purification of souls, when separated from the body, will be easier. We can set no limits to the agency of the Redeemer; to redeem, to rescue, to discipline, is his work, and so will he continue to operate after this life." [118]

> "Punishment is, in its operation, like medicine; it dissolves the hard heart, purges away the filth of uncleanness, and reduces the swellings of pride and haughtiness; thus restoring its subject to a sound and healthful state." [119]

> "God's punishments are saving and disciplinary leading to conversion…and especially since souls, although darkened by passions, when released from their bodies, are able to perceive

---

[116] http://www.tentmaker.org/books/

[117] Clement de Alexandria, *Comentary of 1John Adumbrat.* in Ep. I Johan., printed at the end of his Treatise, Quis dives salvetur, p.1009, Potter´s Edit.

[118] Clement of Alexandria, *Strom.* lib. vi. cap. 6m p. 763, Ed. Potter.

[119] Clement of Alexandria, *Paedagogus* 1.8 as cited in Thayors Léxicon.

more clearly because of their being no longer obstructed by the paltry flesh." [120]

Origen AD 184 to AD 254.

"But our belief is that the Word shall prevail over the entire rational creation, and change every soul into his own perfection; in which will choose what he desires, and obtain what he chooses. For although, in the diseases and wounds of the body, there are some which no medical skill can cure, yet we hold that in the mind there is no evil so strong that it may not be overcome by the Supreme Word and God. For stronger than all the evils in the soul is the Word, and the healing power that dwells in him; and this healing he applies, according to the will of God, to every man. The consummation of all things is the destruction of evil..." [121]

"But he that despises the purification of the word of God and the doctrine of the Gospel only keeps himself for dreadful and penal purifications afterward; that so the fire of hell may purge him in torments whom neither apostolical doctrine nor gospel preaching has cleansed, according to that which is written of being "purified by fire." But how long this purification which is wrought out by penal fire shall endure, or for how many periods or ages it shall torment sinners, He only knows to whom all judgment is committed by the Father." [122]

Theofilus of Antioch AD 186.

"And God showed great kindness to man, in this, that He did not suffer him to continue being in sin forever; but, as it were, by a kind of banishment, cast him out of Paradise, in order that, having by punishment expiated, within an appointed time, the sin, and having been disciplined, he should afterwards be recalled. Wherefore also, when man had been formed in this world, it is

---

[120] Clement of Alexandria, Hanson, *John Wesley, Universalism: The Prevailing Doctrine of the Christian Church During Its First Five Hundred Years.* p. 117

[121] Origin, *Contra Selsum* 8.72.

[122] Origin, *Commentary In Epist. Ad Rom. lib viii. cap. xi.*

mystically written in Genesis, as if he had been twice placed in Paradise; so that the one was fulfilled after the resurrection and judgment. Nay further, just as a vessel, when on being fashioned it has some flaw, is remolded or re-made, that it may become new and entire; so also it happens to man by death. For he is broken up by force, that in the resurrection he may be found whole, I mean spotless, and righteous, and immortal." [123]

Irenaeus AD 182.

"Wherefore also He drove him out of Paradise, and removed him far from the tree of life, not because He wanted to deprive him of the tree of life, as some dare to assert, but because He pitied him, (and desired) that he should not continue always a sinner, and that the sin which surrounded him should not be immortal, and the evil interminable and irremediable." [124]

Ambrose of Milan AD 340 to AD 397.

Commenting on Ephesians 1 Ambrose says the following: *"This seemed good to God...to manifest in Christ the mystery of His will ... namely, that He should be merciful to all who had strayed, whether in Heaven or in earth... Every being, then, in the heavens and on earth, while it learns the knowledge of Christ, is being restored to that which it was created,"* [125]

In his commentary on 1Corintios 15:27 he says: *"When every creature learns that Christ is its head, and that Christ's head is God the Father, then God is all in all; that is to say, that every creature should believe alike, that with one voice every tongue of things in Heaven and earth and under the earth, should confess that there is one God from Whom are all things."* [126]

---

[123] http://www.tentmaker.org/books/

[124] Iranio, *Contr. Hoer. lib. iii. c. 23, para. 6.*

[125] Allin, *Universalism Asserted, p. 133.*

[126] Allin, *Universalism Asserted, p. 133.*

"It is necessary that all should be proved by fire, whosoever they are that desire to return to Paradise. For not in vain is it written, that, when Adam and Eve were expelled from Paradise, God placed at the outlet a flaming sword which turned every way. All therefore must pass through these fires, whether it be that Evangelist John whom the Lord so loved...or Peter, who received the keys of the kingdom of heaven." [127]

"Our Savior has appointed two kinds of resurrection, in accordance with which John says, in the Apocalypse, 'Blessed is he that hath part in the first resurrection'; for such come to grace without the judgment. As for those who do not come to the first, but are reserved until the second resurrection, these shall be burnt, until they fulfill their appointed times, between the first and the second resurrection; or, if they should not have fulfilled them then, they shall remain still longer in punishment." [128]

Gregory of Nyssa AD 330 to AD 394.

"Wherefore that at the same time liberty of free-will should be left to nature and yet the evil be purged away, the wisdom of God discovered this plan, to suffer man to do what he would, that having tasted the evil which he desired, and learning by experience for what wretchedness he had bartered away the blessings he had, he might of his own will hasten back with desire to the first blessedness,...either being purged in this life through prayer and discipline, or after his departure hence through the furnace of cleansing fire." [129]

"For it is needful that evil should someday be wholly and absolutely removed out of the circle of being. For inasmuch as it is not in the nature of evil to exist without the will, when every will comes to be in God, will not evil go on to absolute extinction, by reason of there being no receptacle of it left?" [130]

---

[127] Ambrose, *in Psalm i. para. 54, p. 763, Ed. Paris. 1686.*

[128] Psalm . i. para. 54, p. 763, Ed. Paris. 1686

[129] Gregorio de Niza, *Orat. pro Mortuis, ad. fin. p. 634, Ed. Paris. 1638.*

[130] Gregorio de Niza, *Dial. de Anima et Resurrect. tom.iii. p. 227, Ed. Paris. 1638*

"the One who both delivers man from evil, and who heals the inventor of evil himself." [131]

"When every created being is at harmony with itself…and every tongue shall confess that Jesus Christ is Lord; when every creature shall have been made one body… Now the body of Christ, as I have often said, is the whole of humanity. And again he writes, Everything shall be subdued to Christ, and they shall be subdued by a full knowledge of Him, and by a remodeling… Now God will be all in all at the time of restitution." [132]

Gregory Nazianzen AD 328 to AD 389.

"These, if they will, may go our way, which indeed is Christ's; but if not, let them go their own way. In another place perhaps they shall be baptized with fire, that last baptism, which is not only very painful, but enduring also; which eats up, as if it were hay, all defiled matter, and consumes all vanity and vice." [133]

"For all things shall be subject to Him, and all things shall acknowledge His empire; and when God shall be all in all, those who now excite discords by revolts, having been quite pacified, shall praise God in peaceful concord." [134]

---

[131] Gregorio de Niza, *Catechetical Oraciones, Cap. 26.*

[132] Gregorio de Niza, *Catechetical Oraciones, (36)*

[133] Gregorio, el Nazianceno, *Orat. xxix. par.19, p.690. Ed. Paris 1778*

[134] Basil the Great (c. 329 – c. 379) Commentary on Isaiah
Crowder, John (2013-09-28). Cosmos Reborn : Happy Theology on the New Creation (Kindle Locations 3788-3789). Sons of Thunder Ministries & Publications - Digital version by Ten10 Ebooks. Kindle Edition.

Marcellus of Ancyra AD 315 to Ad 374.

"For what else do the words mean, 'until the times of the restitution' (Acts, iii: 21), but that the apostle designed to point out that time in which all things partake of that perfect restoration?" [135]

Titus of Bostra AD 338 to AD 378.

"The very abyss of torment is indeed the place of chastisement, but it is not eternal (aionioti) nor did it exist in the original constitution of nature. It was afterwards, as a remedy for sinners, that it might cure them. And the punishments are holy, as they are remedial and salutary in their effect on transgressors; for they are inflicted, not to preserve them in their wickedness, but to make them cease from their wickedness. The anguish of their suffering compels them to break off their vices… If death were an evil, blame would rightfully fall on him who appointed it." [136]

Theodore of Mopsuestia AD 359 to AD 429.

"The wicked who have committed evil the whole period of their lives shall be punished till they learn that, by continuing in sin, they only continue in misery. And when, by this means, they shall have been brought to fear God, and to regard him with good will, they shall obtain the enjoyment of his grace. For he never would have said, 'until thou hast paid the uttermost farthing,' unless we can be released from suffering after having suffered adequately for sin; nor would he have said, 'he shall be beaten with many stripes,' and again, 'he shall be beaten with few stripes,' unless the punishment to be endured for sin will have an end." [137]

---

[135] Marcelo de Anicra, Hanson, John Wesley, *Universalism: The Prevailing Doctrine of the Christian Church During the First Five Hundred Years*, Universalist Publishing House, Boston, 1899, p. 244

[136] Tito de Bostra, *Tillemont*, p.

[137] Gregorio el Nazianceno, *Assemani Bib. Orient. Tom. iii.*

Ambrose of Milan AD 340 to AD 397.

"What then hinders our believing that he who is beaten small as the dust is not annihilated, but is changed for the better; so that, instead of an earthly man, he is made a spiritual man, and our believing that he who is destroyed, is so destroyed that all taint is removed, and there remains but what is pure and clean? And in God's saying of the adversaries of Jerusalem, 'They shall be as though they were not," you are to understand they shall exist substantially, and as converted, but shall not exist as enemies... God gave death, not as a penalty, but as a remedy; death was given for a remedy as the end of evils...How shall the sinner exist in the future, seeing the place of sin cannot be of long continuance?" [138]

Marius Victorinus AD 300.

On 1Corinthians 15:28, he says: *"All things shall be rendered spiritual at the consummation of the world. At the consummation all things shall be one... Therefore all things converted to him shall become one, i.e., spiritual; through the Son all things shall be made one, for all things are by him, for all things that exist are one, though they be different. For the body of the entire universe is not like a mere heap, which becomes a body, only by the contact of its particles; but it is a body chiefly in its several parts being closely and mutually bound together--it forms a continuous chain. For the chain is this, God: Jesus: the Spirit: the intellect: the soul: the angelic host: and lastly, all subordinate bodily existences."* [139]

On Ephesians 1:4: *"The mystery was completed by the Savior in order that, perfection having been completed throughout all things, and in all things by Christ, all universally should be made one through Christ and in Christ.... And because he (Christ) is the life, he is that by whom all things have been made, for all things cleansed by him return into eternal life."* [140]

---

[138] Ambrosio de Milán, *Hanson*, pp. 245,246

[139] Marius Victurinas, *Hanson*, p. 249

[140] Marius Victurinas, *Hanson*, p. 249

Jerome AD 347 to AD 420.

"Your enemies, O God, shall perish,...every man who has been Your enemy shall hereafter be made Your friend; the man shall not perish, the enemy shall perish." [141]

"In the restitution of all things when Christ the true physician shall have come to heal the body of the universal church...every one...shall receive his proper place... What I mean is, the fallen angel will begin to be that which he was created, and man who has been expelled from Paradise will be once more restored to the tilling of Paradise... These things then will take place universally." [142]

"Most persons regard the story of Jonah as teaching the ultimate forgiveness of all rational creatures, even the devil." [143]

"The apostate angels, and the prince of this world, and Lucifer, the morning star, though now ungovernable, licentiously wandering about, and plunging themselves into the depths of sin, shall in the end, embrace the happy dominion of Christ and his saints... No rational creature before God will perish forever." [144]

"Israel and all heretics, because they had the works of Sodom and Gomorrah, are overthrown like Sodom and Gomorrah, that they may be set free like a brand snatched from the burning. And this is the meaning of the prophet's words, 'Sodom shall be restored as of old,' that he who by his vice is as an inhabitant of Sodom, after the works of Sodom have been burnt in him, may be restored to his ancient state." [145]

---

[141] Jerome. In Ps. xcii. 9.22

[142] Allin, *Universalism Asserted*, p. 134.

[143] Jerome. In Ps. xcii. 9.22
[144] Jerome. In Ps. xcii. 9.22

[145] J.W. HANSON, D. D. Universalism The Prevailing Doctrine Of The Christian Church During Its First Five Hundred Years. http://www.tentmaker.org/books/

Theodore the Blessed AD 387 to AD 458.

Regarding Ephesians 1:23, Theodore wrote: *"In the present life God is in all, for his nature is without limits, but is not all in all. But in the coming life, when mortality is at an end and immortality granted, and sin has no longer any place, God will be all in all. For the Lord, who loves man, punishes medicinally, that he may check the course of impiety."* [146]

Theodore Olympiodorus AD 495 to AD 570.

"Do not suppose that the soul is punished for endless eons. The soul is not punished to gratify the revenge of the divinity, but for the sake of healing. The soul is punished for an eonian period (aionios) calling its life and its allotted period of punishment its eon." [147]

---

[146] Teodoro el Bendecido, *Hanson*, p.254.

[147] http://brazenchurch.com/how-hell-invaded-church-doctrine/

Summary of the History of Universalism

In 1895 James Strong, who compiled *The Strong's Exhaustive Concordance of the Bible,* together with John McClintock, published the encyclopedia called *The Cyclopedia of Biblical, Theological, and Ecclesiastical Literature*, which includes an extensive summary of the history of Universalism. Neither of these men were Universalists and nevertheless they present an objective summary, and for this reason I am including it even though it is rather lengthy. It clearly demonstrates that Universalism was not the belief of just a fringe group and has always had those who held to the teaching throughout history; at times with great cost to themselves.

Universalism:

1. In The Early Centuries.

In 195 Clemens Alexandrinus, who was president of the Catechetical School at Alexandria, advocated Universalism on the ground of the remedial character of all punishment. His pupil and successor in the school, Origen Adamantius, famous alike for his learning, piety, and zeal, taught Universalism on the ground of the ever-continuing freedom of the will, the deep mental and spiritual anguish occasioned by the light and knowledge of the truth until it leads to repentance, and then the harmony of the soul with God. Origen's position, abilities, and untiring efforts for the spread of the Gospel gave him great influence with his pupils, and with the Church at large, in whose behalf he became a voluminous writer. In addition to his position and work in the school of Alexandria, he also had care for several years, in connection with Pamphilius, of the theological school at Caesarea, one of whose distinguished pupils was the celebrated Gregory Thaumaturgus, a great admirer of his master's theories, and finally, about A.D. 235, his strong defender and ardent eulogist. Pamphilius, and Eusebius, the first Church historian, also defended Origen's doctrines from charges brought against them by the Western Church, and in answering the complaint that he denied all future punishment they quote from his writings in contradiction thereof, not only his positive assurances of future and severe punishment, but his equally positive assertion that such correction is purifying and salutary. In A.D. 364, Titus, bishop of Bostra, wrote in advocacy of Universalism, contending that, although there are torments in the abyss of hell, they are not eternal, but that their great severity will lead the wicked to repentance and so to salvation. Gregory of Nyssa, A.D. 380, also advocated Universalism on the same grounds. Contemporary with him was the justly celebrated defender of orthodoxy, Didymus the Blind, a successor of Origen in the school at Alexandria, and a zealous Universalist. Prominent among his scholars was Jerome, eminent alike for his abilities, his inconsistencies, and instability. Universalism as taught by Origen is clearly and ably set forth by Jerome in his commentaries on the epistles, and in his letters. John, bishop of Jerusalem at this period, was also an advocate of Universalism on Origen's theory. Another contemporary, Diodorus, a teacher of great repute in the school at Antioch, and afterwards bishop of Jerusalem, was also a Universalist, who, in opposition to the then general prevalence of allegorical interpretation, strictly adhered to the natural import of the text in his many commentaries on the Scriptures. He defended Universalism on the ground that the divine mercy far exceeds all the effects and all the desserts of sin. His pupil and successor in the school, Theodore of Mopsuestia, A.D. 420, called "the crown and climax of the school of Antioch," and by the Nestorians, whose sect he founded, "the interpreter of the Word of God," and whose writings were text-books in the schools of Eastern Syria, was a prominent and influential Universalist. His theory was that sin is an incidental part of the development and education of the human race; that, while some are more involved in it than others, God will overrule it to the final establishment of all in good. He is the reputed author of the liturgy used by the Nestorians, a Church which at one time equaled, in its membership the combined adherents of both the Greek and Latin communions, and which has had no rival in military zeal. In the addresses and prayers of this liturgy Universalism is distinctly avowed. Theodoret, A.D. 430, bishop of Cyprus in Syria, a pupil of Theodore of Mopsuestia, was also a Universalist, holding the doctrine on the theory advocated by the Antiochian school. For some time prior to this, certain opinions of Origen on pre-existence and on the salvation of the devil had been in dispute and pronounced heretical by a synod; but his doctrine of the universal salvation of the human race had not been involved in this condemnation. At a local council called by the emperor Justinian at Constantinople, A.D. 544, Origen's doctrine of universal salvation was declared heretical. Nine years later another council was held by the same authority at the same place, when condemnation was pronounced on the Nestorians, although their belief in Universalism was not mentioned. It has been common to call this an ecumenical council, but without warrant (see the action of the Latin Church in refusing to recognize it or to send a legate to it). Doderlein, in his Institutes of Christian Theology, after quoting the decree of Justinian against Origen, says, 'That was not the belief of all, and in proportion as any one was eminent in learning in Christian antiquity, the more did he cherish and defend the hope of the termination of future 'torments.' Drexelius, in his defense of eternal punishment, gives this testimony, 'That God should doom the apostate angels and men at the day of retribution to eternal torments seemed so hard and incredible a doctrine to some persons that even Origen himself who was mighty in the Scriptures, and no less famous for his admirable wit and excellent learning, presumed to maintain in his book of principles that both the devils and the damned, after a certain period of years, the fire having purged or cleansed them from their pollutions, should be restored to grace. Augustine and others set forth his error and condemned him for it. But, notwithstanding their condemnation, this error has found a great many in the world who have given it a kind of civil reception. The Anti-heretics so called, dispersed this error throughout all Spain under various interpretations." Gieseler, the ecclesiastical historian, says, 'The belief in the inalienable capacity of improvement in all rational beings and the limited duration of future punishment, was so general, even in the West, and among the opponents of Origen, that, even if it may not be said to have arisen without the influence of Origen's school, it had become entirely independent of his system.' And Augustine bears this testimony: 'Some - nay, very many - from human sympathy commiserate the eternal punishment of the damned and their perpetual torture without intermission, and thus do not believe in it; not, indeed, by opposing the Holy Scriptures, but by softening all the severe things according to their own feelings, and giving a milder meaning to those things which they think are said in them more terribly than truly. Universalism almost wholly disappeared during the period known as the Dark Ages, although there are occasional glimpses of it even in the mutilated records which the papal Church has permitted to descend to us. In the 7th century, Maximus, the Greek monk and confessor taught Universalism; in the 8th, Clement of Ireland was deposed from the priesthood for teaching that when Christ descended into hell he restored all the damned; while in the 9th, John Scotus Erigena, a famous philosopher who stood at the head of the learned of the court of France, was a bold defender of Universalism. In the 11th century, the Albigenses were, according to papal authorities, Universalists; In the 12th, Raynold, abbot of St. Martin's, in France, was charged before a council with holding "that all men will eventually be saved;" In the 13th, Solomon, bishop of Bassorah, discussed the question of universal salvation, answering it in the affirmative. The Lollards in the 14th century taught Universalism in Bohemia and Austria; and at the same period a council convened by Langman, archbishop of Canterbury, gave judgment against Universalism as one of the heresies then taught in that province. In the early part of the 15th century, a sect called 'Men of Understanding' taught Universalism in Flanders, advocating it on the ground of the German Mystics, as did Tauler of Strasburg, and John Wessel, who, with others, have been called 'the Reformers before the Reformation,' whose writings Luther industriously studied and greatly admired.

2. In Modern Times.

With the Reformation, Universalism made a fresh appearance early in the 16th century, chiefly among some of the Anabaptist sects. The seventeenth article of the Augustine Confession, 1530, was expressly framed to 'condemn the Anabaptists, who maintain that there shall be an end to the punishments of the damned and of the devils.' Denk, Hetzer, and Stanislaus Pannonius were the most eminent defenders of Universalism at this period. Later in the century, Samuel Huber, divinity professor at Wittenberg, taught Universalism, it is alleged by Spanheim; and because, says Musheim, he would not go back to the old methods of teaching, "he was compelled to relinquish his office and go into exile.' Early in the 17th century, Ernest Sonner, professor of philosophy at Altorf, published 'a theological and philosophical demonstration that the endless punishment of the wicked would argue, not the justice, but the injustice, of God.' John William Petersen, at one time court preacher at Lutin, and subsequently superintendent at Lunenberg, adopted and defended Universalism with such zeal that he was cited before the consistory, and, as he could not conscientiously renounce his convictions, was deprived of his office and forced into private life. In his retirement he wrote and published three folio volumes on Universalism, entitled Musterion Apokatastaseos Paltan, in which he mentions many who had defended that doctrine. The volumes appeared between the years 1700 and 1710. They opened a century of spirited controversy, of which Mosheim says, 'The points of theology which had been controverted in the 17th century were destined to excite keener disputes in the 18th, such 'as the eternity of hell torments, and the final restoration of all intelligent beings to order, perfection, and happiness.' Dietelmair, an opponent of Universalism, wrote on its history about the middle of this century. In the preface to his work he speaks of the contests which raged vehemently enough within the very bounds of the orthodox Church in the end of the last century 'the' beginning of the present." Among the defenses of Universalism contained in the first volume of Petersen's work was the Everlasting Gospel, attributed to Paul Siegvolk, which was but an assumed name of George Klein-Nicolai, deposed for his Universalism as preacher of Friessdorf. He published other works in defense of Universalism, but the most rapid and lasting popularity belonged to the Everlasting Gospel, which in forty-five years passed through five editions in Germany. In 1726 John Henry Haug, professor at Strasburg, having procured the assistance of Dr. Ernest Christoph Hochman, Christian Dippel, Count De Marcey, and others, commenced the publication of the Berleburger Bibel, an entirely new translation and commentary of the Holy Scriptures. They made themselves familiar with all the writings of the Mystics, and in their great work taught and defended Universalism from the Mystical standpoint. Their work fills eight large folio volumes, the last of which was published in 1742. Strong persecution assailing them, and no printer being willing to risk his office in doing their work, they were compelled to purchase their own type and a small press. When the Church they had established was at last broken up by their enemies, the members fled to America, taking their press with them, and it was set up by Christopher Sower in Germantown, Pa. One of De Marcey's intimate friends was George De Benneville, born of French parents in London in 1703. Before he was twenty years of age he commenced preaching in France, where he was arrested and condemned to die, but was reprieved on the scaffold by Louis XV. Making his way into Germany, he there preached Universalism several years, and then came to America. In 1727 appeared Ludvig Gerhard's Complete System of the Everlasting Gospel of the Restoration of All Things, together with the Baseless Opposite Doctrine of Eternal Damnation. The author was at one time professor of theology in the University of Rostock, and his publication called forth, according to Walch, no less than fourteen volumes in reply. Jung, Stilling in the latter part of the 18th century, an able defender of Christianity against German rationalism, was an ardent and eminent Universalist. Prof. Tholuck wrote, in 1835, that this doctrine "came particularly into notice through Jung-Stilling, that eminent man who was a particular instrument in the hand of God for keeping up evangelical truth in the latter part of the former century, and at the same time a strong patron to that doctrine. 'During the present century, Universalism has made rapid progress in Germany. Olshausen says of it that it 'has, no doubt, a deep root in noble minds, and is the expression of a heart-felt desire for a perfect harmony of the creation.' Dr. Dwight wrote in 1829, 'The doctrine of the eternity of future punishment is almost universally rejected...' In England the Protestants, in drawing up their Forty-two Articles of Religion, in 1552, condemned Universalism. Ten years later, when the convocation revised the doctrines of the Church, the number of articles was reduced to thirty-nine, omitting, among others, the one condemning Universalism. Since that time Universalism has not been a forbidden doctrine in the Church of England, but has been advocated and defended by some of the most eminent members of its communion-such men as Dr. Henry More, Sir George Stonehouse, Bp. Thomas Newton, Dr. David Hartley, William Whiston, Dr. Thomas Burnet, Revs. Frederick W. Robertson, Charles Kingsley, Stopford Brooke, and canon Farrar, and indirectly by archbishop Tillotson. The Presbyterian Parliament of 1648, which temporarily overthrew Episcopacy, passed a law against all heresies, punishing the persistent holders of some with death, and of others with imprisonment. 'That all men shall be saved' was among the heresies punishable in the latter manner. This law was not long operative, for the Independents, headed by Cromwell, soon overthrew the law-makers. Gerard Willstanley published a work in advocacy of Universalism only a few days after the passage of the law, which was soon followed by similar works from his pen. William Earbury fearlessly preached Universalism. Richard Coppin was active in its advocacy, publishing largely in its exposition and defense, and was several times tried for his offence. Samuel Richardson, an eminent Baptist, also wrote strongly in its behalf. Sir Henry Vane (the younger), member of the Parliament dissolved by Cromwell, and in 1636 governor of Massachusetts, was a Universalist. Jeremy White, one of Cromwell's chaplains, preached Universalism, and published a work which has passed through several editions. Jane Lead, a

Mystic, was the author of several Universalist books. Henry Brooke, a literary writer, avowed his belief in Universalism in his Fool of Quality, and in a poem on the Messiah. William Law, author of the Serious Call, declared in his Letters, 'As for the purification of all human nature, I fully believe it, either in this world or some after ages.' The English literary reviews of the last century contain many notices of works in defense of Universalism. In 1750 James Relly, who had been a preacher in Whitefield's connection, shocked at the doctrine of reprobation, was by meditation and study led into another scheme of redemption, some of the peculiarities of which may be said to have had their origin with him. Accepting as true the common theory that all men, having sinned in Adam, justly incurred eternal damnation, and that Christ had borne this infinite guilt and punishment in behalf of all who should be saved, Relly was moved to find, if possible, some ground of justice in such a scheme. The divine law explicitly declares that "the soul which sinneth, it shall die," and that the innocent shall not suffer for the guilty. How could a transfer of human sin and penalty to Christ be consistent with that law? How could it be reconciled with equity? The divine sovereignty, without regard to inherent justice in the plan, could not account for it for the absoluteness that could set justice aside might just as easily, and more mercifully, have gone straight to its aim by remitting instead of transferring sin and its deserts. To say that the sufferings of Christ were merely accepted as satisfaction for human deserts, only reckoned as such, by God's sovereign pleasure, was no adequate explanation, since they were thus only a fictitious, not a real, satisfaction; and, further, any sufferings whatsoever, even those of a man, would have answered just as well as an arbitrary acceptance of the coequal of God. The perfect consistency of God's procedure, its absolute harmony with justice and equity, Relly found, as he claimed, in such a real and thorough union of Christ with the human race as made their acts his, and his theirs. All men, he held, were really in Adam and sinned in him, not by a fictitious imputation, but by actual participation; equally so are all men in the second Adam, 'the head of every man,' and he is as justly accountable for what they do as is the head in the natural body, accountable for the deeds of all the members united to that head. Accordingly Christ, in his corporate capacity, was truly guilty of the offence of the 'human race, and could be, as he actually was, justly punished for it; and the race, because of this' union, really suffered in him all the penalty which he endured, and thus fully satisfied justice. There is no more punishment, therefore, due for sin, nor any further occasion for declaring the demands of the law, except to make men feel their inability to obey, and thus compel them to an exclusive reliance on Christ the head. He has effected a complete and finished justification of the whole world. When man believes this he is freed from the sense of guilt, freed also from all doubt and fear. Until he believes it he is, whether in this world or in another, under the condemnation of unbelief and darkness, the only condemnation now possible to the human race. In illustration and defense of this theory, Relly wrote and published several books, preached zealously in London and vicinity, and gathered a congregation in the metropolis. After his death in 1778, two societies were formed from his congregation; but both have now ceased to exist, as has the society gathered by Winchester about 1789, and the Church founded by David Thom, D.D., in Liverpool in 1825. The Unitarians in England are all believers in Universalism, as are also many of the Congregationalists.

3. In America

Universalism is the result of the proclamation of a variety of theories, some of them at a very early date, all resulting in one conclusion - the final holiness of the human race. Sir Henry Vane as was said above, was a Universalist. It is not known that while in America he made any public avowal of that belief; but the presumption is that he did not stand alone. In July, 1684, Joseph Gatchell, of Marblehead, Mass., was brought before the Suffolk County Court for discoursing "that all men should be saved," and, being convicted, was sentenced 'to the pillory and to have his tongue drawn forth and pierced with a hot iron.' Dr. George DeBenneville, also mentioned above, came to America in 1741, expressly called of God, as he believed, to preach the Gospel in the New World. For more than fifty years he preached in various parts of Pennsylvania, Maryland, Virginia, and the Carolinas. He was not an organizer, but simply a preacher, and quite a voluminous writer, though only a few of his productions were published. For several years he was welcomed to the pulpits of the 'Brethren' (Dunkers). It was no doubt at his suggestion that Siegvolk's Everlasting Gospel was translated into English, and published by Christopher Sower, printed, probably, on the identical press on which the Berleburger Bibel had been struck off. This edition was reviewed by Rev. N. Pomp, a German minister in Philadelphia. Alexander Mack, an eminent preacher among the Dunkers, replied to Pomp, defending Siegvolk's views. This work was never published, but the MS. is still preserved. There was found among Dr. De Bonneville's papers, after his death, in 1793, a Commentary on the Apocalypse, which was printed in German, at Lebanon, Pa., in 1808. There was also Universalism in the Episcopal Church. Rev. Richard Clarke, rector of St. Philip's in Charleston, S. C., from 1754 to 1759, was a pronounced advocate of it; as was Rev. John Tyler, rector of the Church in Norwich, Conn., who wrote a work in its defense, which was published by someone to whom he had loaned his MS., about 1787. Some of the Congregationalists of New England were believers in Universalism; among them Dr. Jonathan Mayhew, minister of the West Church in Boston from 1747 to 1766, who distinctly avowed his belief in it in a published Thanksgiving Sermon, Dec. 9, 1762. Dr. Charles Chauncy, minister of the First Church in Boston from 1727 to 1787, issued a pamphlet on the subject in 1782, which was reviewed by Dr. Samuel Mather. In 1784 his larger work The Salvation-of All Men was published, a second edition following in 1787. Dr. Joseph Huntington, minister in Coventry, Conn., from 1762 to 1794, left a work in favor of Universalism, entitled Calvinism Improved, which was published in 1796." [End Article] [148]

Conclusion

Therefore, in summary, we can see that Universalism is not a new doctrine. In fact, it was the predominant doctrine in the early Church until entering into the Dark Ages in the fifth and sixth centuries. Even in the Dark Ages there were voices in the darkness proclaiming the pure gospel of restoration of all things, at the risk of their own ecclesiastical position and even their own lives. With the invention of the printing press, placing the Bible in the hands of the people, the reformation began and the number of individuals who broke with the tradition of eternal punishment for the majority and embraced Universalism greatly increased.

In the last few years there seems to be a restoration of this forgotten doctrine. The reformation of the sixteenth century restored the truth of Justification by faith and other doctrines of the Bible which

---

[148] John McClintock, James Strong, *Enciclopedia de la Literatura, Bíblica, Teológica y Eclesiástica*, 1895, Toma 10 páginas 109-133

the Church had lost sight of. In my opinion we are seeing the beginnings of a new reformation and this time it is the rediscovering of the truth of Universal restoration. The Church needs to awaken to this truth in order that, in the time of the manifestation of the sons of God, we might have the vision for the liberation and restoration of all of creation as prophesied *(Rom 8:18-23)*. If we do not want to repeat the history of the Jews, we must expand our vision so as to see that salvific work of the cross does not end with us – that we are just the firstfruits, the church of the prototypes, and that all the rest will be made alive in due time *(James 1:18; 1Cor 15:22,23)*. It is time that we comprehend that *we who first trusted in Christ* are His workmanship, destined to be manifested to the praise of the glory of His grace in the coming ages *(Eph 1:12; 2:7-10)*.

Chapter thirteen
The Unadulterated Gospel

> *"For we are not as many, adulterating the word of God:*
> *but with sincerity: but as from God,*
> *before God, in Christ we speak."*
> *(2Corinthians 2:17 DRB)*

Since I came to understand the glorious gospel of universal reconciliation, I have struggled to find an apt title to describe it. I thought that "full gospel" would have been a good term if it were not for the fact that that expression has already acquired its own unique connotations. The term "full gospel" was coined upon rediscovering the reality that the gospel not only includes our salvation from sin but also physical healing – a reversal of the consequences of sin in our physical bodies. The redemptive work on the cross not only made it possible for God to be just and at the same time show mercy, justifying the ungodly *(Rom 3:25,26)*. It also made it possible for a just and holy God to reverse His own declared consequences for Adam's sin - healing the sick and even raising the dead. God cannot be just and at the same time simply overlook sin or arbitrarily reverse the curse of death in consequence of sin. Only His redemptive work on the cross made it possible for Him to be just and at the same time show mercy towards unworthy sinners like us.

All forgiveness on the part of God towards men and all divine healing against the declared curse of death - both under the Old and New Testament, are only possible because of the propitiatory sacrifice of Christ on the cross. God was only able to be merciful and at the same time just, healing the children of Israel in the desert and foregoing pronounced judgment, in light of the cross.

The healing revival and the rediscovered truth of the "full gospel" of divine healing, enabled many to begin to appropriate by faith - not only forgiveness of sin, but also physical healing. Prior to that time many suffered physical infirmities unnecessarily, not knowing that the gospel was also inclusive of physical healing. The discovery that divine healing could be appropriated by faith in the same way as spiritual salvation (by grace through faith), added a whole new dimension to the gospel which had been lost since the Church entered into the Dark Ages.

For some time I was frustrated because I now knew that the "full gospel" was really much more *"full"* than what many in the healing revival were able to comprehend. I wanted to be able to use the term "full gospel" to refer to universal salvation, but I knew I couldn't because the expression was already limited by its association with the healing gospel.

Then, one day while I was pondering this, I felt that the Lord unveiled to me an even more apt expression: *"The Unadulterated Gospel"* or *"The Pure Gospel."* From the very beginnings of the Church, the first and foremost focus of Satan has been to dilute and veil the glory of the gospel so that mankind cannot discover and experience it's saving, transforming power:

> "But even if **our gospel is veiled**, it is veiled to those who are perishing, 4 whose minds the god of this age has blinded, who do not believe, **lest the light of the gospel of the glory of Christ, who is the image of God, should shine on them**." (2Cor 4:3-4)

In the cross, we discover the wisdom of God and the power of God unto salvation. The wise of this age regard it as foolishness; the strong see it as unnecessary; the legalists have leavened it with the works of the flesh; entrepreneurs have exploited it for personal gain; libertines have adapted it to their licentious lifestyles. It has been diluted, banned, mocked, modified, reduced to an image, used as an ornament and trampled upon. But it still continues to be the wisdom of God and the power of God to all who see and embrace it in all its purity.

The pure gospel has always been under assault since the day that the Great Commission was commended to the Church. Much space in the New Testament epistles is dedicated to the defense of the gospel in its purity. Paul declared to the Galatians:

> "I marvel that you are turning away so soon from Him who called you in the grace of Christ, to **a different gospel**, 7 **which is not another**; but there are some who trouble you and want to **pervert the gospel** of Christ. 8 **But even if we, or an angel from heaven, preach any other gospel to you than what we have preached to you, let him be accursed**. 9 As we have said before, so now I say again, if anyone preaches any other gospel to you than what you have received, **let him be accursed**." (Gal 1:6-9)

Paul's missionary journeys to the Gentiles were usually followed up by a group of Judaizers. The Judaizers were Jews who professed faith in Jesus the Messiah but, at the same time, insisted upon following in the law and the tradition of the Pharisees. Jesus warned his disciples against the leaven of the Pharisees and of the Sadducees; referring to the doctrine of the Pharisees and the doctrine of the Sadducees *(Matt 16:6,12)*. Both the exclusivism and legalism of the Pharisees as well as the unbelief and rationalism of the Sadducees continue adulterating the gospel and denying its power to save, until this very day.

Paul, in Galatians 1:8,9, pronounced a double curse upon anyone who preaches another gospel. He says that if anyone preaches another gospel other than the pure gospel of justification by grace through faith; apart from works of the law which he preached, then it wasn't the gospel at all. There is no other gospel or "good news" other than the glorious good news of a universal reconciliation, which will eventually be received by all, by grace through faith in the blood of His cross.

The elitist doctrine of the Judaizers, who followed in the tradition of the Pharisees, taught salvation by faith in Jesus plus the works of the law, rather than by grace through faith apart from works. Paul taught that Christ is *the Savior of all men, especially of those who believe,* and he proclaimed the ultimate reconciliation of all through Christ *(1Tim 4:10; Col 1:20)*. The Pharisees, on the other hand, taught that the final destiny of all mankind, except for the best of the best and the strongest of the strong, is eternal torment in a never-ending lake of fire. Paul emphasizes that that is not the gospel; no matter what they may call it.

The Leaven of the Pharisees - The Good News, Bad News Gospel

Sadly, some variation of the *"good news, bad news gospel"* of the Judaizers, is what many still proclaim even to this day. But Paul said it isn't really good news at all, but rather "bad news" being passed off as the gospel. Many missionaries have been unsuccessful in selling their *"good news, bad news gospel"* to the unreached and for good reason. Let me illustrate. Imagine a missionary's first encounter with a member of a remote tribe in the heart of the jungle who has never heard of Jesus. Traditional missionaries usually start out essentially in the following manner:

Missionary: *"I have good news for you but first I must tell you the bad news. The bad news is that you are a sinner and are headed for hell."*

The tribesman interrupts: *"What is hell?"*

Missionary: *"Hell is a place of never-ending fiery torment." "Everyone who does not believe the good news before dying will spend eternity burning in hell."*

The tribesman: *"Now, that **is** bad news! A foreigner visited our village a couple of months back and many of us fell sick from a virus he brought with him. I lost my dear wife and two children. Does that mean that they are now burning in this fiery hell and that they will be there forever and ever?"*

Missionary: *"I hate to be the one to have to break the bad news to you but, yes. Unless one believes the good news before dying, they will spend eternity in hell."*

The tribesman: *"Then pray tell, what is the good news?"*

Missionary: *"The good news is that God loves **you** so much that He sent His Son so that you may have eternal life."*

Tribesman: *"That is a whole lot to take in all at once. Let me think about it. Tomorrow I will let you know what I have decided."*

Missionary: *"Now is the day of decision. If you wait until tomorrow you could die in your sleep. Then God's **eternal wrath** will be poured out upon you, along with your wife and two children. You need to believe the good news today because there may never be a tomorrow."*

Although most traditional Christians would be a little more tactful in their presentation of the *"good news, bad news gospel,"* and although there are various differing versions of this *"good news, bad news gospel,"* they always fall far short of the pure undiluted gospel of the ultimate salvation of all through the redemptive work of the cross. Another version often presented is as follows:

Missionary: *"I have good news for you but first I must tell you the bad news. The bad news is that you are a sinner and are headed for hell"*

The tribesman interrupts: *"What is hell?"*

Missionary: *"Hell is a place of never-ending fiery torment." "You must believe the good news before dying or you will spend eternity burning in hell."*

The tribesman: *"Now, that **is** bad news! A foreigner visited our village a couple of months back and many of us fell sick from a virus he brought with him. I lost my dear wife and two children. Does that mean that they are now burning in this fiery hell and that they will be there forever and ever?"*

Missionary: *"I believe that they will be in heaven, since they didn't have an opportunity to hear the good news before dying. But now you have heard the gospel, so there will be no second opportunity for you."*

The tribesman: *"You mean to tell me that all who died in our village without hearing the good news will go to heaven, but that from now on all of us must believe the good news before we die or we will go to an eternal hell?"*

Missionary: *"That's it exactly."*

Tribesman: *"Then, why in heaven's name did you come here in the first place? I, for my part, will believe so I don't go to this hell, but I don't know what decision the rest of my tribe will make. We would have all gone to heaven if you just hadn't come here. Now many of us will probably go to this never-ending hell!"*

So, we see that no matter what form one chooses to present the *"good news, bad news gospel,"* it always ends up being bad news for the great majority. That is why Paul said that any other gospel, other than the pure unadulterated gospel which he preached, is not really another gospel at all. It is simply "bad news" covered in a "good news" wrapping. The *unadulterated gospel* of Jesus Christ is *good tidings of great joy which will be to **all** people (Luke 2:10)*. Anything less is another gospel which Paul says is really not a gospel at all. A missionary who is an ambassador of reconciliation to all of God's creation has the privilege of proclaiming an unadulterated gospel. It would be in somewhat the following manner:

Missionary: *"I have good news for you. We were all created in the image of God to enjoy communion with Him. Our first parents disobeyed God and all of us since that time have lived in disobedience to Him – all of us have sinned and come short of the glory of God and His good purposes for our lives. God's kingdom is a kingdom of love, light and truth. When man does not walk with God who is light, we become lost in darkness, separated from our Creator. We have all erred from the truth in this way, falling into hatred, envy and strife. Separated from our God we have brought upon ourselves suffering and death. Separated from our Father God we live as spiritual orphans. In our emptiness man has become enslaved to many self-destructive vices.*

(Note that this is not part of the gospel. It is simply a description of the plight of mankind apart from God, in the far country.)

"But the good news is that God did not leave us in our lost condition. In the fullness of time God sent His Son to live as one of us. In contrast with our first father, Adam, who disobeyed God, He lived a life of perfect obedience to the Father but offered himself up to die in our place, taking the guilt for all our disobedience. On the third day after His death God raised Him up from the dead. His resurrection demonstrated that the sacrifice of His innocent blood for us as our substitute was sufficient to satisfy the justice of God for all our sinful, disobedient acts put together. Even as in our first parent, Adam, all of us stood guilty and condemned before the Most Holy God; now in the Last Adam - Christ, all are justified through faith in Him, being born-again into the New Creation which God began in Him.

"God the Father, Son and Holy Spirit, reconciled all of fallen sinful creation to Himself through the blood of His cross and He entreats you through us to now become reconciled to Him in your hearts. Even as in our father, Adam, all of us die, in the last Adam, Christ Jesus, all will be made alive, but each in his own order. Now is the best time to bow the knee to Him in loving surrender. Christ is the Savior of all but especially of those who believe now.

"Receive Christ as your Savior now and let Him come into your life and transform you, making you into a new creation, of which

He is the prototype. God's kingdom is a kingdom of pure light, love and righteousness. Without the holiness that comes from walking in union with Christ no one will be able to enter into His kingdom or even bear to look upon Him in all His glorious splendor.

"Surrender your life to Him now so that He may transform you into His own image in this life. Then when He comes for you, you will be found to be like Him. If you are found in Him when He comes for you, you will be taken into His very presence and you will become one with Him as a wife becomes one with her husband. If you are not found in Him when He comes for you – if you haven't yet died out to your old way of living as a child of Adam, then you will have to be set aside for judgment and submitted to fiery afflictions, being hurt by the second death which you were unwilling to undergo in this life. Receive Him into your life now, allowing Him to transform you into His image so that it will not be necessary for God to separate you for judgment and fiery correction in that day while the sons of the kingdom are rejoicing in the presence of the Lord.

The tribesman: *"Now I understand that all our suffering is because we have turned, every one of us, to our own way. Now I repent and receive Christ into my heart that He may transform me into a new person. I want to abide in Him so that when He comes for me, I will look just like Him and will not be ashamed in His presence."*

The truth of the pure unadulterated, *everlasting* gospel is the grace of God leading us to repentance and a vital faith in Christ. It is not bad news wrapped in good news wrappings. It is universal in its scope, being good tidings of great joy for **all** people *(Lu 2:10)*. It declares without apology that ultimately all in heaven, on earth and under the earth will confess Jesus as Lord and bow their knee in humble, willful submission. This is the gospel that we must defend and proclaim.

The Leaven of the Sadducees

As we have seen, the leaven of the Pharisees converts the good news into bad news. Jesus accused the scribes and Pharisees of making the kingdom of heaven unattainable for those who desired to enter in, and without realizing it they excluded themselves as well

(Matt 23:13). The Judaizers bad news gospel tried to combine two incompatible elements: grace and works, making any assurance of salvation impossible *(Rom 11:6).* Combining this bad news gospel with the doctrine of eternal torments, they only managed to leave their proselytes feeling more hopeless than ever, going back into the world two times worse than before receiving their leaven *(Matt 23:15).*

While the leaven of the Pharisees converted the gospel into bad news by adding works to grace and by adding the word **eternal** to punishment, the leaven of the Sadducees manifests in the form of unbelief concerning the essential elements of the gospel, rendering it powerless to save.

This form of leaven has sought to undermine the substance and foundation of the pure gospel of Jesus Christ. This began to rise in the earliest forms of Gnosticism which denied that Jesus was the Christ. They maintained that the "Christ Spirit" came upon the man, Jesus, at His baptism and ascended before the man, Jesus, died. In other words, they denied that Jesus was Himself the Christ; the Son of God born of a virgin. According to these Gnostics, when Jesus died on the cross it was only the perfect man, Jesus, and not the God-man, Jesus Christ, who gave His life for mankind.

The implications of this doctrine should be obvious: One perfect man can only act as substitute for one other individual, at best. If He was not God, in Christ, reconciling the world to Himself on the cross, then His blood shed as a propitiatory sacrifice could not have been of sufficient worth to expiate for our sins, not to mention the sins of the whole world *(cf. 1Jn 2:2).* That is why John so sternly warns: *"Who is a liar but he who denies that Jesus is the Christ? He is antichrist who denies the Father and the Son." (1Jn 2:22).* This is why Paul adamantly warns against any argument that would in any way undermine the full divinity of Jesus Christ:

> *"Beware lest anyone cheat you through philosophy and empty deceit, according to the tradition of men, according to the basic principles of the world, and not according to Christ. 9* ***For in Him dwells all the fullness of the Godhead bodily****; 10 and you are complete in Him, who is the head of all principality and power." (Col 2:8-10)*

If Jesus Christ was merely a man and not the God-man, *in whom dwells the fullness of the Godhead bodily*, then those who have placed their hope of salvation in Him alone, are of all, the most to be pitied. We would yet be in our sins because the substitutionary sacrifice of a mere man – however perfect, would not be of sufficient worth to save all of mankind.

The leaven of the Sadducees laces the pure gospel with rationalistic humanism which manifests a condescending distain for those who hold fast to the biblical teaching of the substitutionary, propitiatory value of Christ's death on the cross. They would reduce His life and even His death to nothing more than an example for us to follow. However, the entire Old Testament sacrificial system was designed to foreshadow His expiatory sacrifice of Himself as our substitute on the Cross. Christ's substitutionary death through His blood, shed in the place of ours, is a recurring theme throughout the entirety of the Scriptures. The following are just a few key examples:

*"All we like sheep have gone astray; we have turned, every one, to his own way; and **the Lord has laid on Him the iniquity of us all**." (Isa 53:6)*

*"For He made Him who knew no sin **to be sin for us, that we might become the righteousness of God in Him**." (2Cor 5:21)*

*"for all have sinned and fall short of the glory of God, 24 being justified freely by His grace through the redemption that is in Christ Jesus, 25 **whom God set forth as a propitiation by His blood**, through faith, to demonstrate His righteousness, because in His forbearance God had passed over the sins that were previously committed, 26 to demonstrate at the present time His righteousness, that He might be just and the justifier of the one who has faith in Jesus." (Rom 3:23-26)*

*"Therefore, in all things **He had to be made like His brethren**, that He might be a merciful and faithful High Priest in things pertaining to God, **to make propitiation** for the sins of the people." (Heb 2:17)*

*"And **He Himself is the propitiation for our sins**, and **not for ours only but also for the whole world**." (1Jn 2:2)*

"In this is love, not that we loved God, but that He loved us and sent His Son to be the propitiation for our sins." (1Jn 4:10)

In spite of these passages and many more like them, they insist that justice does not permit any individual to pay the debt of another. They insist that each must pay his own debt. Nevertheless, we see that God made provision in the law, giving one the right to pay the redemptive price for another's freedom from slavery. The only stipulation was that the redeemer must be one of his brothers:

"Now if a sojourner or stranger close to you becomes rich, and one of your brethren who dwells by him becomes poor, and sells himself to the stranger or sojourner close to you, or to a member of the stranger's family, 48 after he is sold he may be redeemed again. **One of his brothers may redeem him.***" (Lev 25:47-48)*

According to the law of God, if one were to become a slave, then a brother or kinsman of the slave had the right to redeem him (buy his freedom). That is why it was necessary for Jesus Christ to be made *in all things like His brethren.* Only in this manner could God the Son qualify as our kinsman Redeemer or "Brother Redeemer." The entirety of Adam's race has been slaves to the foreigner; Satan. The Son of God had to take the form of human flesh, similar to ours, in order to qualify as our Brother Redeemer. God, having foreseen the redemptive work of Christ on the cross, established the law of the "kinsman redeemer" to be a shadow of our Great Kinsman Redeemer, Jesus Christ, who would become like unto His brethren and redeem us with His own blood. Peter warns us of those who would deny the redemptive value of the sacrifice of Christ's blood for us:

"But there were also false prophets among the people, even as there will be false teachers among you, who will secretly bring in destructive heresies, **even denying the Lord who bought them***, and bring on themselves swift destruction." (2Peter 2:1)*

Many Universalists, (as well as Traditionalists, who still believe in eternal punishment or conditional mortality), preach a false humanistic gospel, having been contaminated with the leaven of the Sadducees. They deny that the only way to God is through the substitutionary death and resurrection of Jesus Christ the Son of God. Many of them even deny the divinity of Jesus Christ as the Son of God.

I must emphasize that not all who have broken with tradition in favor of Universalism are biblical Universalists who would insist that the only way to God is through faith in the substitutionary sacrifice of Jesus Christ. Universalism is just as appealing to the modern Libertines today who use the grace of God as a cloak for their immoral lifestyles, as it was in the days of the apostles *(Rom 3:8; 6:15)*. Jude says:

*"For certain men have crept in unnoticed, who long ago were marked out for this condemnation, ungodly men, who **turn the grace of our God into lewdness and deny the only Lord God and our Lord Jesus Christ**." (Jude 4)*

The apostles, however, did not modify the pure gospel of the grace of God in order to protect it against being misused by those who would abuse it. Because of their insistence upon the pure unadulterated gospel of grace they were falsely accused by the Pharisaic Judaizers:

"And why not say, 'Let us do evil that good may come'? — as we are slanderously reported and as some affirm that we say. Their condemnation is just." (Rom 3:8)

The fact that some would pervert the gospel of universal reconciliation, diluting it to fulfill their own selfish ends, does not justify us restricting it or amending it. When I began to discover the biblical doctrine of universal reconciliation, I began to read everything I could find on the subject – both for it and against it. Nevertheless, those that I could recommend, which were entirely faithful to the Scriptures, I could count on my fingers.

Unbiblical forms of Universalism abound. Many today espouse a syncretistic version of Universalism which is inclusive of all religions. Beginning with Modernism in the 19th Century with its liberal theology, the leaven of the Sadducees has now shifted into high-gear, morphing into Post-Modernism and Progressivism. Many within today's Emerging Church Movement have drifted from the Faith once and for all delivered to the saints to a subjective relativism *(Jude 4)*. Anyone making a claim to absolute truths based upon biblical doctrine is now considered by many as being arrogant and small-minded. There is a rapid departure from faith in the objective Word of God to a relativism conducive to a syncretistic conglomerate One-World Church, now being referred to by other, more palatable names, such as the "Emergent Church." The brand of Universalism presented by some within that movement is inclusive of all faiths and is overtly antagonistic to the pure unadulterated gospel. They like to selectively quote some of the sayings of Jesus but not such declarations as, *"It is written, 'Man shall not live by bread alone, but by EVERY word that proceeds from the mouth of God,"* or *"I am THE way, the truth, and the life. No one comes to the Father except through Me."* (Matt 4:4, Jn 14:6).

It is my conviction that we must return to the pure, unadulterated gospel of the reconciliation of all through the blood of the cross of Jesus Christ. The Church Fathers in the times of Augustine adulterated the gospel, amending it to include the Pharisee's doctrine of eternal punishment in order to protect it from being taken lightly by the unregenerate who were joining the ranks of the Church. That only introduced the Church into the Dark Ages, during which time the glorious gospel was replaced with the *"good news, bad news gospel."* We more than any other generation must insist upon the pure gospel preached by the Apostles and the early Church. We must take to heart the words of Paul:

"But even if we, or an angel from heaven, preach any other gospel to you than what we have preached to you, let him be accursed. 9 As we have said before, so now I say again, if anyone preaches any other gospel to you than what you have received, let him be accursed." (Gal 1:8-9)

INDEX OF PASSAGES IMPLYING A UNIVERSAL RESTORATION

The following is a list of texts which, to me, clearly indicate that hell is not eternal and that there will be a universal restoration of all that which is in heaven, in earth and under the earth. There are others which could have been included here, but in my opinion these are the most conclusive.

Passages that imply a Total Restoration:

Acts 3:21,25
Whom heaven must receive until the times of <u>restoration of all things</u>, which God has spoken by the mouth of all His holy prophets since the world began…. 25 You are sons of the prophets, and of the covenant which God made with our fathers, saying to Abraham, 'And in your seed <u>all the families of the earth shall be blessed</u>.

- Each time we see "all things" in the translations we must keep in mind that "things" does not have an equivalent in Greek and has been added by the translators.

Colossians 1:16,20
For by Him <u>all things were created</u> that are in <u>heaven</u> and that are on <u>earth</u>, <u>visible</u> and <u>invisible</u>, whether thrones or dominions or principalities or powers. All things were created through Him and for Him…and by Him <u>to reconcile all things to Himself</u>, by Him, whether things <u>on earth</u> or things <u>in heaven</u>, having made peace through the blood of His cross.

- The same all that was created by Christ was also reconciled by Him.

2Corinthians 5:19
that is, that God was in Christ <u>reconciling the world to Himself</u>, not imputing their trespasses to them, and has committed to us the word of reconciliation.

Philippians 3:21
...He is able even to subdue <u>all</u> ~~things~~ to Himself.

2Corinthians 5:14
...that if <u>One died for all</u>, then <u>all died</u>.

Romans 5:12-21
Therefore, just as through <u>one man</u> sin entered the world, and death through sin, and thus death spread to <u>all men</u>, because <u>all sinned</u> — 13 (For until the law sin was in the world, but sin is not imputed when there is no law. 14 Nevertheless, <u>death reigned from Adam to Moses</u>, even over those who had not sinned according to the likeness of the transgression of Adam, who is a type of Him who was to come. 15 <u>But the free gift is not like the offense</u>. For if <u>by the one man's offense many died</u>, much more the grace of God and the gift <u>by the grace of the one Man, Jesus Christ, abounded to many</u>. 16 And the gift is not like that which came through the one who sinned. For the judgment which came <u>from one offense resulted in condemnation</u>, but <u>the free gift</u> which came from many offenses <u>resulted in justification</u>. 17 For if by the one man's offense death reigned through the one, much more those who receive abundance of grace and of the gift of righteousness will reign in life through the One, Jesus Christ.) 18 Therefore, as <u>through one man's offense judgment came to all men</u>, resulting in condemnation, <u>even so through one Man's righteous act the free gift came to all men</u>, resulting in justification of life. 19 For as by <u>one man's disobedience</u> <u>many were made sinners</u>, so also by <u>one Man's obedience</u> <u>many will be made righteous</u>. 20 Moreover the law entered that the offense might abound. But <u>where sin abounded, grace abounded much more</u>, 21 so that as sin reigned in death, even so grace might reign through righteousness to eternal life through Jesus Christ our Lord.

- The sin *abounded* by one – Adam, but the grace *much more abounded* by One – Christ. The work Christ accomplished much more than restoring what Adam lost. Could that be true if 90% of mankind were to be eternally lost?

1Corinthians 15:21-28
For since by man came death, by Man also came the resurrection of the dead. 22 <u>*For as in Adam all(100%) die,*</u> <u>*even so in Christ all (100%)*</u> <u>*shall be made alive.*</u> *23* <u>*But each one in his own order:*</u> *Christ the firstfruits, afterward those who are Christ's at His coming. 24 Then comes the end, when He delivers the kingdom to God the Father, when He puts an end to all rule and all authority and power. 25 For He must reign till He has put all enemies under His feet. 26 The last enemy that will be destroyed is death. 27 For "He has put all things under His feet." But when He says "all things are put under Him," it is evident that He who put all things under Him is excepted. 28 Now* <u>*when all things are made subject to Him, then the Son Himself will also be subject to Him who put all things under Him, that God may be all in all*</u> *(10%?).*

- Are we to understand that all who will end up in God are 10% whereas in Adam it is 100%? How can we call that "much more"?

Ephesians 1:9-12
having made known to us the mystery of His will, according to His good pleasure which He purposed in Himself, 10 <u>*that in the dispensation of the fullness of the times He might gather together in one all*</u> ~~things~~ <u>*in Christ*</u>*, both which are* <u>*in heaven*</u> *and which are* <u>*on earth*</u> *— in Him. 11 In Him also we have obtained an inheritance, being predestined according to the purpose of Him who works all things according to the counsel of His will, 12* <u>*that we who first trusted in Christ should be to the praise of His glory.*</u>

- The Church is only the firstfruits. In the dispensation of the fullness of times all in the heaven and in the earth will put their trust in Christ. We are just the first.

Ephesians 2:7
<u>*that in the ages to come He might show the exceeding riches of His grace in His kindness toward us in Christ Jesus.*</u>

- To whom will we be showing the exceeding riches of His grace, and why will it be displayed? Just to show it to the angels who don't need it?

James 1:18
Of His own will He brought us forth by the word of truth, that we might be a kind of <u>firstfruits of His creatures</u>.

- We are the firstfruits. Firstfruits imply that the rest will follow.

Romans 8:18-23
For I consider that the sufferings of this present time are not worthy to be compared with the glory which shall be revealed in us. 19 For <u>the earnest expectation of the creation eagerly waits for the revealing of the sons of God.</u> 20 For the creation was subjected to futility, not willingly, but because of Him who subjected it in hope; 21 because <u>the creation itself also will be delivered from the bondage of corruption into the glorious liberty of the children of God</u>. 22 For we know that the whole creation groans and labors with birth pangs together until now. 23 Not only that, but we also who have <u>the firstfruits of the Spirit</u>, even we ourselves groan within ourselves, eagerly waiting for the adoption, the redemption of our body.

1Timothy 2:3-6
For this is good and acceptable in the sight of God our Savior, 4 <u>who desires all men to be saved</u> and to come to the knowledge of the truth. 5 For there is one God and one Mediator between God and men, the Man Christ Jesus, 6 <u>who gave Himself a ransom for all, to be testified in due time.</u>

- All, but in due time.

Acts 3:25,26
You are sons of the prophets, and of the covenant which God made with our fathers, saying to Abraham, 'And <u>in your seed all the families of the earth shall be blessed</u>. 26 <u>To you first</u>, God, having raised up His Servant Jesus, sent Him to bless you, in turning away every one of you from your iniquities."

1Peter 2:12
having your conduct honorable among the Gentiles, that when they speak against you as evildoers, they may, by your good works which they observe, glorify God <u>in the day of visitation</u>.

- Each one "in his own order" will have his "day of visitation."

1Timothy 2:4
Who <u>desires all men to be saved</u> and to come to the knowledge of the truth.

- Could it possibly be that in the end God doesn't get what He desires?

cf. Isa 46:10 ...My counsel shall stand, and I will do all My pleasure,

1Timothy 4:9-10
*This is a faithful saying and worthy of all acceptance. 10 For to this end we both labor and suffer reproach, because we trust in the living God, <u>who is the Savior of</u> **all men, especially of those who believe**.*

Acts 10:34
...In truth I perceive that God shows no partiality.

Romans 5:8
But God demonstrates His own love toward us, in that while we were still sinners, Christ died for us.

- His love towards the whole world. (1John 2:2)

Romans 11:15,16, 26,29,33-36)
For if their being cast away is the reconciling of the world, what will their acceptance be but life from the dead? 16 For if the firstfruit is holy, the lump is also holy; and if the root is holy, so are the branches. has come in. 26 <u>And so all Israel will be saved</u>....29 For the gifts and the calling of God are irrevocable.... 32 <u>For God has</u>

committed ~~them~~ [149] *all to disobedience, that He might have mercy on all. 33 Oh, the depth of the riches both of the wisdom and knowledge of God! How unsearchable are His judgments and His ways past finding out! 34 "For who has known the mind of the Lord? Or who has become His counselor?" 35 'Or who has first given to Him and it shall be repaid to him?" 36 <u>For of Him and through Him and to Him are all things, to whom be glory forever</u>. Amen.*

Romans 12: 21
Do not be overcome by evil, but <u>overcome evil with good</u>.

- How will God overcome evil? With eternal vengeance? Would that overcome evil or perpetuate it?

Romans 15:9-12
and that the Gentiles might glorify God for His mercy, as it is written: "For this reason I will confess to You among the Gentiles, and sing to Your name." 10 And again he says: "Rejoice, O Gentiles, with His people!" 11 And again: "<u>Praise the Lord, all you Gentiles! Laud Him, all you peoples!</u>" 12 And again, Isaiah says: "There shall be a root of Jesse; And He who shall rise to reign over the Gentiles, in <u>Him the Gentiles shall hope</u>."

1Corinthians 13:5-8 RSV
Love is patient and kind; love is not jealous or boastful; 5 it is not arrogant or rude. Love does not insist on its own way; it is not irritable or resentful; 6 it does not rejoice at wrong, but rejoices in the right. 7 Love bears all things, believes all things, hopes all things, endures all things. 8 <u>Love never ends</u>. (cf. 1John 4:16)

1John 4:16
So we know and believe the love God has for us. <u>God is love</u>....

- Since God is love and He is eternal, love never ends.

Ephesians 4:8-10

---

[149] *"them"* is not in the original Greek text, but was added by the translators.

Therefore He says: "<u>When He ascended on high, He led captivity captive</u>, and gave gifts to men." 9 (Now this, "He ascended" — what does it mean but that He also <u>first descended into the lower parts of the earth</u>? 10 He who descended is also the One who ascended far above all the heavens, that He might fill all things. (c.f. 1Peter 3:18-20 and 4:6)

1Peter 3:18-20
For Christ also suffered once for sins, the just for the unjust, that He might bring us to God, being put to death in the flesh but made alive by the Spirit, 19 by whom also <u>He went and preached to the spirits in prison</u>, 20 <u>who formerly were disobedient</u>, when once the Divine longsuffering waited <u>in the days of Noah</u>, while the ark was being prepared, in which a few, that is, eight souls, were saved through water.

1Peter 4:6
For this reason <u>the gospel was preached also to those who are dead</u>, that they might be judged according to men in the flesh, but live according to God in the spirit.

Philippians 2:10-11
that at the name of Jesus <u>every knee should bow</u>, of those <u>in heaven</u>, and of those <u>on earth</u>, and of those <u>under the earth</u>, 11 and that <u>every tongue should confess that Jesus Christ is Lord</u>, to the glory of God the Father. (cf. 1Cor 12:3)

1Corinthians 12:3
...no one can say that Jesus is Lord except by the Holy Spirit.

1Timothy 1:19-20
having faith and a good conscience, which some having rejected, concerning the faith have suffered shipwreck, 20 of whom are Hymenaeus and Alexander, whom I delivered to Satan <u>that they may learn</u> not to blaspheme.

Titus 2:11-12 NIV
For the grace of God that brings salvation <u>has appeared to all men</u>.

Titus 3:4-6
But when the kindness and the love of God our Savior toward man appeared, (toward every man cf. 2:11) 5 not by works of

righteousness which we have done, but according to His mercy He saved us, through the washing of regeneration and renewing of the Holy Spirit

Hebrews 2:2
For if the word spoken through angels proved steadfast, and every transgression and disobedience received <u>a just reward</u>.

- The law prescribed a "just reward." Should we believe that a "just reward" will be followed by eternal torments?

Hebrews 2:8,9
You have put <u>all ~~things~~</u> in subjection under his feet. For in that He put all in subjection under him, He left nothing that is not put under him. But now <u>we do not yet see all ~~things~~</u> put under him. 9 But we see Jesus, who was made a little lower than the angels, for the suffering of death crowned with glory and honor, that He, by the grace of God, might taste death <u>for everyone</u>.

- Does all and everyone mean 100% or only 10%?

Hebrews 2:14-15 ASV
*Since then the children are sharers in flesh and blood, he also himself in like manner partook of the same; that through death he might bring to nought him that had the power of death, that is, the devil; 15 and might <u>deliver **all them** who through fear of death were all their lifetime subject to bondage</u>.*

Hebrews 5:6
As He also says in another place: "<u>You are a priest forever</u> (ton aiona) according to the order of Melchizedek."

Hebrews 7:25
Therefore He is also able to save to the uttermost those who come to God through Him, since He <u>always lives to make intercession</u> for them.

- His priestly intercession does not end at death, but continues as long as necessary for all who wish to draw near to God by Him.

1John 2:2
And He Himself is the propitiation for our sins, and not for ours only but <u>also for the whole world</u>.

1John 3:8
...For this purpose the Son of God was manifested, that He might destroy the works of the devil.

- As the last Adam He destroyed the Works of the devil. The devil's Works will not continue going on forever in hell.

1John 4:14
And we have seen and testify that the Father has sent the Son as <u>Savior of the world</u>.

Revelation 5:13-14
And <u>every creature</u> which is <u>in heaven</u> and <u>on the earth</u> and <u>under the earth</u> and such as are in the sea, and all that are in them, I heard saying: "Blessing and honor and glory and power be to Him who sits on the throne, and to the Lamb, forever and ever!" (cf. Phil 2:10-11)

> *Philippians 2:10-11*
> *that at the name of Jesus <u>every</u> knee should bow, of those <u>in heaven</u>, and of those <u>on earth</u>, and of those <u>under the earth</u>, 11 and that every tongue should confess that Jesus Christ is Lord, to the glory of God the Father.*

Revelation 15:4
*Who shall not fear You, O Lord, and glorify Your name? For You alone are holy. For **all nations** <u>shall come and worship before You</u>, for Your judgments have been manifested.*

Revelation 21:5
Then He who sat on the throne said, "Behold, <u>I make all things new</u>."

Revelation 21:24-27
And <u>the nations of those who are saved shall walk in its light</u>, and the kings of the earth bring their glory and honor into it. 25 <u>Its gates shall not be shut</u> at all by day (there shall be no night there).

26 And they shall bring the glory and the honor of the nations into it. 27 <u>But there shall by no means enter it anything that defiles, or causes an abomination or a lie, but only those who are written in the Lamb's Book of Life</u>.

Revelation 22:1-2
And he showed me a pure river of water of life, clear as crystal, proceeding from the throne of God and of the Lamb. 2 In the middle of its street, and on either side of the river, was the tree of life, which bore twelve fruits, each tree yielding its fruit every month. The leaves of the tree were <u>for the healing of the nations</u>.
Revelation 22:14-15 NIV
<u>Blessed are those who wash their robes, that they may have the right to the tree of life and may go through the gates into the city</u>. 15 Outside are the dogs, those who practice magic arts, the sexually immoral, the murderers, the idolaters and everyone who loves and practices falsehood.

- The gates of the New Jerusalem will always be open. No one who has not washed his robes and is not found written in the book of life can enter, but the Bride invites all who desire to enter and drink of the water of life within the city.

Genesis 12:3 NIV
I will bless those who bless you, and whoever curses you I will curse; and <u>all peoples on earth will be blessed through you</u>.

Job 23:13 Job 23:13 NIV
But he stands alone, and who can oppose him? He does whatever he pleases (thelo).

Job 42:2
I know that <u>You can do everything</u>, and that <u>no purpose of Yours can be withheld</u> from You.

Psalm 2:8 NIV
Ask of me, and I will make the nations your inheritance, the ends of the earth your possession.

- Christ receives the nations as an inheritance.

Psalm 22:27

All the ends of the world shall remember and turn to the Lord, and *all the families of the nations shall worship before You.*

Psalm 66:3-4
Say to God, "How awesome are Your works! Through the greatness of Your power *Your enemies shall submit themselves to You.* 4 *All the earth shall worship You* and sing praises to You; They shall sing praises to Your name."

Psalm 72:11
Yes, *all kings* shall fall down before Him; *All nations* shall serve Him.
Psalm 86:9
All nations whom You have made shall come and worship before You, O Lord, and shall glorify Your name.

Psalm 90:3
You turn man to destruction, and say, "Return, O children of men."

Psalm 138:4
All the kings of the earth shall praise You, O Lord, when they hear the words of Your mouth.

Psalm 145:8-10
The Lord is gracious and full of compassion, slow to anger and great in mercy. 9 *The Lord is good to all*, and *His tender mercies are over all His works*.

Proverbs 16:9
A man's heart plans his way, but *the Lord directs his steps*.

Proverbs 19:21
There are many plans in a man's heart, nevertheless *the Lord's counsel — that will stand*.

Proverbs 20:24
A man's steps are of the Lord; How then can a man understand his own way?

Psalm 135:6
Whatever the Lord pleases He does, in heaven and in earth,

Isaiah 14:24
The Lord of hosts has sworn, saying, "<u>Surely, as I have thought, so it shall come to pass</u>, and <u>as I have purposed, so it shall stand</u>."

Isaiah 46:10-11
Declaring the end from the beginning, and from ancient times things that are not yet done, saying, 'My counsel shall stand, and I will do all My pleasure,' calling a bird of prey from the east, the man who executes My counsel, from a far country. Indeed I have spoken it; I will also bring it to pass. I have purposed it; I will also do it.

Ecclesiastes 3:11
He has made everything beautiful in its time. Also <u>He has put eternity in their hearts</u>, except that no one can find out the work that God does from beginning to end.

Isaiah 14:27
For the Lord of hosts has purposed, and who will annul it? His hand is stretched out, and who will turn it back?"

- He desires that all be saved and He has all the time necessary to bring it to pass. cf. 2Peter 3:8,9

2Peter 3:8,9
But, beloved, <u>do not forget this one thing, that with the Lord one day is as a thousand years, and a thousand years as one day</u>. 9 The Lord is not slack concerning His promise, as some count slackness, but is longsuffering toward us, <u>not willing that any should perish but that all should come to repentance</u>.

Isaiah 25:6-8
And in this mountain the Lord of hosts will make for all people a feast of choice pieces, a feast of wines on the lees, of fat things full of marrow, of well-refined wines on the lees. 7 <u>And He will destroy on this mountain the surface of the covering cast over all people, and the veil that is spread over all nations</u>. 8 <u>He will swallow up death forever</u>, and the Lord God will wipe away tears from all faces; the rebuke of His people. He will take away from all the earth; for the Lord has spoken.

Isaiah 45:21-24

Tell and bring forth your case; yes, let them take counsel together. Who has declared this from ancient time? Who has told it from that time? Have not I, the Lord? And there is no other God besides Me, a just God and a Savior; There is none besides Me. 22 "<u>Look to Me, and be saved, all you ends of the earth</u>! For I am God, and there is no other. 23 <u>I have sworn by Myself</u>; the word has gone out of My mouth in righteousness, and shall not return, <u>that to Me every knee shall bow, every tongue shall take an oath</u>. 24 <u>He shall say, 'Surely in the Lord I have righteousness and strength</u>. To Him men shall come, and all shall be ashamed who are incensed against Him.

Jeremiah 31:34
No more shall every man teach his neighbor, and every man his brother, saying, 'Know the Lord,' for they <u>all shall know Me, from the least of them to the greatest of them</u>, says the Lord. For <u>I will forgive their iniquity, and their sin I will remember no more</u>."

Ezekiel 16:53-56, 61
When I bring back their captives, <u>the captives of Sodom and her daughters, and the captives of Samaria and her daughters, then I will also bring back the captives of your captivity among them</u>, 54 that you may bear your own shame and be disgraced by all that you did when you comforted them. 55 When <u>your sisters, Sodom and her daughters, return to their former state, and Samaria and her daughters return to their former state, then you and your daughters will return to your former state</u>.... 61 Then you will remember your ways and be ashamed, <u>when you receive your older and your younger sisters</u>; for I will give them to you for daughters, but not because of My covenant with you.

Daniel 7:14
Then to Him was given dominion and glory and a kingdom, <u>that all peoples, nations, and languages should serve Him</u>. His dominion is an everlasting dominion, which shall not pass away, and His kingdom the one which shall not be destroyed.

Matthew 12:11-12
Then He said to them, "What man is there among you who has one sheep, and if it falls into a pit on the Sabbath, will not lay hold of it and lift it out? 12 <u>Of how much more value then is a man than a sheep</u>? Therefore it is lawful to do good on the Sabbath."

Matthew 12:20-21
A bruised reed He will not break, and smoking flax He will not quench, <u>till He sends forth justice to victory</u>; 21 And <u>in His name Gentiles will trust</u>."

Matthew 13:33
Another parable He spoke to them: "The kingdom of heaven is like leaven, which a woman took and hid in three measures of meal <u>till it was all leavened</u>."

Matthew 14:14
And when Jesus went out He saw a great multitude; and He was moved with compassion for them, and healed their sick.

- *Wouldn't their sickness be unimportant in in the light of an eternal hell, if that was in fact what awaited them?*

Matthew 18:11
For the Son of Man has come to save that which was lost.

- *How many are lost? Will He achieve His objective to save all who are lost?*

Matthew 19:28
So Jesus said to them, "Assuredly I say to you, that <u>in the regeneration</u>, when the Son of Man sits on the throne of His glory, you who have followed Me will also sit on twelve thrones, judging the twelve tribes of Israel.

Matthew 23:1, 9
Then Jesus spoke to the multitudes and to His disciples, saying:... 9 Do not call anyone on earth your father; for One is your Father, He who is in heaven.

Luke 3:38
the son of Enosh, the son of Seth, <u>the son of Adam, the son of God</u>.

- *Isn't God the Father of all humanity?*

Acts 17:28-31
for in Him we live and move and have our being, as also some of your own poets have said, '<u>For we are also His offspring</u>.' 29

Therefore, since we are the offspring of God, we ought not to think that the Divine Nature is like gold or silver or stone, something shaped by art and man's devising. 30 Truly, these times of ignorance God overlooked, but now commands all men everywhere to repent, 31 because He has appointed a day on which He will judge the world in righteousness by the Man whom He has ordained. He has given assurance of this to all by raising Him from the dead."

- Though the Athens were fallen and in need of the new birth in order to enter the Kingdom of God, all are His sons because they were created by Him

Malachi 2:10
Have we not all one Father? Has not one God created us?

Luke 2:10-11
Then the angel said to them, "Do not be afraid, for behold, I bring you good tidings of great joy which will be to all people. 11 For there is born to you this day in the city of David a Savior, who is Christ the Lord.

- All the people means *all flesh* – both Jews and Gentiles. (cf. 30-32, 3:6)

Luke 2:30-32
For my eyes have seen Your salvation 31 which You have prepared before the face of all peoples, 32 A light to bring revelation to the Gentiles, and the glory of Your people Israel."

Luke 12:57-59
Yes, and why, even of yourselves, do you not judge what is right? 58 When you go with your adversary to the magistrate, make every effort along the way to settle with him, lest he drag you to the judge, the judge deliver you to the officer, and the officer throw you into prison. 59 I tell you, you shall not depart from there till you have paid the very last mite. (cf. 1 Tess 5:21-22)

1Thessalonians 5:21-22
Test all things; hold fast what is good. 22 Abstain from every form of evil.

Luke 15:4-5
What man of you, having a hundred sheep, if he loses one of them, does not leave the ninety-nine in the wilderness, and go after the one which is lost until he finds it?

- Will the Good Shepherd keep searching until He finds the last lost sheep or will He conform Himself with the 10% already in the fold?

Luke 23:34
Then Jesus said, "Father, forgive them, for they do not know what they do."

- Do you think God answered this prayer? What about the rest?

John 1:7-9
This man came for a witness, to bear witness of the Light, that all through him might believe…. 9 That was the true Light which gives light to every man coming into the world.

- Will His mission that all be saved through Him be fulfilled? Will all ultimately believe, or will His mission end in failure with only 10% having heard and believed?

John 1:29
Behold! The Lamb of God who takes away the sin of the world!

- Not just of a few chosen ones.

John 4:42
…and we know that this is indeed the Christ, the Savior of the world.

- Is He really the Savior of the whole world or of just a few?

John 6:33
For the bread of God is He who comes down from heaven and gives life to the world.

John 6:37-40

All that the Father gives Me will come to Me, and the one who comes to Me I will by no means cast out. 38 For I have come down from heaven, not to do My own will, but the will of Him who sent Me. 39 *This is the will of the Father who sent Me, that of all He has given Me I should lose nothing*, but should raise it up at the last day. 40 And this is the will of Him who sent Me, that everyone who sees the Son and believes in Him may have everlasting life; and I will raise him up at the last day.

John 6:51
I am the living bread which came down from heaven. If anyone eats of this bread, he will live forever; and the bread that I shall give is My flesh, which I shall give for the life of the world.

John 12:32
And I, if I am lifted up from the earth, *will draw* **all** ~~peoples~~ *to Myself*. [150]

- "Forcefully draw," Gr. *elkoúo*. cf. John 18:10; 21:11; Acts 16:19; James 2:6.

John 17:20-23
I do not pray for these alone, but also for those who will believe in Me through their word; 21 *that they all may be one*, as You, Father, are in Me, and I in You; that they also may be one in Us, that the world may believe that You sent Me. 22 And the glory which You gave Me I have given them, that they may be one just as We are one: 23 I in them, and You in Me; that they may be made perfect in one, and *that the* **world** *may know* that You have sent Me, and *have loved them* as You have loved Me.

Passages which indicate that Punishment is Not Eternal:

Genesis 1:31
Then God (who declares the end from the beginning Isa 46:10) saw everything that He had made, and indeed *it was very good*. So the evening and the morning were the sixth day.

---

[150] The word *"peoples"* is not in the Greek text but was added by the translators, allowing Calvinists to say it only refers to *"all peoples"* or *"people groups"* rather than everyone.

- How would it be possible for Father God to say that everything He had made was good, knowing that the majority of mankind, created in His image and likeness would spend eternity in hell?

Genesis 2:17
but of the tree of the knowledge of good and evil you shall not eat, for in the day that you eat of it you shall surely die.

- Why didn't He explain from the beginning that the consequences would be eternal punishment? God pronounced temporal curses on Adam and Eve and their descendants after the fall. Why didn't He ever mention eternal punishment? If eternal punishment is what awaits the majority, why isn't it emphasized from the very beginning of the Old Testament? Why are there only warnings of temporal judgments?

Genesis 4:11-15
So now you are cursed from the earth, which has opened its mouth to receive your brother's blood from your hand. 12 When you till the ground, it shall no longer yield its strength to you. A fugitive and a vagabond you shall be on the earth." 13 And Cain said to the Lord, "My punishment is greater than I can bear! 14 Surely You have driven me out this day from the face of the ground; I shall be hidden from Your face; I shall be a fugitive and a vagabond on the earth, and it will happen that anyone who finds me will kill me." 15 And the Lord said to him, "Therefore, whoever kills Cain, vengeance shall be taken on him sevenfold." And the Lord set a mark on Cain, lest anyone finding him should kill him.

- This would have been a good moment to tell Cain that an eternal hell awaited him, but instead God put a seal of protection upon him.

Genesis 18:25
…Shall not the Judge of all the earth do right?

- Would it be right for a judge to give infinite punishment for a finite offense? What would you think of a judge who gives a death sentence for a traffic violation? Even God's law limits punishment saying "an eye for an eye and a tooth for a tooth" because anything beyond that wouldn't be a just punishment.

Deuteronomy 25:3
<u>Forty blows he may give him and no more</u>, lest he should exceed this and beat him with many blows above these, and your brother be humiliated in your sight.

Exodus 21:23-25
...<u>life for life</u>, 24 <u>eye for eye</u>, <u>tooth for tooth</u>, hand for hand, foot for foot, 25 burn for burn, wound for wound, stripe for stripe.

1Chronicles 21:12,13
either three years of famine, or three months to be defeated by your foes with the sword of your enemies overtaking you, or else for three days the sword of the Lord — the plague in the land, with the angel of the Lord destroying throughout all the territory of Israel.' Now consider what answer I should take back to Him who sent me." 13 And David said to Gad, "I am in great distress. <u>Please let me fall into the hand of the Lord, for His mercies are very great; but do not let me fall into the hand of man</u>."

- We see that David chose the judgment of God over falling into the hands of man, because the mercies of God are very great. Nevertheless, the consequences were great.

1 Samuel 2:6 NASU
The Lord kills and makes alive; He brings down to Sheol (Gr. Hades) and raises up.

2 Samuel 14:14
For we will surely die and become like water spilled on the ground, which cannot be gathered up again. Yet God does not take away a life; but <u>He devises means, so that His banished ones are not expelled from Him</u>.

1 Chronicles 16:34
Oh, give thanks to the Lord, for He is good! For <u>His mercy endures forever</u>.

1 Chronicles 16:41
...because His mercy endures forever

- Repeated 41 times in the Old Testament.

Psalm 30:5
For His anger is but for a moment, His favor is for life; Weeping may endure for a night, but joy comes in the morning.

Psalm 65:2-3
*O you who hear prayer, <u>to you **all** men will come</u>. 3 When we were overwhelmed by sins, <u>you forgave our transgressions</u>.*

Psalm 66:1-4
Make a joyful shout to God, all the earth! 2 Sing out the honor of His name; Make His praise glorious. 3 Say to God, "How awesome are Your works! Through the greatness of <u>Your power your enemies shall submit themselves to You</u>. 4 <u>All the earth shall worship You and sing praises to You</u>; They shall sing praises to Your name."

Psalm 66:11-12
You brought us into the net.... We went through fire and through water; But You brought us out to rich fulfillment.

Psalm 83:16
Fill their faces with shame, that they may seek Your name, O Lord.

Psalm 90:3,4
<u>You turn man to destruction, and say, "Return, O children of men."</u>
4 For a thousand years in Your sight are like yesterday when it is past, and like a watch in the night.

Psalm 98:4-9
Shout joyfully to the Lord, <u>all the earth</u>; Break forth in song, rejoice, and sing praises.... 7 Let the sea roar, and all its fullness, <u>The world and those who dwell in it</u>... 9 <u>For He is coming to judge the earth. With righteousness He shall judge the world</u>, and the peoples with equity.

Psalm 103:8-9
The Lord is merciful and gracious, slow to anger, and abounding in mercy. 9 He will not always strive with us, <u>nor will He keep His anger forever</u>. (cf. Lam 3:31-33)

Lamentations 3:31-33
For <u>the Lord will not cast off forever</u>. 32 Though He causes grief, <u>yet He will show compassion according to the multitude of His mercies</u>. 33 For <u>He does not afflict willingly</u>, nor grieve the children of men.

Psalm 107:1
Oh, give thanks to the Lord, for <u>He is good! For His mercy endures forever</u>.

Joel 2:13
So rend your heart, and not your garments; Return to the Lord your God, for <u>He is gracious and merciful</u>, <u>slow to anger, and of great kindness</u>; and <u>He relents from doing harm</u>.

Psalm 136:1-26
Repeats "His mercy endures forever" in 26 times.

Isaiah 26:9 Isa 26:9
...For when <u>Your judgments</u> are in the earth, the inhabitants of the world will <u>learn</u> righteousness.

- Judgment is in order that we may learn. It is not simply for vengeance.

Isaiah 33:10, 14-16 NIV
Now will I arise," says the Lord. Now will I be exalted; now will I be lifted up.... 14 The sinners in Zion are terrified; trembling grips the godless: "Who of us can dwell with the consuming fire? Who of us can dwell with everlasting burning?" 15 He who walks righteously and speaks what is right, who rejects gain from extortion and keeps his hand from accepting bribes, who stops his ears against plots of murder and shuts his eyes against contemplating evil — 16 this is the man who will dwell on the heights....

- Here we see that only those who walk righteously and with integrity will be able to dwell in God´s presence which is a consuming fire and eonian flames. Here both the fire and the chaff and straw of the unjust *(11,12)* are symbolic – The fire is God and the chaff and straw are the dead works of the wicked. Why should we think that the eonian fire of Matthew 25:41 is distinct from this consuming fire and eonian burning?

Isaiah 49:15
Can a woman forget her nursing child, and not have compassion on the son of her womb? Surely they may forget, yet I will not forget you.

Isaiah 50:2
Is My hand shortened at all that it cannot redeem? Or have I no power to deliver?
- Is God limited by man in His ability to save?

Isaiah 52:10
The Lord has made bare His holy arm in the eyes of all the nations; And all the ends of the earth shall see the salvation of our God.

Isaiah 54:8
With a little <u>wrath</u> I hid My face from you <u>for a moment</u>; <u>But with everlasting kindness I will have mercy</u> on you, says the Lord, your Redeemer.

- We see that it is His mercy which is eternal and not His wrath.

Isaiah 55:7-9
Let the wicked forsake his way, and the unrighteous man his thoughts; Let him return to the Lord, and He will have mercy on him; And to our God, for He will abundantly pardon. 8 "For My thoughts are not your thoughts, nor are your ways My ways," says the Lord. 9 "For as the heavens are higher than the earth, so are My ways higher than your ways, and My thoughts than your thoughts.

- Traditionalists often cite this passage when one says that it is incomprehensible that a God of love would torment His creatures forever; "His thoughts are higher than our thoughts" they respond. But in the context Isaiah is speaking of the incomprehensibility of God's mercy – not the incomprehensibility of His severity.

Isaiah 57:16
For I will not contend forever, nor will I always be angry; for the spirit would fail before Me, and the souls which I have made.

- Where do we find eternal wrath in the Bible?

Jeremiah 10:23
O Lord, I know the way of man is not in himself; it is not in man who walks to direct his own steps.

Daniel 9:24
Seventy weeks are determined for your people and for your holy city, to finish the transgression, to make an end of sins, to make reconciliation for iniquity, to bring in everlasting righteousness, to seal up vision and prophecy, and to anoint the Most Holy.

- "To finish" and "to make an end of" do not harmonize with an eternal hell where sin would be perpetuated.

Hosea 13:14 ASV
I will ransom them from the power of Sheol; I will redeem them from death: O death, where are thy plagues? O Sheol, where is thy destruction? Repentance shall be hid from mine eyes. (i.e. "I will not even consider repenting of this")

Jonah 4:2
So he prayed to the Lord, and said, "Ah, Lord, was not this what I said when I was still in my country? Therefore I fled previously to Tarshish; for I know that You are a gracious and merciful God, slow to anger and abundant in loving-kindness, One who relents from doing harm.

Malachi 3:6
For I am the Lord, I do not change; therefore you are not consumed, O sons of Jacob.

- Could it be that His love which "never ceases" ends with a heartbeat at one's death but His wrath endures forever?

Jeremiah 23:20
*The anger of the Lord will not turn back **Until** He has executed and performed the thoughts of His heart. In the latter days you will understand it perfectly.*

Jeremiah 17:4
And you, even yourself, shall let go of your heritage which I gave you; And I will cause you to serve your enemies in the land which you do not know; For you have kindled a fire in My anger which shall burn forever (olam a-ad). (cf. Jer 30:3)

Jeremiah 25:9
behold, I will send and take all the families of the north,' says the Lord, 'and Nebuchadnezzar the king of Babylon, My servant, and will bring them against this land, against its inhabitants, and against these nations all around, and will utterly destroy them, and make them an astonishment, a hissing, and perpetual (olam) desolations. (cf. Jer 30:3)

Jeremiah 30:3
For behold, the days are coming,' says the Lord, 'that I will bring back from captivity My people Israel and Judah,' says the Lord. 'And I will cause them to return to the land that I gave to their fathers, and they shall possess it.

Jeremiah 48:42,47
And Moab shall be destroyed as a people, because he exalted himself against the Lord.... 47 Yet I will bring back the captives of Moab in the latter days," says the Lord. Thus far is the judgment of Moab.

Habakkuk 1:12
Are You not from everlasting, O Lord my God, my Holy One? We shall not die. O Lord, You have appointed them for judgment; O Rock, You have marked them for correction.

Matthew 5:22,26
*...whoever says ,'You fool!' shall be in danger of hell fire (Gehenna pur).... 26 Assuredly, I say to you, you will by no means get out of there **till** you have paid the last penny.*

Matthew 18:34-35

And his master was angry, <u>and delivered him to the torturers</u> **<u>until</u>** <u>he should pay all that was due to him</u>. 35 <u>So My heavenly Father also will do to you</u> if each of you, from his heart, does not forgive his brother his trespasses.

- The punishment continues "until." If God would never forgive us even after we have forgiven, than He would be requiring of us something He wouldn't do Himself.

Matthew 5:43-45
You have heard that it was said, 'You shall love your neighbor and hate your enemy.' 44 But I say to you, <u>love your enemies, bless those who curse you, do good to those who hate you, and pray for those who spitefully use you and persecute you</u>, 45 **that you may be sons of your Father in heaven**; for He makes His sun rise on the evil and on the good, and sends rain on the just and on the unjust.

- Would He tell us to do something He himself would not do? No. Loving our enemies makes us like our Father in Heaven.

Matthew 7:2
For with what judgment you judge, you will be judged; and <u>with the measure you use, it will be</u> **measured** <u>back to you.</u>

- Is God's justice measured, according to the offense, or is it infinite?

Matthew 10:15
Assuredly, I say to you, it will be <u>more tolerable</u> for the land of Sodom and Gomorrah in the Day of Judgment than for that city!

Matthew 21:31-32
Which of the two did the will of his father? They said to Him, "The first." Jesus said to them, "Assuredly, I say to you that <u>tax collectors and harlots enter the kingdom of God</u> **before you**. 32 For John came to you in the way of righteousness, and <u>you did not believe</u> him; but tax collectors and harlots <u>believed him;</u> and when you saw it, you did not afterward relent and believe him. (cf. Lu 13:28-30)

Luke 13:28-30
There will be weeping and gnashing of teeth, when you see Abraham and Isaac and Jacob and all the prophets in the kingdom of God, <u>and yourselves thrust out</u>. 29 They will come from the east and the west, from the north and the south, and sit down in the kingdom of God. 30 And indeed <u>there are last who will be first, and there are first who will be last</u>.

- They will be excluded but not eternally. The tax collectors and harlots enter before them – they will be last to enter but nevertheless will finally enter.

1Timothy 4:10
*For to this end we both labor and suffer reproach, because we trust in the living God, <u>who is the Savior of **all** men, **especially** of those who believe</u>.*

- The self-righteous religious leaders did not believe and therefore do not enter with those who were quick to believe. Nevertheless, they too will ultimately be saved because He is the Savior of **all**.

Luke 12:46-48
*the master of that servant will come on a day when he is not looking for him, and at an hour when he is not aware, and will cut him in two (lash him severely) and <u>appoint him his **portion** (meros) with the unbelievers</u>. 47 And that servant who knew his master's will, and did not prepare himself or do according to his will, <u>shall be beaten with many stripes</u>. 48 But he who did not kno[151]w, yet committed things deserving of stripes, <u>shall be beaten with few</u>.*

- Throughout Scripture we see that punishment is meted out with a just measure and not infinite. "Portion" is from the Greek word *meros* which means "that which is merited." "Few" and "many" lashes indicate measured time of duration and not just severity. (Compare with the following texts)

Matthew 24:51
*and will cut him in two (lash him severely) and <u>appoint him his</u> <u>**portion**</u> (meros) with the hypocrites. There shall be weeping and gnashing of teeth.*

Revelation 21:8
*…<u>shall have their **part** (meros) in the lake</u> which burns with fire and brimstone, which is the second death.*

- Even the lake of fire is not infinite in duration, but rather measured to each one according one's Works or merits.

Mark 9:49
For everyone will be salted with fire.

Mark 10:26-27
And they were greatly astonished, saying among themselves, <u>"Who then can be saved?</u>" 27 But Jesus looked at them and said, "With men it is impossible, but not with God; for <u>with God all things are possible</u>."

Revelation 1:18
I am He who lives, and was dead, and behold, I am alive forevermore. Amen. And <u>I have the keys of Hades and of Death</u>.

CONTACT THE AUTHOR

Contact: http://www.triumphofmercy.com
Author: George Sidney Hurd